"Joy Davidman: secular Jew, then Communist, then married with children, then Christian, then married to C. S. Lewis — all of these metamorphoses Don King traces in this book, evaluating her writing throughout. Davidman was a poet first and near the last, and a poet best. King has built the foundations for any future evaluations of her as writer."

— JOE R. CHRISTOPHER
coauthor of *C. S. Lewis: An Annotated Checklist of Writings about Him and His Works*

"King's best insights into Joy Davidman come from where they ought to — a careful reading of her works and letters. His analysis of the implications of Davidman's newly discovered sonnet cycle on our biographical understanding of C. S. Lewis is reason alone to buy this book!"

— CHARLIE W. STARR
author of *Light: C. S. Lewis's First and Final Short Story*

Yet One More Spring

A Critical Study of Joy Davidman

Don W. King

WILLIAM B. EERDMANS PUBLISHING COMPANY

GRAND RAPIDS, MICHIGAN / CAMBRIDGE, U.K.

Published 2015 by

Wm. B. Eerdmans Publishing Co.

2140 Oak Industrial Drive N.E., Grand Rapids, Michigan 49505 /

P.O. Box 163, Cambridge CB3 9PU U.K.

Printed in the United States of America

21 20 19 18 17 16 15   7 6 5 4 3 2 1

Library of Congress Cataloging-in-Publication Data

King, Don W., 1951-

    Yet one more spring: a critical study of Joy Davidman / Don W. King.

        pages   cm

    Includes bibliographical references and index.

    ISBN 978-0-8028-6936-4 (pbk.: alk. paper)

    1. Davidman, Joy — Criticism and interpretation.   2. Davidman, Joy.

    3. Authors, American — 20th century — Biography.

    4. Christian converts — United States — Biography.

    5. Lewis, C. S. (Clive Staples), 1898-1963.   I. Title.

    PS3507.A6659Z75   2015

    811'.52 — dc23

        [B]

                    2015014138

www.eerdmans.com

To Bobbie and Kathy

Contents

Acknowledgments

I have many persons to thank for assistance in writing this book. First and foremost, I thank David and Douglas Gresham who graciously gave me permission to cite from their mother's published and unpublished works. Dr. Judith Priestman of the Bodleian Library has been a faithful supporter in all my efforts, as has her colleague, Colin Harris, Reader Services Librarian & Superintendent of the Modern Papers and John Johnson Reading Room. Elizabeth Pearson, the Library Director at Montreat College, and her staff have been endlessly patient and helpful in securing materials, especially Nathan King and Sue Diehl. I also thank my student assistants, including Mary Willis Bertram, Laura Davidson, Molly-Kate Garner, Corrie Greene, Alyssa Klaus, and Mackenzie May. I am grateful as well to the staff at the Marion E. Wade Center, particularly Laura Schmidt, Heidi Truty, the late Christopher W. Mitchell, and Marjorie Mead, who encouraged my research and made me comfortable during my many visits to the Wade Center. I owe debts of gratitude to Montreat College for awarding me research grants to work on this book, and the Appalachian College Association for awarding me two summer research grants. I am most appreciative of the excellent editorial advice of Wm. B. Eerdmans Publishing Company, especially Jon Pott, Vice President and Editor-in-Chief, and my editor, Jenny Hoffman. Finally, I owe my wife, Jeanine, a great debt since I spent so many hours away from her while working on this book.

All published and unpublished works by Joy Davidman are copyrighted by David and Douglas Gresham and are used by their permission. Throughout this study I refer to the Joy Davidman Papers, 1926-1964, held at the Wade Center. Unless otherwise noted, all italics in quoted material are in the original.

Acknowledgments

Portions of this book have appeared in the following journals and are used by permission: "Fire and Ice: C. S. Lewis and the Love Poetry of Joy Davidman and Ruth Pitter," *SEVEN: An Anglo-American Literary Review* 22 (2005): 60-88; "Joy Davidman and the *New Masses:* Communist Poet and Reviewer," *The Chronicle of the Oxford C. S. Lewis Society* 4, no. 1 (February 2007): 18-44; "The Early Writings of Joy Davidman," *The Journal of Inklings Studies* 1, no. 1 (March 2011): 47-67; "Into the Lion's Den: Joy Davidman and Metro-Goldwyn-Mayer," *Mythlore* 30 (Fall/Winter 2011): 91-106; "Joy Davidman, Poet: *Letter to a Comrade*," *Christianity and Literature* 62, no. 1 (Autumn 2012): 63-94; and "A Naked Tree: The Love Sonnets of Joy Davidman to C. S. Lewis," *SEVEN: An Anglo-American Literary Review* 29 (2012): 79-102.

Introduction

In some ways it is unfortunate that Joy Davidman (1915-1960) is best known as the woman C. S. Lewis married in the last decade of his life. Davidman's relationship with Lewis has been explored on multiple levels, perhaps most famously in the 1993 film *Shadowlands,* starring Anthony Hopkins and Deborah Winger. While this attention has kept her name in the public eye, Lewis's reputation has obscured Davidman's own accomplishments as a writer. Although her letters, collected in *Out of My Bone: The Letters of Joy Davidman* (2009), have shed new light on important biographical details of Davidman's life, *Yet One More Spring* brings Davidman out of Lewis's shadow through an analytical study of her poetry, fiction, and nonfiction.

Davidman was an award-winning poet; in 1938 she received the Russell Loines Memorial award for poetry, given by the National Institute of Arts and Letters, for her *Letter to a Comrade* (1938). Her poems also appeared in journals such as *Poetry: A Magazine of Verse; Accent: A Quarterly of New Literature; Fantasy: A Literary Quarterly with an Emphasis on Poetry; New Masses; New Republic;* and in two book collections of verse: *Seven Poets in Search of an Answer* (1944), and *War Poems of the United Nations* (1943). She also published two novels, *Anya* (1940) and *Weeping Bay* (1950). In addition, she was a prolific book, theater, and film reviewer during the late 1930s and early 1940s for the *New Masses,* the semi-official magazine of the Communist Party of the United States of America. Her last book, *Smoke on the Mountain: An Interpretation of the Ten Commandments* (1955), is a fascinating exploration of the Decalogue. Despite this body of work, little critical work has been done on Davidman. For instance, there is no book-length study of her work, the few articles and reviews of her work are very dated, and the first biography of her life, by Lyle W. Dorsett, *And God Came In: The Extraordinary Story of Joy Davidman* (1983), is over thirty years old. Fortuitously, Abigail Santamaria's new biography, *Joy: Poet, Seeker, and the Woman Who Captivated C. S. Lewis,* was published in 2015.

Yet One More Spring intends to address this critical inattention through a chronological study of her writings, including both her published and unpublished works. As I was writing this book, a cache of her heretofore unknown manuscripts became available through Douglas Gresham, Davidman's younger son. In brief, the story of how these new manuscripts have come to light is as follows. In the early summer of 2010, Gresham was contacted by an ailing Jean Wakeman. Wakeman, who was Davidman's closest friend in England, spent a career as a motoring journalist. She often drove Davidman to various spots around Oxford, especially once Joy's bone cancer developed. As a young man Gresham often stayed with Wakeman, particularly after the death of his mother. Subsequent to Lewis's death she opened her home to Gresham for three years between 1963 and 1966. According to Gresham, Wakeman asked him to come and clean out her house after she moved into a caregiving facility. During the process of cleaning out Wakeman's house Gresham discovered not only a large number of his mother's unknown manuscripts, but also several manuscripts by Lewis.[1]

These new manuscripts, along with those previously collected, are available in The Joy Davidman Papers, 1926-1964, housed at the Marion E. Wade Center at Wheaton College. This treasure trove of material includes, among other things, twenty-seven previously unknown letters from Davidman to her husband, William Lindsay Gresham; to her sons, David and Douglas; and to her cousin, Renée Pierce, all written during her initial visit to England between August and December 1952 — the trip during which she first met C. S. Lewis.[2] Even more intriguing are manuscript versions of dozens of short stories; her unpublished novella, "Britannia over Brooklyn"; and over 250 previously unknown poems.[3] In particular, there is an

---

1. Regrettably, Wakeman died on August 16, 2010, at St. Luke's Nursing Home in Headington, England. For more on Wakeman's relationship with Gresham, see "Jean Wakeman (1920-2010)," *SEVEN: An Anglo-American Literary Review* 27 (2010): 5.

2. I discuss these letters in Chapter 8.

3. In the Joy Davidman Papers, Box 1, Series 4, Folder 27, there is her own index of over 230 poems that she wrote between August 1933 and January 1941. She lists the poems in chronological order; in addition, she indicates the number of lines contained in each poem. Of this group, thirty-two were published either in the literary journal *Poetry* or in her only published volume of poetry, *Letter to a Comrade* (New Haven: Yale University Press,

astonishing and beautiful sequence of forty-five love sonnets that Davidman wrote to Lewis.[4]

In moving through Davidman's work chronologically, I hope to accomplish several aims. First, in using this chronological approach I am making a critical case that Davidman's place in the canon of twentieth-century American literature deserves more attention than it has heretofore received, particularly because of her poetry. For instance, her poems — those appearing in *Letter to a Comrade* and elsewhere — give evidence of her efficacy as a poet; she uses irony effectively, her imagery is evocative and striking, and her subject matter exposes her profound understanding of the human condition. In addition, her work as a novelist and reviewer is also noteworthy and illustrates much about her intellectual, aesthetic, and artistic development.

Second, this chronological approach shows something of her religious, philosophical, and intellectual journey from secular Judaism to atheism to Communism to Christianity; her very personal engagement with these issues offers key insights into the historical milieu of America in the 1930s and 1940s. Despite the fact that Davidman later rejected the ideas she espoused as a fervent Communist, many readers will benefit from understanding her beliefs in the context of her published works. In fact, a number of once-active American Communists became disenchanted; while other studies exist documenting this disaffection, exploring Davidman's rejection of Communism provides important insights into her intellectual honesty and personal integrity.

Third, this chronological exploration of Davidman shows how she matured as a writer. I explore her commitment to the craft of writing, especially her voice, her rhetoric, her style, and the literary influences informing her work. She was very much a conscious craftswoman, spending the summers of 1938, 1940, 1941, and 1942 at the MacDowell Colony, a writers' retreat in

---

1938). A second index of sixty-five poems, this time in the form of a table of contents for an unpublished volume of poetry that may have been entitled "Courage," is found in folder 21. Sixteen of these poems were published between June 27, 1939, and July 31, 1945, in journals or books, including *Accent: A Quarterly of New Literature; Fantasy: A Literary Quarterly with an Emphasis on Poetry; New Masses; New Republic; Seven Poets in Search of an Answer*, ed. Thomas Yoseloff (New York: Bernard Ackerman, 1944); and *War Poems of the United Nations*, ed. Joy Davidman (New York: Dial Press, 1943). Several dozen additional poems not listed in either of these indices are scattered throughout folders 20-40; although Davidman dated some of these poems — some as late as 1954 — others are impossible to date with certainty. I discuss many of these poems in Chapter 5. Davidman's poetry is now collected in *A Naked Tree: Love Sonnets to C. S. Lewis and Other Poems* (Grand Rapids: Eerdmans, 2015).

4. I discuss this sonnet sequence in Chapter 8.

New Hampshire, where she honed her skills. For instance, her best piece of fiction, *Anya,* is a direct result of her time at the colony. She understood the intellectual energy it takes to become an effective writer of poetry, fiction, and nonfiction, and she never backed away from hard work.

Finally, this chronological survey reveals Davidman's literary influence upon Lewis, something that has not been sufficiently noted until now. In addition to examining the forty-five love sonnet sequence she wrote to Lewis, I argue that Lewis's autobiography, *Surprised by Joy* (1955), was influenced by his reading of Davidman's autobiographical essay, "The Longest Way Round" (1949), and that several other of Lewis's later works show the influence of Davidman.

At her best, Joy Davidman is a formidable poet. Her poem from *Letter to a Comrade,* "Yet One More Spring," gives striking evidence of this, suggesting that hers is a voice that is insistent and hard to forget:

> What will come of me
> After the fern has feathered from my brain
> And the rosetree out of my blood; what will come of me
> In the end, under the rainy locustblossom
> Shaking its honey out on springtime air
> Under the wind, under the stooping sky?
> What will come of me and shall I lie
> Voiceless forever in earth and unremembered,
> And be forever the cold green blood of flowers
> And speak forever with the tongue of grass
> Unsyllabled, and sound no louder
> Than the slow falling downward of white water,
> And only speak the quickened sandgrain stirring,
> Only the whisper of the leaf unfolding,
> Only the tongue of leaves forever and ever?
>
> Out of my heart the bloodroot,
> Out of my tongue the rose,
> Out of my bone the jointed corn,
> Out of my fiber trees.
> Out of my mouth a sunflower,
> And from my fingers vines,
> And the rank dandelion shall laugh from my loins
> Over million seeded earth; but out of my heart,

Core of my heart, blood of my heart, the bloodroot
Coming to lift a petal in peril of snow,
Coming to dribble from a broken stem
Bitterly the bright color of blood forever.

But I would be more than a cold voice of flowers
And more than water, more than sprouting earth
Under the quiet passion of the spring;
I would leave you the trouble of my heart
To trouble you at evening; I would perplex you
With lightning coming and going about my head,
Outrageous signs, and wonders; I would leave you
The shape of my body filled with images,
The shape of my mind filled with imaginations,
The shape of myself. I would create myself
In a little fume of words and leave my words
After my death to kiss you forever and ever.[5]

I hope this critical exploration of her poetry, fiction, and nonfiction advances the argument that Joy Davidman is a writer deserving of much more scholarly attention and discussion. Moreover, for those interested in her relationship with Lewis, *Yet One More Spring: A Critical Study of Joy Davidman* provides new insights into how she won the heart of the most important Christian apologist of the twentieth century.

June 2015
Montreat College
Montreat, NC

---

5. *Naked Tree,* 134-35.

Chronology of Joy Davidman's Life (1915-1960)

April 18, 1915. Helen Joy Davidman is born to Joseph and Jeannette Davidman.

1919. Joy's brother Howard is born.

Joy is brought up in and around New York City with summer vacations to Maine and other New England sites.

By age twelve she is an atheist and a writer.

As a young teenager she suffers from early thyroid problems and is treated with a radium-laced collar that she wears to bed.

1929. Joy finishes high school at age fourteen.

1930. She matriculates at Hunter College in 1930 and becomes an associate editor for the *Echo,* the college's literary magazine.

1934. She graduates from Hunter College, begins teaching English in local high schools, and matriculates at Columbia University for an MA in English.

1935. She earns her MA from Columbia University. Her master's thesis is titled "My Lord of Orrery."

1936. She continues high school teaching and publishes poems in the important literary journal, *Poetry.*

1938. Joy's volume of poetry, *Letter to a Comrade,* is published to favorable reviews and wins the Russell Loines Memorial award for poetry given by the National Institute of Arts and Letters. Also, after several abortive attempts, she joins the Communist Party of the United States of America (CPUSA) and throws herself into the cause as an editor for its magazine, *New Masses.* She spends the summer at the MacDowell Colony, a writers' retreat in New Hampshire; she returns there in the summers of 1940, 1941, and 1942.

1939. She moves for six months to Hollywood in a failed effort at writing screenplays.

1940. Her novel, *Anya,* is published.

1941-43. Her poems and reviews are appearing regularly in the *New Masses.*

1942. She meets William Lindsay Gresham; they are married near the MacDowell Colony on August 2, 1942.

1943. She edits and publishes the *War Poems of the United Nations,* a collection of poems with a strong pro-Communism bias.

March 27, 1944. David Gresham is born; Joy is gradually becoming disillusioned with Communism.

November 10, 1945. Douglas Gresham is born.

1946. Bill Gresham publishes the very successful novel *Nightmare Alley;* using some of the proceeds, Joy and Bill purchase a large farm house in New York; Joy is no longer active in the CPUSA. Also, she has a mystical experience that leads her from atheism to theism.

1947. Joy begins reading books by C. S. Lewis and eventually converts to Christianity.

1948. She becomes a member of the Pleasant Plains Presbyterian Church.

1949. She begins corresponding with Chad Walsh; Bill Gresham publishes his second novel, *Limbo Tower.*

January 10, 1950. C. S. Lewis receives his first letter from Joy.

1950. Joy's novel, *Weeping Bay,* is published.

1951. The autobiographical essay of her conversion, "The Longest Way Round," is published.

August 1952. Her marriage to Bill falling apart, Joy sails for England to visit friends and to meet Lewis.

September 24, 1952. Joy meets and has lunch with Lewis.

Christmas 1952. She spends Christmas with Lewis and his brother, Warren, at their home near Oxford, the Kilns.

January 1953. She returns to New York and the eventual break-up of her marriage to Bill.

February 1953. She becomes a member of the Episcopal Church.

November 1953. Joy and her sons arrive in London; Joy believes they can live more cheaply in England than in New York.

Christmas 1953. Lewis and Warren invite the three to spend the holidays at the Kilns.

For the next eighteen months Joy and the boys eke out an existence in London with the boys going to a boarding school. At the same time, Joy and

Lewis spend a good deal of time together; he loves her wit, intellect, sense of humor, and sharp mind.

1954. She publishes *Smoke on the Mountain: An Interpretation of the Ten Commandments.*

August 1955. Joy, probably with help from Lewis, rents a house in Headington, about a mile from the Kilns.

September 13, 1955. Lewis writes his lifelong friend, Arthur Greeves, that he is thinking of marrying Joy in a civil ceremony.

April 23, 1956. Lewis marries Joy in a civil ceremony; they live separately.

October 18, 1956. Joy falls when her left femur snaps; she is told she has advanced cancer and that it has spread throughout her body.

December 24, 1956. Lewis publishes a public announcement of his marriage to Joy in the *The Times;* Joy begins to live at the Kilns.

Lewis, now completely in love with Joy, asks the Bishop of Oxford to conduct a religious wedding; he refuses. In desperation, Lewis asks a former pupil and Anglican priest, Peter Bide, to come to the hospital and offer a prayer of healing; while there Lewis asks Bide to marry them; Bide agrees and marries them in the hospital on March 21, 1957.

Joy recovers and for the better part of two and a half years they experience real happiness.

July 1958. Lewis and Joy take a wonderful trip by plane to Ireland.

December 1959. Joy's cancer begins to return.

April 3-14, 1960. Lewis and Joy take another delightful trip, this time to Greece.

May 20, 1960. Joy's cancer returns with a vengeance. She is hospitalized again.

July 13, 1960. Joy dies. Lewis later told a friend: "I never expected to have, in my sixties, the happiness that passed me by in my twenties."

September 1962. Bill Gresham dies.

November 22, 1963. Lewis dies peacefully, the same day that John F. Kennedy is fatally wounded in Dallas.

CHAPTER 1

Early Writings (1929-1938)

Joy Davidman was a brilliant young woman — graduating from high school at fourteen, earning her BA in English from Hunter College at nineteen, and completing her MA in English from Columbia University at twenty. Given her precocious academic accomplishments in literary studies, it comes as no surprise to learn that she was writing poetry from an early age. Although we cannot date precisely her first poem, we do know she was writing creatively as a young teenager since she identified herself as a poet at the age of fourteen in her autobiographical essay, "The Longest Way Round":

> When I was fourteen I went walking in the park on a Sunday afternoon, in clean, cold, luminous air. The trees tinkled with sleet; the city noises were muffled by the snow. Winter sunset, with a line of young maples sheathed in ice between me and the sun — as I looked up they burned unimaginably golden — burned and were not consumed. I heard the voice in the burning tree; the meaning of all things was revealed and the sacrament at the heart of all beauty lay bare; time and space fell away, and for a moment the world was only a door swinging ajar. Then the light faded, the cold stung my toes, and I went home, reflecting that I had had another aesthetic experience. I had them fairly often. That was what beautiful things did to you, I recognized, probably because of some visceral or glandular reaction that hadn't been fully explored by science just yet. For I was a well-brought-up, right-thinking child of materialism. Beauty, I knew, existed; but God, of course, did not. . . . A young poet like myself could be seized and shaken by spiritual powers

a dozen times a day, and still take it for granted *that* there was no such thing as spirit.[1]

Although this passage focuses upon her early atheism, it is marked by several poetic phrases, including "clean, cold, luminous air," "trees tinkled with sleet," and "a line of young maples sheathed in ice" that "burned unimaginably golden." Moreover, she confesses that "a young poet like myself" was often in the grip of overwhelming aesthetic experiences, and poems from this period offer multiple examples of her longing for beauty. For instance, in "What Spur of Gold Is This That Pricks the Dawn?," a poem that dates from January 1929 when she was thirteen, Davidman writes:

What spur of gold is this that pricks the dawn
To further flaming of its fierce desire
Of glory? On the eager winds of morn
Comes blowing down the soul-devouring fire
That keenly lashes the mad spirit higher
And higher yet; the dry hot fever of fame,
The far bright crown to which all slaves aspire —
Need most imperative, to which the name
Of fondest love shows but a flickering flame.[2]

This poem is a modest enough effort, yet her ease in using alliteration, metaphor, alternate rhyme, and iambic pentameter demonstrate her earnest commitment to the craft of verse; in addition, the longing to experience life fully, including the aspiration for fame, marks an early thematic focus in her verse. She also notes in her autobiographical essay that

like most adolescents, I was really two people. The hard, cocksure young atheist was largely what psychologists call a "persona," a mask, a surface personality for dealing with the world. In the greedy, grabbing,

---

1. First printed in *These Found the Way: Thirteen Converts to Protestant Christianity*, ed. David Wesley Soper (Philadelphia: Westminster, 1951). Reprinted in *Out of My Bone: The Letters of Joy Davidman* (hereafter *Bone*), ed. Don W. King (Grand Rapids: Eerdmans, 2009), here 83 and 84. Because *These Found the Way* is difficult to find, all references to "The Longest Way Round" are from *Bone*.

2. *A Naked Tree: Love Sonnets to C. S. Lewis and Other Poems* (hereafter *Naked Tree*), ed. Don W. King (Grand Rapids: Eerdmans, 2015), 1; in this chapter, all page references given in parentheses in the text are from *Naked Tree*.

big-city, middle-class world I knew, this seemed the sort of person that was wanted. But underneath the surface my own real personality stirred, stretched its wings, discovered its own tastes. It was a girl with vague eyes, who scribbled verses — scribbled them in a blind fury, not knowing what she wrote or why, and read them afterward with wonder. We call that fury "poetic inspiration" nowadays; we might be wiser to call it "prophecy."[3]

Over one hundred early poems dating from 1929 to 1938 give full evidence of Davidman's earliest efforts as a poet who "scribbled verses . . . in a blind fury."[4]

After she matriculated at Hunter College in New York City, she soon became an associate editor for the college's literary magazine, the *Echo*. In addition to her editorial duties, she published translations of two French poems — "Clair de Lune" by Paul Verlaine (1844-1896) and "Odelette" by Henri de Regnier (1864-1936) in the Christmas 1932 issue.[5] Both are romantic reveries. "Clair de Lune" honors "conquering love and life" and the "sad light of the calm moon," which makes "the quiet birds" and a tall fountain "sob with its ecstasy, in the silver gleam" (5-6). "Odelette" celebrates nature, especially how a native instrument quickens life in the forest:

> I with just one little reed
> Can make the high trees quiver,
> And the dew-cool meadow,
> And the gentle willow
> And the ever-singing river.
> I with just this hollow reed
> Have awakened the wood to song.

This song evokes love and makes "whoever passes weep" (6-7). The importance of romantic love in Davidman's later poetry first finds expression in these early translations.

Several of her short stories also appeared in the *Echo*. "Reveal the Titan" is the story of Philip, a musician and composer, who finds himself unable

---

3. *Bone,* 86.

4. Poems from this period are in *Naked Tree,* 1-89.

5. Although Verlaine was Davidman's favorite French poet (she translated over a dozen of his poems), she also translated the poems of several others, including Charles D'Orléans (1394-1465), François Villon (1431-1463), and Francis Jammes (1868-1938); see the Joy Davidman Papers (hereafter DP), especially Box 1, Series 4, Folder 39.

to write music after having run away to France; in an effort to rekindle his creativity, he decides to return to Presqu'Isle, the place of his boyhood and early life.[6] After arriving, his muse almost immediately returns: "Philip felt the coming of the tone-poem, 'Prometheus.' The vast waves of the orchestra rose surging through him; this was the place, this loneliness was the temple of his thought. He did not need a woman, or anyone; only sand and the lake, and to be alone." Yet he is quickly drawn again to Marian, the woman he had abandoned there five years earlier when he went to France to write his music. When he finds Marian, he also discovers she has a six-year-old son, Paul, and it takes Philip only a few minutes to realize Paul is his son. However, when Philip begins to recriminate against himself for deserting her, Marian assures him altruistically: "But it was all right, alone. . . . You've been what you should be. What . . . I wanted you to be." Philip begins teaching Paul the piano, impressed that his son has perfect pitch. For several days following, Philip and Marian are often together — happy and in love. But it is a short reprieve: "He could not keep this mood. . . . Her head might be on his shoulder, yet presently one of them would sigh, would turn, and the moment would be flung aside. Presently, his life would go journeying on other pathways. . . . Meanwhile Philip let music blow by on the wind, and clung to his life in the woman and the child."

After Philip takes Paul on an outing — during which Paul accidentally falls into the lake — Marian is furious: "Never take Paul anywhere again. Do you understand? . . . You want him for a toy to make music. I've had him, he's mine — there's no part of you in him!" Even though they try to reconcile, Philip is distraught: "He wandered about the streets; there was no help. Not Marian. And he had lost the Prometheus. . . . Something in him was jarred and sick." But then he finds himself at twilight on Presqu'Isle and throws himself down on the sand: "So softly, so vaguely that it was only the rippling water, a violin awoke at the back of his mind. Light as a feather, the song dipped and circled; and then it grew till it was the full chorus of the strings resounding. There came a deep-voiced answer from the horns. Philip sprang to his feet and stood with arms outstretched. So the dawn parted to reveal the Titan, transpierced upon his rock within the empty sky!" He returns to his hotel room inspired and writes all night, "covering sheets of paper with the swift skeletons of notes." He rushes to Marian the next day and plays key

6. "Reveal the Titan," *Echo,* May 1934, 26-36. For an early version of this story, see DP, Box 1, Series 5, Folder 66. Presqu'Isle is a sandy peninsula that arches into Lake Erie in Erie County, Pennsylvania.

sections for her; she is impressed: "It's going to be wonderful, Philip." Yet despite their affection for each other, that afternoon Philip and Marian agree to part "before we hate each other." The story ends with Philip choosing art over love: "The train climbed eastward. Eyes that were both alien and familiar faded into the distance in his mind, into the blue waters of his youth. There was no crystal glaze of sunlight over his life any longer; Philip sighed. And long chanting phrases of music began to take form in his brain. Philip took out a sheet of paper, and the train wheels beat in his ears the rhythm of a great chorale."

"Reveal the Titan" is noteworthy on several accounts. First, Davidman handles the details of the story — plot, characterization, dialogue, and setting — competently, especially for a nineteen-year-old. Second, she works hard to make us understand what makes Philip tick; that is, she does more than simply create a straw man that she can then take apart. While it is clear her overall attitude toward him is ironic, she avoids making him flat and one-dimensional. He is not the first artist to sacrifice human relationships in pursuit of his muse; perhaps there is something in him that Davidman herself identifies with. Marian is harder to warm to — on the one hand, she readily welcomes Philip back after five years of raising their child alone, but, on the other hand, she reacts in an unreasonably harsh way over the accident. Third, that the great tone-poem Philip is seeking to write is entitled "Prometheus" illustrates Davidman's effort to link her story to a larger mythology.[7] Here, however, she is not entirely successful; why she evokes the name of Prometheus — the Titan who stole fire from heaven in order to give it to humankind and whose punishment from Zeus included being chained to a rock and daily having his liver devoured by an eagle — is never made clear; perhaps irony is intended as Davidman means to undercut Philip's over-inflated sense of his tone-poem's grandeur. Finally, Davidman largely avoids the pitfall of many novice short story writers — she shows rather than tells.

Her second story appearing in the *Echo*, "Apostate" is the story of Chinya — a proud, head-strong, independent young Jewish woman who lives in the kosher enclave of the small Russian village of Toultchin sometime in the last decade of the nineteenth century.[8] The story opens with news of the long-expected return of her three brothers from Odessa — all known thieves. To

---

7. In January 1938, Davidman wrote a poem entitled "Prometheus"; *Naked Tree*, 45.

8. "Apostate," *Echo*, November 1934, 17-26. Toultchin (today Tulchin) is a city in the southern part of Ukraine along the Selnitsa River. It is about 390 km northwest of Odessa. For an early version of this story, see DP, Box 1, Series 5, Folder 44.

celebrate, she begins planning a great *simcha* to mark her brothers' home-coming.[9] Her father is the village goldsmith, "Nachman Goldschmidt, the gonif!"[10] Nachman and Chinya are often at odds; when she will not do as he says, Nachman beats her: "Chinya fought back cheerfully, and upon occasion she tore his shirt or blackened his eye. She was not submissive; at such times Nachman rather regretted his dead wife. Chinya did not resemble her mother, yet Nachman's temper wearied her."

Chinya's unyielding nature creates a crisis when she goes to the *schochet* to secure ingredients for a special *kishkeh* she plans to make for her brothers.[11] Another woman, Surka, fights with Chinya over the prized portion of a recently slaughtered bull's intestines, "clear and glistening, covered with a network of small purple veins and with luscious lumps of fat." Chinya yanks the intestines away and taunts Surka: "Kishkeh you want, fat sow!" She then hurries to a local *yarid* and gets into another tussle, this time over an ornamental shawl, with the local hunchbacked *schadchen*, Enya.[12] Seeing Enya draped with the shawl, Chinya mocks her: "Look, the hunchback makes herself beautiful to catch a man!" When Chinya grabs the shawl, Surka comes up from behind and a battle royale begins, much to the delight of the locals:

> "Ah — a zhidovka fight!" and the moujiks laughed deeply. The two snarled with sharp teeth; their arms whirled fantastically in the air. Enya was knocked over as she tried to kick Chinya from behind. Surka tore the girl's collar; her own shawl was pulled from her head. Her cropped black hair, the hair of a respectable married Jewess, stuck out stiffly in all directions. The moujiks threw back their heads and roared, their bearded throats quivering ecstatically. Now the fat woman bellowed suddenly as Chinya hit her in the stomach.[13]

Chinya walks away from the fight with the shawl while Enya screams "venomous insults after her."

The commotion attracts the notice of a local *moujik*, Ivan Mihailovitch, "a young peasant with bright-colored eyes and a soft beard." He begins

9. A *simcha* is a party or celebration.

10. *Gonif* is Yiddish for thief.

11. A *schochet* (or *skokhet*) is a kosher butcher. *Kishkeh* is a sausage stuffed in part with *kasha* (cereal).

12. A *yarid* is a local market or fair; a *schadchen* (or *shadhken*) is a marriage broker.

13. *Zhidovka* is a derogatory name for a Jewish woman; a *moujik* is a non-Jewish Russian peasant.

walking beside Chinya, attracted by her physical beauty and her resilient character, even though, as he admits to her: "You, you are a zhidovka." In spite of the cultural and religious chasm between them, Ivan cannot help himself; soon they are off to the forest and a quick courtship ensues. Kisses are followed by a proposal from Ivan: "If you will be a Christian, zhidovka . . . I will marry you." At first Chinya coyly turns him down, but she too is drawn to forbidden fruit: "Ivan kissed her again, and she put her hands on his shoulders. She liked the flesh and the heavy hard bones underneath." He presses her for an answer to his proposal and assures her that "it is right to be a Christian." Chinya promises to give him an answer on the morrow, and as they part she calls out "I am Chinya."

When she returns home that evening, she muses over what makes her a Jew: "She could not feel anything in her body that belonged to the synagogue and the Law, anything that was unalterably the enemy of Ivan. If she was baptized by the priest and lived with Ivan Mihailovitch and ate pig meat, her body would still be Chinya. Yet, for her father, being a Jew was real. She was hearing his voice in the back of her mind, the chant of the Sabbath ritual, the undertone of a sorrowing exultation." Her reverie is interrupted when she learns that her father is negotiating with Enya regarding a husband for her. Upon finding out that her intended is the bookish scholar Avrom, Chinya tells her father: "He looks like a wet cat." Their tempers flare, and after Chinya complains that Avrom is "a soft lump of tallow, an ugly worm," Nachman cuffs her and she throws a pot at him. Her final word is that "Avrom should go marry the Talmud." Accordingly, we are not surprised when on the following day she tells Ivan she will marry him. He explains that she must be baptized, take the Christian name Katerina, and do as the priest tells her. At the back of his mind, however, Ivan has doubts and thinks " 'once a Jewess, always a Jewess.' But she tasted sweet to his lips."

Word soon spreads in the village that in five days a Jewess is to be baptized; Chinya hopes that her father will not hear the rumors and that her brothers will "not come home until she [is] safely a Christian." On the day of the baptism, Enya learns that Chinya is the convert; she does not care since both Avrom and Nachman have paid for her services: "It was good, and it was a good joke on Nachman the gonif. . . . A daughter dipped in the brook and turned into a Christian! Enya even laughed. Presently she went to tell her friend Surka." When Nachman learns what is happening, he rushes down to the river. Most of the Christians there are watching Chinya distrustfully (some believe she is a witch who has enchanted Ivan), and none act graciously toward her. In fact, Chinya is forced to eat a piece of bacon: "Chinya took the bacon; the stuff was cold and clung against her skin. There were several boys leaning forward at her; they laughed and urged her to eat. She threw back her head and put the bacon in her mouth." As she kneels for the ceremony, her father and brothers burst on the scene, break up the baptism, and beat Chinya with their belts all the way home. Ivan is tempted to step in, but his cousin grabs him and reminds him that she " 'is only a zhidovka.' . . . In the end, a Jewess was always a Jewess." Chinya's humiliation is compounded by the indifference of the priest, the grinning *moujiks,* and "Surka's mouth of malign satisfaction." Avrom tries to intervene, but Chinya's brothers tell him to come for her later — after the beating. The story ends violently:

> She fell on the path; she fell more than once on the road to the village, her dress was gradually cut to shreds, she had mud in her hair. All the way into the Jewish quarter of Toultchin her brothers beat her, and the whooping, braying crowd of moujiks followed all the way. Chinya turned in fury and cried out at them; then one of the women crossed herself, but the others were in a passion of delight. They whistled, they stamped their feet for pure joy, they leaped high in the air and laughed, how they laughed!

"Apostate" is a significant advance over "Reveal the Titan." The description is more visually (and, to some degree, viscerally) compelling. During the scene when the bull is butchered, we read:

> They had trussed the animal up, so that he was quite helpless as the knife came to cut his throat. . . . There was a brief roar of pain; Chinya elbowed her way to the door. She saw the dead animal in his brown hide, with blood coming from him, a raw and shocking vividness in the sunlight. Chinya felt rather pleased at the shiny pool and at the odor that rose in the air. Then the butcher ripped the bull's hide loose like a peasant pulling off his wife's smock.

And Davidman deftly describes Chinya early on the morning of the young woman's anticipated baptism: "In the vague sweet morning Chinya woke and stood in the center of the room; when she stretched her arms the soft brown hairs on them stirred in the shadowy wind. She felt the cool air on her flesh; then she was warm, a driving warmth spread up through her body and out like a fan through her breasts and up to her lips." The not so subtly implied sexual awakening and yearnings of Chinya come through clearly in this passage.

Another strength is Davidman's effective characterization, particularly the way the antipathy between father and daughter is held in dramatic tension throughout the story; there is never a softening between them. Nachman does not understand his daughter and treats her as chattel, reflecting the patriarchal cultural milieu of the story. At the same time, Chinya sets her will against the machinations conspiring to keep her "in her place," and her rebellion moves well beyond mere childish disobedience; in her willful break with cultural and religious expectations, she sets into motion an inevitable chain of events culminating in her being thwarted and forced back into the very situation from which she is trying to escape. It is worth noting that Davidman's relationship with her father was similarly tense. According to Lyle Dorsett in his biography of Davidman, Joseph Davidman was extremely demanding, insisting that his daughter excel at the highest level, no matter the situation. While the source of the tension between the Davidmans was different from that of Nachman and Chinya, the resulting friction may have found expression in "Apostate."[14]

Still another advance over "Reveal the Titan" is how Davidman handles religious themes in "Apostate." Specifically, Davidman's exploration of the loss of faith in this story — albeit Chinya's understanding of her Jewish faith is superficial and not actualized (another source of tension between father and daughter) — indicates her own subconscious interest in religious matters, something she affirms throughout "The Longest Way Round." There, after noting her conversion to theism, she writes about apostasy:

> All my atheist life I had regarded the "apostate" with traditional Jewish horror. What I wanted was to become a good Jew, of the comfortable "Reformed" persuasion. I had the usual delusion that "all religions mean the same thing." Fortunately I had learned my lesson, and this time I looked before I leaped; I *studied* religions, and found them anything but the same thing. Some of them had wisdom up to a point, some of them had good ethical intentions, some of them had flashes of spiritual insight; but only one of them had complete understanding of the grace and repentance and charity

---

14. Lyle W. Dorsett, *And God Came In: The Extraordinary Story of Joy Davidman* (New York: Macmillan, 1983). Dorsett writes: "Because the perfect father could never be wrong, and because Joy was driven to be perfect, too, there was no way that she and her father could take opposite sides on an issue and leave it at that; agreement to disagree was out of the question. Inevitably, discussions evolved into arguments, and arguments eventually led to long-lasting resentments" (11). See also Abigail Santamaria, *Joy: Poet, Seeker, and the Woman Who Captivated C. S. Lewis* (New York: Houghton Mifflin Harcourt, 2015), ch. 1.

that had come to me from God. And the Redeemer who had made himself known, whose personality I would have recognized among ten thousand — well, when I read the New Testament, I recognized him. He was Jesus.[15]

While "Apostate" makes no overt references to Christ, the fact that Chinya "wondered what made her a Jew" and that she "could not feel anything in her body that belonged to the synagogue and the Law" suggests Davidman's own lack of rootedness in Judaism, almost certainly bolstered by her father's rejection of its theological underpinnings: "My father declared proudly that he had retained the ethics of Judaism, the only 'real' part of it, and got rid of the theology — rather as if he had kept the top floor of our house but torn down first floor and foundation. When I came along, I noticed that there was nothing supporting the ethics; down it crashed."[16] Unlike the irony associated with the self-absorbed Philip in "Reveal the Titan," in "Apostate" Chinya is a complex character who, caught in a cramped, stifling, repressive society, attempts to break free; that she is cruelly prevented — beaten, shamed, and driven home by her father and brothers — is a pointed critique, not of her, but of the patriarchal domination of women in a religious system that values form over substance.[17]

Davidman continued writing poetry and fiction, but in the fall of 1934 she matriculated at Columbia University and began a master's program in English literature. As an important part of completing the requirements for her MA, she had to write a scholarly thesis. The result, "My Lord of Orrery," concerns the life and writings of the Renaissance figure Roger Boyle, Lord Broghill, First Earl of Orrery (1621-79).[18] Boyle is a curious choice as the object of a literary thesis since he is known primarily as a statesman, soldier, and administrator. He served under Oliver Cromwell during the English

---

15. *Bone*, 96. I explore in greater detail Davidman's conversion to Christianity in Chapter 7.

16. *Bone*, 84.

17. It should be pointed out that Davidman's talents as a fiction writer were recognized when "Apostate" appeared: the *Echo* announced it as the winner of the Bernard Cohen Prize Story. In addition, Davidman revived details of the plot, characters, and themes of "Apostate" in "Descent into Darkness," the penultimate chapter of her novel *Anya* (1940). Specifically, Chinya, her father, and her thieving brothers have a central place in this chapter. For more on this, see Chapter 6.

18. The cover sheet of her thesis includes her name, the date the degree was to be conferred — December 1935 — and this statement: "Submitted in partial fulfillment of the requirements for the degree of Master of Arts in the Department of English and Comparative Literature, Faculty of Philosophy, Columbia University."

Civil War, yet after the Restoration of Charles II in 1660 Boyle became a popular poet and dramatist at the court. In the foreword, Davidman explains why she has written her thesis on Boyle:

> Some men, it has been remarked, are poems; others only make poems. Lord Orrery was a litterateur only in his spare time; the formidable bulk of his writings represents unconsidered trifles cast off by his energetic mind; but his life was a lively adventure far more vital than any he could have written. It is therefore necessary, in his biography, to focus much attention upon matters not primarily literary, yet the cause of literature does not thereby suffer; for to convey a spirited idea of high life in the seventeenth century to the reader is sufficient aim in itself, and, also, in Orrery's life helps to explain the somewhat surprising influence which his works exercised upon English literature. A man who wrote the first romance [*Parthenissa,* 1676] and the first heroic play [*The Generall,* 1663] in English, in his spare moments, does indeed deserve some attention; and what significance his story has may be found not only in the debatable value of his writing, but in the picturesque and unquestionable color of my lord's personality.

Moreover, she justifies her thesis by saying "here, for the first time, is an attempt to tell Orrery's story as amusingly as possible."

As a piece of scholarly writing, "My Lord of Orrery" is not very good. On the one hand, at 269 pages with 1,326 footnotes, it is a massive effort; on the other hand, it is highly derivative — often every sentence in a paragraph is footnoted. In addition, it is neither critical nor analytical since for the most part it relies on standard sources in order to retell Orrery's life. Yet we never get to know Orrery beyond the external facts — Davidman provides no "inside view" of Orrery, and she offers little discussion of his interior life. The writing is colloquial and pedestrian at best. For example, in describing an attack of gout Orrery experienced in June 1664, she writes: "This was not the sort of gout that annoys one's great toe. It traveled up my lord's legs, played a military tattoo on his spine, paralyzed his wrists and exploded terrifically inside his skull." Later she says that Orrery sent an underling a "message which would have blistered the skin of a rhinoceros."[19] The most interesting thing about the thesis concerns the fifteen chapter titles; all are phrases from *As You Like It* — fourteen come from Jaques's famous "All the world's a stage" speech in Act II, scene 7, and one comes from Touchstone's catalog of

19. "My Lord of Orrery," 164, 260.

quarrelling styles in Act V, scene 4. Perhaps coming up with the chapter titles was a creative coping mechanism Davidman employed while performing her obligatory academic writing and research assignment. Moreover, that Davidman selected Orrery as the subject of her thesis is ironic since she was on the verge of becoming a fervent Communist.

With her thesis out of the way, Davidman concentrated her efforts on her chief literary gift: writing poetry. Her continued devotion to verse was rewarded in 1936 when two poems were published in the highly regarded literary journal, *Poetry: A Magazine of Verse.* "Resurrection" and "Amulet" appeared in the January 1936 issue. "Resurrection" is written in six-line stanzas of iambic tetrameter with an *abbacc* rhyme scheme.[20] While Davidman had touched in a general way upon lost religious faith in "Apostate," in this poem she focuses upon the person of Christ. Here she considers the dead and unrisen Jesus, who has been "stripped of [his] body to the bone":

> This is the kingdom that you find
> When the brave empty eye-holes stare
> Impartially against the air;
> A little universe defined
> By infinite white ribs for bars
> Against the struggles of the stars. (15)

Yet Davidman does not mock this mistaken savior; rather, her tone is one of pity over a wasted life: "This is the glory that you have: / A broad sun

---

20. Later Davidman commented about the occasion of writing "Resurrection":

This inner personality was deeply interested in Christ, and didn't know it. As a Jew, I had been led to feel cold chills at the mention of his name. Is this strange? For a thousand years Jews have lived among people who interpreted Christ's will to mean floggings and burnings, "gentleman's agreements," and closed universities. If nominal Christians so confuse their Master's teaching, surely a poor Jew may be pardoned a little confusion. Nevertheless I had read the Bible (for its literary beauty, of course!) and I quoted Jesus unconsciously in everything I did, from writing verse to fighting my parents. My first published poem *was* called "Resurrection" — a sort of private argument with Jesus, attempting to convince him (and myself) that he had never risen. I wrote it at Easter, of all possible seasons, and never guessed why.

The cross recurs through most of my early poems, and I seem to remember explaining that Jesus was "a valuable literary convention." Those verses were mainly the desperate question: Is life really only a matter of satisfying one's appetites, or is there more? (*Bone*, 86)

See also the discussion in Chapter 2, below, of the poem "Againrising" from *Letter to a Comrade* (New Haven: Yale University Press, 1938); *Naked Tree*, 148-49.

standing overhead / To shape a halo for your head" (15-16). The poem ends with a final vision that underscores the futile belief that Jesus could conquer physical death:

> Symbols for the celebrant
> Are your sharp and silver feet,
> Syllables he shall repeat;
> So your light bones lie aslant
> The mystical and sacred sun —
> Infinity in skeleton. (16)

The bleak image of the wind and sun playing over the exposed bones of Jesus lends the poem its final irony.[21]

"Amulet" is a sonnet that contains both a threat and an anodyne. The threat comes in the octave as a lover promises to be "a serpent that will suck your blood, / Sting your bare eyes, or pleasurably drain / Sweet fiery thought and honey from your brain, / And find the savor of your heartstrings good" (22). The lover intends to "unclothe your spirit of your skin" in relentless and obsessive pursuit of the beloved. The anodyne comes in the sestet where the beloved is told how to counter the incantatory power of the magical ornament:

> This is the way to keep your soul from me;
> Let the sweet lure and the entangled guile
> Crumble before your tolerant clear smile;
> And let your cold and lovely honesty
> Within my semblance made of shallow glass
> Read my desires of you as they pass. (22)

Obsessive lovers appear often in Davidman's love poetry as we will see below (and also in *Letter to a Comrade*). However, the difference in "Amulet" is that the lover offers the beloved an out; in the later poems, the lover offers no such possibility — indeed, the lover's obsession becomes an intractable possessiveness.

In March 1937 more poems appeared in *Poetry*. In lines of rhyming iambic trimeter couplets, "Variations on a Theme" considers several different impli-

---

21. Davidman initially considered including a longer version of "Resurrection" in *Letter to a Comrade;* for more on this see Bone, 3, 6-8, and 12.

cations of the Latin phrase *non omnis moriar*, I shall not wholly die.[22] After her death, the speaker affirms that her soul will be "too tenuous for fate, / And too bereft of blood / For the abhorrent God / To tatter and mar" (28). Instead she imagines her soul, "floating and alone," free of pain and released from the confines of her body. Wordsworth-like, she will ascend above the earth, and "flit out of death; / The tinsel soul shall go / Higher than mountain snow / Into the windy air" (28-29). In the end she insists that "I shall not wholly die / While death begets a flower" (29). In an irony she is blind to, while Davidman cannot have it that Jesus lives on in "Resurrection," she can insist via the speaker in this poem that her spirit will live on and not wholly die.

"The Half-Hearted," written in lines of alternating iambic pentameter rhyme, portrays another obsessive lover.[23] Here a woman, intent on winning the man she loves, contrives many ways to win him: "I have created mountains and designed / Cold flowerings of frost to please my love" (23). She, like the obsessive lover in "Amulet," is not above using magic in order to obtain him: "I give the sorceries that I have written, / My sharp and subtle arabesques of wit; / Is there an alchemy I have forgotten? / Is there a sacrament that I omit?" (23-24).[24] Even the half-heartedness of her beloved does not thwart her obsession: "The harsh imperial carving of his head / Will never turn its marble to a kiss / Though my soft mouth were singing or were dead; / And yet I love my love no less for this" (24). "Odi et Amo" explores the paradox of the Latin phrase that means "I hate and I love."[25] Throughout most of this terza rime poem yet another obsessive lover catalogs what she would have done to win her beloved: "I would have given you this flower or that, / Tears for your pleasures, roses for your grief, . . . / A flare of laughter, and a fancy rife with spirits to inform the silver breath; / All this for love" (20). However, no matter her intentions, her beloved appears oblivious to her passion. As a result, her desire turns to hate: "For this ungentle strife / I shall find present ways to give you death" (20).[26]

---

22. "Variations on a Theme," *Poetry* 49 (March 1937): 323-24.

23. "The Half-Hearted," *Poetry* 49 (March 1937): 325.

24. Several poems in *Letter to a Comrade* also employ the idea of using sorcery or black magic in order to secure the beloved. See especially "Sorceress Eclogue" and "Night-Piece," *Naked Tree*, 129-31, 116-17.

25. "Odi et Amo," *Poetry* 49 (March 1937): 327.

26. A fourth poem appeared at the same time as these three: "Shadow Dance," *Poetry* 49 (March 1937): 326; *Naked Tree*, 29-30. Davidman initially considered including "Shadow Dance" in *Letter to a Comrade*; see *Bone*, 3, 10, 12. Perhaps one explanation for Davidman's many poems dealing with romantic love stems from an affair she had with one of her profes-

I turn now to offering an assessment of Davidman's other poems written between 1929 and 1938; in this regard I will be selective with an eye for pieces that either illustrate thematic foci already discussed or offer insights into the direction her later published poetry would go. I begin with two critical observations. First, she experimented a good deal with the sonnet. This is significant because it contrasts dramatically with the paucity of sonnets in her published work. Moreover, she has a facile hand with the sonnet, and it proves to be a natural medium for much of her love poetry. Second, while some of her poems celebrate nature's beauty ("Midsummer Madness" [4], written in summer 1930), emphasize the tawdriness of city life ("Office Windows" [68-71]; August 1938), and muse upon the human condition ("Whom They Destroy" [13]; October 1933), the primary focus is upon romantic love, including not only sexual longings but also the anticipation of sexual consummation as well as the anguish of a scorned lover.

The sonnet "In a Moment of Ecstasy" (winter 1930) is the recollection of an older person intent on retaining her days of passion: "When I am old beside a sheltered fire, / When the dim blue shadow fills my passive years, / I would not look upon the sun-desire / Of my keen sunlit youth with helpless tears" (2). "And Rainbow Wings" (May 1934) is a dream reverie in which a young woman anticipates sexual consummation: "If your strong semblance came [in my dream] in lust to rape / A flesh that flowers to this consummation, / Or brought an illusory adoration, / Sleep would become enchantment and escape" (17). "Miss Briggs' Farm" (December 1935) is notable for its use of overtly charged sexual words, images, and metaphors: "The heavy flesh of farmland like a nipple / Breaks into pointed rooftops and sharp towers / Discreetly phallic"; "In the cool copulating world, forsaken / Of male thigh and sinew"; "She is well served tonight by flame and passion / . . . For she will feed in an ecstatic fashion / Her secret body . . . / . . . naked and shuddering and white / . . . spread out in cruciform delight, / Upon a hill her body clasps the ground / Devising for her an ambiguous sinning" (24-25).

"The Gypsy's Song" (January 1936) celebrates the physical beauty and sexual prowess of men that for this gypsy woman sends "hot bubbles through my blood":

I love men for little things;
Hands as delicate as wings,

---

sors at Hunter College. For more on this, see Dorsett, *And God Came In,* 19, and Santamaria, *Joy,* ch. 2.

> Hands as strong as yellow fire
> Strike a spark to my desire;
> Curve of eyebrow, cut of cheek
> Make my supple knees grow weak;
> Dagger slapping on his thighs,
> Murderous splendor in his eyes,
> Twisted laughter at his mouth
> Prove my blood is of the south. (26)

"Regrets" (May 1936) is a straightforward argument that a young woman should give herself sexually to the first man who asks: "Let the first comer / Make you his lover" (30). "Elizabethan" (March 1937), on the other hand, concerns a scorned lover who disdains ever to love again: "I never will bleed / Precious dribbles of pain / For a lover again; / Let me sleep, let me eat, / My sole body tastes sweet, / If I live I am free; / You get no more of me" (36).

However, the most striking illustration of Davidman's focus upon sexual love comes in a sequence of ten love sonnets she dates as being written in August 1933.[27] In "I Hate You for Your Kind Indifference," which appeared in the Christmas 1933 issue of *Echo,* the pervading tone of the sequence is established: a scorned lover angrily — and often ironically — reacts to her former lover. The opening quatrain is indicative: "I hate you for your kind indifference / That tiptoes past the naked thing who cries / A shocking lust; and, like a man of sense, / Stares at my passion with a mild surprise." More sarcasm fails to hide the pathos of the scorned woman:

> I meant to rouse you till your flesh divined
> Behind my eyes the hot and hostile woman;
> But you are gentle and I am not human;
> The clarity of your Hellenic mind
> Knows me a pitiable amusing thing,
> A trivial insect with a tattered wing. (9)

The next sonnet, "The Difficult Ritual of Your Adoration," continues this pathetic mode, describing how the scorned woman has done everything she can think of to keep her beloved, including creating a "ritual" of adoring poetry: "Whatever light and lovely thing is mine / I burn in pleasant incense for your praise; / My body and my brain, my nights and days, / In sacrificial

---

27. The first two sonnets of this sequence have not survived.

torture at your shrine." The poem ends with a desperate plea: "Pity me / In any way that is without a smile" (9-10).

"The Green and Silken Summer Passes Me" notes how with the passage of time the scorned woman's anguish appears to have ameliorated somewhat; that is, she has managed to forget the physical attractions of her beloved. Yet the poem ends with a return to an emphasis upon her suffering:

> It is the pleasant image of your mind
> That I have lost; a lithe malignant pain
> Rattles my dry and brittle heart; above
> The glassy sky is hollow, bright, and blind;
> My flesh is still unanswered, and my brain
> Still dark and dark. I have not lost my love. (10)

The pathetic tone of the entire sequence climaxes in the next sonnet, "I Know My Eyes Are Like a Dog's": "I know my eyes are like a dog's, and plead / Too humbly; still, you fling the dog a bone. / You will not toss me for my eager need / Even the bitter answer of a stone. / I am your starving and devoted slave, / Thus hate you sometimes." The poem ends with her promise to create a sepulcher for their love and a grave "for a proud corpse that would not be my friend" (10-11).

Following this flood of pathos, "If I Contrived Myself a Diamond Death" suggests that the scorned lover might find some relief for her loss in death, pain, or self-inflicted suffering ("It would be pretty artistry to spill / My splendid blood in jewels for your sake") if it were not for the banality of everyday things: "I am destroyed unbeautifully here / By hard and little things rubbed cold and clean; / At spotless tiny tasks I sit between / Cold tea and toast, and with a casual ear / Beneath a clock-face in a shiny room / I hear the crystal ladies tinkling doom" (11). In the next sonnet, "Unwary Thirst within My Withering Brain," she thinks about devising ways to cause her beloved pain and suffering since "I half believe I am your enemy; / I plan a variegated agony / To recompense you for my writing pain." But her longing for his body mitigates such action: "Your body is as precious as the sun, / A sacred and a salt communion / Denied my loving self, whom to console / I play with hate of you, devising horror, / Nor fear to face within the naked mirror / This aspect of my particolored soul" (12).

The last two sonnets in the sequence reveal an easing off of her intense emotional pain, though her sense of loss is still there. The penultimate sonnet, "Let the Red Image of My Agony," is no testimony of hatred; instead, she is resolved to resist the pathetic: "Let the red image of my agony / Move you no more than to a cool regret / For inconsiderable sorrow." Although she has suffered much, she affirms that she can go on: "I will not have you tainted by my pain; / I am scarred and sculptured to a hollow mask / Of vivid torture; yet I am not slain / By sharp contrivances of your disdain" (157).[28] The final sonnet, "To Decorate My Sorrows," is a poignant conclusion as she argues that she will use the writing of poetry about her loss as an anodyne: "I find a jeweled word for every wound, / Mellow and delicate words which I array / In silken arabesques of tiny sound; / Artist's diversion for a rainy day." But the solace she finds in this argument does not completely convince:

> Yet while despair anatomizing passion
> Shapes hard and shining poetry, and while
> I use my sobbing thought of you to fashion
> A sonnet from your casual slight smile,
> — An art I try to value high above you —
> Even while I write about you, sir, I love you. (12-13)

This sonnet sequence, written when she was eighteen and about to begin her senior year at Hunter College, is striking for many reasons, including the strong narrative motif running through the sequence (that is, it is a story told in verse), her intensity of emotion (admittedly spilling over into bathos at times), her recognition that writing can offer a therapy (albeit a limited one) for pain, the ease of composition, and the seeming artlessness of the poems. This ten-sonnet sequence illustrates her tendency toward writing love sonnet sequences; in fact, she writes three more sequences.[29]

Davidman's most sexually charged poem of this period, "Postscript: But All I Want" (June 1938), is a poem celebrating the pleasure of sexual intercourse:

---

28. Published as "An Absolution" in *Letter to a Comrade,* 92; *Naked Tree,* 157.

29. Davidman wrote two other love sonnet sequences at about this time. The first, a five-sonnet sequence titled "Rough Sonnets," Davidman dates as being written in September 1938. In this sequence a young woman is haunted by visions, images, and fantasies of the man she longs to be intimate with; *Naked Tree,* 73-75. The second is a sequence of three poems, "Sonnets for Proteus," and she dates the sequence as being written November 1939; *Naked Tree,* 176-78. These sonnets recount the painful internal recriminations a female lover makes against herself as she suffers the anguish of unrequited love. The third and most stunning of these is a sequence of forty-five love sonnets that Davidman wrote to C. S. Lewis; *Naked Tree,* 282-307. I discuss this sequence in detail in Chapter 8.

. . . but all I want is the sense of your mouth
but all I want is the look of your mouth and eyes
but all I want is the hair on the back of your head
to run my finger over;

your body the great and bare and splendid creation
come down upon me like the weight of god
descended upon me like the thunderbolt
eating me wholly

but all I want is your presence your possession
the shaft of fire the great agony the great beauty
the lifting up and using of my body
to give you pleasure;

I would embrace you with my hands and fingers
clasped across the strong bones of your spine
and feel the joints of your body with my fingers
and I would

and I would love you beloved who leave me here breathless
lying without knowledge of the muscles of your body
but all I want is the sun, but I want earthquake,
but all I want
all I want . . . (55-56)[30]

This poem needs little comment; however, it is notable since its focus upon physical passion and sexual consummation underscores Davidman's earnest enjoyment of sensual experiences. If Ursula Brangwen of D. H. Lawrence's *The Rainbow* had written a poem, this is the kind she might have written.

Joy Davidman's early work suggests she was on the verge of being a significant writer. Her facile handling of the short stories in the *Echo* demonstrates she was an able writer of fiction. Her master's thesis, "My Lord of Orrery," while not compelling reading, is notable because it illustrates her tenacity and potential as a researcher. Its chief contribution to her development as a writer was to prepare her later for the reviews of more than two hundred movies and books she published in the *New Masses* from 1938 to

30. The ellipsis marks are in Davidman's typescript version of the poem.

1944.[31] In her early published poems we see a poet in training. Not only does Davidman experiment with meter and form, but also she practices other important elements of prosody, including enjambment, caesura, assonance, and consonance, showing herself a capable and adept young poet. More importantly, the early success of her poems, especially those appearing in *Poetry* — she was not yet twenty-one — must have been heady and certainly inspired her later to publish *Letter to a Comrade.* The other poems of this period are chiefly important for their insights into Davidman's personal life; since she did not keep a journal where we might have expected her to write about her interior life, many of these poems are journal-like; they reflect upon the important personal events of that inner life, revealing that sexual love was profoundly important to her. As we move to an exploration of her subsequent work, these early pieces hint at the promise of her literary corpus.

31. For more on this see Chapter 3.

CHAPTER 2

Letter to a Comrade (1938)

In December 1935 Davidman completed her MA in English at Columbia University. Eager to use her degree and driven by a desire to share her enthusiasm for literature, she joined the English faculty at Roosevelt High School in fall 1936.[1] During what turned out to be a disenchanting year of teaching high school English, Davidman found solace in her writing, especially poetry. After resigning her teaching position in the summer of 1937, she threw herself into writing verse: between September 1937 and December 1938 she wrote more than one hundred poems.[2] Because of her earlier success in publishing poems in *Poetry,* Davidman decided to write Stephen Vincent Benét, then editor of the Yale Series of Younger Poets and the person most responsible for helping Davidman to publish *Letter to a Comrade.*[3] Accord-

1. For more on this, see Lyle W. Dorsett, *And God Came In: The Extraordinary Story of Joy Davidman* (New York: Macmillan, 1983), 24-26; and Abigail Santamaria, *Joy: Poet, Seeker, and the Woman Who Captivated C. S. Lewis* (New York: Houghton Mifflin Harcourt, 2015), ch. 3.

2. See the index of poems (including dates of composition) that Davidman compiled in DP Box 1, Series 4, Folder 27.

3. Stephen Vincent Benét (1898-1943) published poetry, including *Heavens and Earth: A Book of Poems* (1920); novels, including *Young People's Pride* (1922), *Spanish Bayonet* (1926), and *The Devil and Daniel Webster* (1937); and short stories, including *Thirteen O'Clock: Stories of Several Worlds* (1937). His narrative poem about the American Civil War, *John Brown's Body* (1928), won the Pulitzer Prize for poetry in 1929. He was editor of the Yale Series of Younger Poets from 1933 to 1942. *Letter to a Comrade* won the 1938 Russell Loines Memorial award for poetry given by the National Institute for Arts and Letters. Since Benét had been elected to the National Institute for Arts and Letters in 1929, almost certainly his endorsement of *Letter to a Comrade* ensured its winning the award.

ingly, my interests in this chapter are to explore in more detail the letters Davidman wrote during this time to Benét concerning the development of *Letter to a Comrade,* to offer a thematic discussion of the poems, and to make a critical assessment of the volume as a whole.[4]

Davidman was in correspondence with Benét by the summer of 1936 about both her poetry and the Yale competition. On August 18, 1936, she wrote: "I did not receive your letter discussing my manuscript *Ashes and Sparks* until my recent return from a vacation trip, and therefore there has been some delay in answering on my part; but I am very glad you thought highly of my work, and I should like to thank you for your encouragement."[5] She further thanked Benét for his promise of future assistance: "If I am still unpublished in two years' time, I shall take advantage of your invitation to submit another manuscript for the Yale Series of Younger Poets, and I trust I shall then send a manuscript more worthy of your consideration. I'll not weary you with any more conclusion than to say again I am grateful" (*Bone,* 1-2). That she was working so diligently on a volume of poetry at this time underscores her determination to achieve acclaim as a poet.

Given Benét's kindness to Davidman — perhaps verging on being her poetic mentor — it is not surprising that two years later she sent him a second manuscript, asked for his critical opinion, and wondered if he believed it worthy of submitting to the Yale competition.[6] After receiving his praise

4. For contemporary reviews of *Letter to a Comrade,* see R. P. Blackmur, "Nine Poets," *Partisan Review,* Winter 1939, p. 112; Dorothy Emerson, "Three Young Poets," *Scholastic* 34 (May 27, 1939): 27E; Desmond Hawkins, Review of Joy Davidman's *Letter to a Comrade, Spectator* 162 (May 19, 1939): 868; Ruth Lechlitner, Review of Joy Davidman's *Letter to a Comrade, New York Herald Tribune Books,* December 25, 1938, p. 2; C. A. Millspaugh, "Among the New Books of Verse," *Kenyon Review* 2 (1940): 363; Review of Joy Davidman's *Letter to a Comrade, Times Literary Supplement* [London], October 14, 1939, p. 599; Muriel Rukeyser, Review of Joy Davidman's *Letter to a Comrade, New Republic* 98 (March 8, 1939): 146; Dorothy Ulrich, Review of Joy Davidman's *Letter to a Comrade, New York Times Book Review,* August 6, 1939, p. 4; Oscar Williams, Review of Joy Davidman's *Letter to a Comrade, Poetry* 54 (April 1939): 33.

5. In DP there is no evidence that *Ashes and Sparks* survived; it was likely an early version of *Letter to a Comrade.*

6. After Benét's death on March 13, 1943, Davidman's tribute to him appeared as "Stephen Vincent Benét," *New Masses* 46 (March 30, 1943): 23-24. In the tribute Davidman praised Benét as her mentor:

> To a whole generation of young writers, like Norman Rosten, Margaret Walker, and myself, Stephen Vincent Benét's name was literally synonymous with poetry. It was he who, as editor of the Yale Series of Younger Poets, selected our work for first publication. The critical introductions he wrote seized upon our half-formed meanings and made passion-

for the manuscript in a subsequent letter, she wrote: "I have to thank you not only for your very kind letter of recommendation [endorsing her submission of *Letter to a Comrade* to the Yale competition] but also for something more subtle. When one is beset with rejection slips and tormented by distrust of one's work and ability, it is a comforting thing to receive encouragement from a man who knows. And so I am very grateful for your letter; it will justify the sunny moments in which I tell myself how good I am" (April 2, 1938; *Bone*, 3). Every writer who has received a rejection slip can appreciate Davidman's confession and understand how Benét's commendation of her work bolstered her view of herself as a poet. Accordingly, on the same day but in a separate letter she submitted her manuscript, *Letter to a Comrade*, to the Yale Series of Younger Poets competition.[7]

Subsequent letters from Davidman to Benét in late July 1938 illustrate that they were in conversation about which poems in the original manuscript needed to be excised and possible substitutions. On July 21 she wrote: "I am sending you eight new poems for inclusion in the manuscript." In addition, she responded to Benét's uncertainty about the manuscript's title: "I have been thinking hard about the question of a title; I quite see the limitations of *Letter to a Comrade*. But the only other possibilities that occur to me are *In Praise of Iron* and the titles of two poems: 'Survey Mankind' and 'Waltzing Mouse.' I do not like any of these, and I have been wondering if you could help me out by suggesting a suitable name for the book."[8] She was also uncertain about whether she needed to secure permission from the editors of

---

ate sense of them; seized our groping emotions, our uncertain technique, and showed us the way toward growth. There never was an editor at once so kind and so brilliant. We knew him first through his illuminating letters; meeting him later, we found a slight, quiet man with an extraordinary warmth of personality and glitter of wit. It was characteristic of him that he put us at our ease at once. . . . I do not speak for myself alone in saying that his poetry was exactly that which a young poet of this America would sell their souls to write.

In her April 14, 1943, letter to Benét's widow, Rosemary, Davidman enclosed a copy of the tribute and said: "You probably won't remember meeting me, and I scarcely knew your husband personally; but he did a great deal for me, both through being my editor and through being what he was and writing what he did" (*Bone*, 33-34).

7. DP does not contain a draft manuscript of the version of *Letter to a Comrade* that was eventually published. However, the draft of the table of contents of this version of *Letter to a Comrade* appears in her submission letter of April 2, 1938 (*Bone*, 3-4), and is reproduced in *Bone*, 4-5. I offer an analysis of this table of contents as well as a discussion of the poems she eventually excised and replaced with substitute poems in *Bone*, 6-14.

8. In May 1938 Davidman had written a poem entitled "In Praise of Iron"; *Naked Tree*, 52-53. For "Survey Mankind" and "Waltzing Mouse" see *Naked Tree*, 117-20 and 151-52.

the journals where several of the poems in the manuscript had already been published, noting: "I'm sorry to give you so much trouble, but you know I am quite inexperienced in these things and need a good deal of assistance" (*Bone,* 11-12). On July 25 she agreed with Benét's suggestion about dropping four poems: "By all means leave them out. They are all, I am glad to say, early work." In addition, it is clear that the manuscript was in flux: "I am sending you so much additional work — I have written thirty poems since submitting the manuscript — that I wish I could find more of the old stuff that I don't like at all." And the question of the volume's title was still up in the air: "I'm still racking my brains over titles; how about *Bitter Shouting*?" (*Bone,* 12-13). On July 26 Davidman gushed with thanks after reading the foreword Benét provided for the manuscript: "Thank you very much for the preface, which, speechless with pride, I have been showing to my friends here. I do not think any more could be said for my poetry than you have done."[9] She also left it to Benét to make the final decision about which poems would appear: "I am sending you a revised table of contents, and I should like to give you a free hand in making any rearrangements or omissions you think necessary." The letter also reveals that the matter of the title is finally resolved: "I am glad you prefer the original title [*Letter to a Comrade*], for I find myself unable to think of the book by any other" (*Bone,* 13-14).[10] In the published version of *Letter to a Comrade* forty-five poems appear, covering work she did between August 1933 ("An Absolution") and July 1938 ("Totentanz").[11]

Davidman's letters to Benét illustrate that she was very much interested in the craft of her art — now liking one poem, now rejecting another, and ever looking to make her verse better, more powerful, and more engaging. When we turn to the poems found in *Letter to a Comrade,* we see her ambitions largely realized. However, an important contextual matter needs to be mentioned here: during the development of *Letter to a Comrade* Davidman

9. See "Foreword," in *Letter to a Comrade,* 7-9.

10. The letters of July 21, 25, and 26, 1938, were written while Davidman was in residence at a writer's retreat. The MacDowell Colony, established in 1907, exists "to nurture the arts by offering creative individuals of the highest talent an inspiring environment in which to produce enduring works of the imagination" (see http://www.macdowellcolony.org). Davidman spent time there in the summer of 1938, 1940, 1941, and 1942. In the summer of 1938 while at the colony she was working on not only *Letter to a Comrade* but also what came to be her first novel, *Anya* (1940). In the July 26 letter she indicated this to Benét: "And thank you for your good wishes about the novel; it's practically done."

11. See the index of poems (including dates of composition) Davidman compiled in DP Box 1, Series 4, Folder 27. For "An Absolution" see *Naked Tree,* 157, and for "Totentanz" see *Naked Tree,* 147-48.

became an ardent Communist and active member of the Communist Party of the United States of America (CPUSA). Her connection to Communism was a gradual process that began sometime in the mid 1930s. Although many Jews had been drawn to membership in the CPUSA, Davidman's Jewish heritage apparently had little to do with attracting her to the Party. Instead it was the injustices she saw around her that prompted her decision. Unlike Vivian Gornick, who knew early on she would be drawn toward the Party, writing, "before I knew that I was Jewish or a girl I knew that I was a member of the working class,"[12] Davidman was only slowly drawn into the Party. In "The Longest Way Round," she says that although she came from a financially secure, middle-class family, the terrible social conditions brought about by the Great Depression moved her to action — albeit action without much reflection:

> To live entirely for my own pleasures, with hungry men selling apples on every street corner, demanded a callousness of which I seemed incapable. Maybe no rational person would worry about the rest of the world; I found myself worrying, all the same. And I wanted to *do* something, so I joined the Communist Party. . . . I entered the Party in a burst of emotion, without making the slightest effort to study Marxist theory. All I knew was that capitalism wasn't working very well, war was imminent — and socialism promised to change all that. And for the first time in my life I was willing to be my brother's keeper. So I rushed round to a Party acquaintance and said I wanted to join. (*Bone*, 90)

While her decision to join the Party was not completely impulsive, by her own admission it was one driven not by reflection and sustained study of Communist books, pamphlets, ideas, or principles; instead, it was a reaction against the social inequalities she saw around her.

However, joining the Party was not as easy as she thought. According to Oliver Pilat, she first joined the CPUSA at a large meeting of a downtown West Side branch: "The ceremony verged on the casual. The chairman intoned: 'Any new members, any outsiders?' " Joy and several others took the oath; she waited for something to happen, but no one from the Party contacted her. She took the oath again during a big Communist rally in Madison Square Garden, but again she heard nothing from Party officials. Still

---

12. Vivian Gornick, *The Romance of American Communism* (New York: Basic Books, 1977), 3.

determined, on a third attempt at a branch meeting on lower Fifth Avenue she finally received her membership card in 1938.[13] In addition to the social and economic crises she saw, her own situation at the time as a "permanent substitute teacher" in the New York City high school system, a designation that effectively blocked her path to a permanent teaching license (in effect, she was chattel in the excess teacher labor pool), also contributed to her movement toward the CPUSA.

By 1939 Davidman had also joined the League of American Writers (LAW); formed in 1935, it was a writers' organization closely aligned with the CPUSA.[14] After joining LAW she began aggressively recruiting others — evidence of her lifelong tendency to throw herself completely into each new cause she embraced. In a letter of March 31, 1939, she invited Kenneth Porter to join the League: "By the way, would you be interested in joining the League of American Writers? It's the logical organization for writers with leftwing sympathies, the only one which really takes United Front action. We've just published, for instance, a pamphlet listing anti-Semitic people and publications in this country with their interrelations; a shocking list" (*Bone*, 21).[15] She also invites Porter to a writer's event she was organizing on behalf of LAW: "You may be interested in the [W. H.] Auden-[Louis] MacNeice-[Christopher] Isherwood symposium . . . that the League of American Writers is holding on April 6. . . . I'm arranging it myself, so I yell about it everywhere. Auden is the curiousest specimen of English method

---

13. Oliver Pilat, "Girl Communist [Joy Davidman]: An Intimate Story of Eight Years in the Party," *The New York Post,* November 2, 1949. Pilat also relates how furious Davidman's parents were when they learned of her decision to join the CPUSA, especially when she began to go by the Party name of Nell Tulchin. See also Dorsett, *And God Came In,* 21-57, and Santamaria, *Joy,* ch. 4.

14. Part of LAW's platform was the following:

> To fight against imperialist war and fascism, defend the Soviet Union against capitalist aggression; for the development and strengthening of the revolutionary labor movement; against white chauvinism (against all forms of Negro discrimination or persecution) and against persecution of minority groups and of the foreign-born; solidarity with Colonial people in their struggles for freedom; against the influence of bourgeois ideas in American liberalism; against the imprisonment of revolutionary writers and artists, as well as other class-war prisoners throughout the world.

Cited in Larry Ceplair and Steven Englund, *The Inquisition in Hollywood: Politics in the Film Industry, 1930-1960* (Garden City, NY: Anchor, 1980), 56. For more, see Franklin Folsom, *Days of Anger, Days of Hope: A Memoir of the League of American Writers, 1937-1942* (Boulder: University Press of Colorado, 1994).

15. Kenneth W. Porter (1905-1981) was a poet and historian.

it has ever been my luck to encounter" (*Bone,* 21). In another instance she wrote Stephen Vincent Benét on June 3, 1940: "The League wants me to ask you if you'd care to appear at an antiwar poetry meeting, to be held on Thursday, June 20, at 8:30 in the evening. We're going on record, while we can, against America's entering the war; and we should be grateful if you would consent to read some appropriate poems of your own (some of those in *Burning City,* for instance)" (*Bone,* 30).[16]

It comes as no surprise, then, that one thematic focus of *Letter to a Comrade* concerns poems having to do with politics — capitalism, Fascism, Communism, and revolution.[17] Davidman's political poems in *Letter to a Comrade* are largely examples of what has been called proletarian literature; that is, poems, short stories, novels, and dramas written by those "who have clearly indicated their sympathy to the revolutionary cause."[18] Writing in the *Partisan Review* in February 1936, Arvin Newton argued that "all proletarian writers . . . are under a solemn obligation to fight tooth and nail against philistinism in all its nauseating forms; to rise above parochialism both of time and place; and to save from the black night of fascism all of the past that is really humane and of good report."[19] Proletarian literature supported the revolutionary aims of the CPUSA in the 1930s, and Davidman, anxious to contribute to the cause, wrote some poems reflecting the ideals of the CPUSA.

The volume's title (and longest) poem, "Letter to a Comrade (to Ellen Weinberg)," is indicative. Written in free verse and divided into four sections, the poem traces an imaginary trip out of New York City taken by a "comrade." Part I begins:

Leaving New York, leaving the triple rivers
netted in ships; turn again,
wanderer, turn the eyes homeward. Remember the city
settled in the eastward sky stiff with towers

16. Stephen Vincent Benét, *Burning City* (New York: Farrar & Rinehart, 1936).

17. Even the book's dedication has a political edge: "To Ernst Thaelmann who will not know." Ernest Thaelmann (1886-1944), born in Hamburg, Germany, helped form the German Communist Party in 1920. A fierce anti-Fascist, he publicly opposed Nazism, was arrested by the Gestapo in 1933, and was executed in Buchenwald concentration camp on August 18, 1944.

18. Daniel Aaron, *Writers on the Left* (New York: Harcourt, 1961), 283.

19. Arvin Newton, "A Letter on Proletarian Literature," *Partisan Review,* February 1936, p. 14.

crested and curved in the tight circle of home
cupped excellently in the sky. Possess understanding;
see this is your heart, turn and perceive these towers
sprung from the syllables of your mouth, this iron this crowding
and lighted fury of the trains emerging
out of the roaring tunnels of your veins.[20]

The imperative for the comrade — perhaps Ellen Weinberg — to remember the centrality of the city gives the poem its thematic center:

Here remain the brothers of your heart, salute them;
here are the picket lines and the bright jangle
of children fighting, the glitter of streets, the houses in windrows,
here also the broken stairs and the fire and the rat
and here the impenetrable sheen of office windows;
but also you shall find here understanding for your speech
among many of the same flesh as your flesh
spoiled by the same poison. (91)

Although we do not get an exact sense of what the imaginary journey will encompass, the opening section casts a politically charged shadow over all that follows.

The imaginary journey then turns south in part II, north in part III, and finally east in part IV. We never know precisely how far south the imaginary journey takes the comrade, but we can intuit at least as far as the farm land of northern Maryland since the Susquehanna River is cited and perhaps as far as West Virginia since we read that "the pulpy flesh of men makes war upon coal in the mines / and grapples with iron" (92). Yet these men appear to be happy and at peace:

In these pastures
there are no stones, there are no enmities.
Tender earth turns easily under the plow,
fecund under the male blade of the plow,
seeded and starred with young blades, later thick and singing

---

20. *Naked Tree,* 90. Because the original edition of *Letter to a Comrade* is difficult to find, all references to the poems are from *Naked Tree*. Ellen Weinberg and Davidman were fellow contributors to *New Masses*.

and the wind moves in the wheat like many snakes.
Clotted on furry stems in the hedge
sweetly the blackberries darken. The land loves its men.
These are the enjoyers of the earth . . .
. . . .
They wear the earth in the creases of their hands. (92)

How, the poem asks, can the comrade connect with these seemingly happy and content people? "How shall you speak the speech of these men how meet them / how read the meanings in their eyes how find them / how come to an understanding with their eyes? . . . / How shall you speak to them, comrade, flesh of metal and jangling, quick flesh of the city?" (92). The answer, Davidman implies, is political revolution:

Say then to these, there is no miracle of help
fixed in the stars, there is no magic, no savior
smiling in blatant ink on election posters;
only the strength of men, only the twigs bound together
invent the faggot, only the eyes that go seeking
find help in brother eyes. Say only
the spirit of men builds bridges of the spirit,
the hands of men contrive united splendors,
the need of men shall awaken thunderous answers;
and so fall silent. Leave silence among them. (93)

Part II ends with the admission that while such men will not listen or perhaps be "diverted with lies," the comrade will have done well to "leave thought among them, / say to them your word and leave the word among them and leave them" (93-94).

Part III goes north into Canada; there the comrade will find "forgotten French laughter" and men at enmity with each other: "And every whisper / makes war on brother whisper. Here divided / men have no voice more than the muted wave / unending on the shores" (94). The source of distrust and dissension is, in part, the ineffectual but pervasive power of Catholicism: "Here whispers lonely breath here find humility / marked on the map, written in the towns with saints' names / by the thin rivers and the stink of fish / and the yellow bricks of the true church" (94). These French Canadians ask for prayer, not for spiritual growth and nourishment, but because of their economic destitution:

> Pray for us
> pray for us; we sons of the French adventurers
> salt and dry codfish beside a salty stream
> here with no buyers; here our bread
> stands to the flies; here our children
> have no teeth, live on the thin flesh of fishes
> and the pallid taste of Christmas berries plucked by the roadside
> while waiting for the cars and money of tourists;
> and because we have no teeth in our heads with which to bite
> therefore priest pray for us, you sitting in the house of yellow bricks
> which we have made beside the church of yellow bricks
> which we have built and made bright with decorations of metal
> and three white saints, and which we have given a tower
> sheeted with tin, and of which we are proud because it is fine.
> Priest give us good words and make intercession
> to the Virgin that she may make intercession
> since now every hour is the hour of our death. (94-95)

We should not miss the irony of the last three lines; that is, Catholicism in particular and religion in general offer vain spiritual promises that do nothing to fill the empty stomachs of the poor.[21] The obvious implication of this is that only political revolution — a breaking of the status quo — offers these poor French Canadians relief from their economic plight and personal misery.

The final section of the poem takes the comrade east to the ocean ("this is land's end") where Davidman creates an analogy between the shrill cries of the sea birds and those imagined cries of the suffering poor: "Come birdcry here is the heart here is the heart's cry, answer / along the ultimate and starving beaches / birdcry the voice of men" (95). A second analogy compares the poor to birch trees that have been ravaged by fire:

> Here to the sea's edge, to the salt and bitter water,
> descend the narrow birches left naked by fires,
> the birch most tender and human flesh of all trees
> reduced to essential bones of destruction; ah they are dead,
> the white birch is dead and never again

---

21. Davidman's novel *Weeping Bay* (New York: Macmillan, 1950) is in part a critique of Catholicism and is set in a French Canadian town; several of its key characters are Catholic priests. I discuss *Weeping Bay* in Chapter 7.

puts forth the silver underside of leaves on the wind
or springtime tassels of the birch. They are dead,
the white trees, human birches; who shall call them
to lift the slaughtered branches upon the sky,
the murdered root to rise again by the sea's edge
at the world's end. (96)

The answer to the question of who shall call them to life utilizes still another
analogy: fireweed, a perennial herbaceous plant that aggressively colonizes
burn sites — especially after forest fires — is compared to revolutionaries
like the comrade who will rise to avenge the murdered poor. The poem then
ends with something of a prophetic imperative:

Only remember,
wanderer, under the murdered and slender trees
white bodies given over to slaughter, remember
only the fireweed, comrade, the glory in burnt places,
the sharply colored torchbearers, the new warriors,
the green and flowery resurrection, the fireweed
marching over burnt hills down to the sea's edge. Remember
resurrection riot among the roots of the birches, resurrection
out of the white and black bones of burnt trees, resurrection.
    Remember
with what a brave necessity the fireweed
answers birdcry down the desolate beaches
speaks to the aimless wind the heart's red syllable,
blooms on our bones. Let the fireweed answer,
comrade, and so we may lie quiet in our graves. (96)

Davidman's employing the word "resurrection" to describe the political rev-
olution she envisions is a telling revelation of the religious fervor she has at
this time in support of the aims of the CPUSA.[22]

Other politically charged poems push Davidman's Communist and rev-
olutionary agenda. For instance, "Spartacus 1938" ends: "Assault the door,

---

22. This fervor later also took the form of teaching poetry classes at a school sponsored
in part by the League of American Writers, the School for Democracy, an anti-Fascist, pro-
Communist institution in New York City. On April 28, 1939, Davidman wrote a friend: "By
the way, I'm planning to give a poetry-writing course in the League's Writers School next
fall" (*Bone,* 24). For more on the School for Democracy, see Chapter 3.

break down the door, break open the door" (100).[23] "Twentieth-Century Americanism" sarcastically critiques the shallow thinking she ascribes to most Americans in the 1930s:

> Give us the World Series,
> the ballplayer with thick nostrils and the loose jaw
> hanging heavily from a piece of chewing gum,
> and when the baseball is over give us no time;
> fill our mind with the Rose Bowl and Yale and Notre Dame
> leaving no time for thought between the baseball and football seasons.
> Feed us music to rot the nerves, make us twitch with music,
> burrow with music beneath the comfortless brain and beneath
> the aching heart and the worn heart and beneath
> the honest gut and rot the gut with music
> in the snake of nerve that sits in the knee reflexes,
> wriggle in the dust with the snake's belly. All night
> delight us with the yellow screaming of sound. (102)

"Survey Mankind" is a call for political activism with a revolutionary aim: "Now with me / bow and set your mouth against America / which you will make fine and the treasure of its men, / which you will give to the workers and to those who turn land over with the plow" (120). "Prayer against Indifference" uses a hard-edged voice, asking that she be castigated if she ever fails to be outraged at injustices such as wars, ruined men, and "bloody children lying dead." Instead, she prays for "eyes that will not shut; / Let me have truth at my tongue's root; / Let courage and the brain command / The honest fingers of my hand" (106).[24] If ever she fails these — of particular note is the allusion to her craft as a writer and its demand that she write and publish the truth — she begs that she be destroyed: "And when I wait to save my skin / Break roof and let my death come in" (106).[25]

Still other political poems by Davidman are less confrontational. For instance, several poems illustrate sympathy for the loyalists' efforts against the Fascist forces during the Spanish Civil War (1936-1939). "Snow in Madrid" is perhaps the most lyrical of all Davidman's political poems:

---

23. First published in *New Masses* 27 (May 24, 1938): 19.

24. First published in *New Masses* 28 (August 9, 1938): 17.

25. Other politically charged poems with a pointed message are "For the Revolution" (*Naked Tree*, 127-28), "In Praise of Fascists" (143), and "Apology for Liberals" (155).

Softly, so casual,
Lovely, so light, so light,
The cruel sky lets fall
Something one does not fight.

How tenderly to crown
The brutal year
The clouds send something down
That one need not fear.

Men before perishing
See with unwounded eye
For once a gentle thing
Fall from the sky. (115)[26]

The tender poignancy of this poem contrasts markedly with the hard-edged revolutionary ones. In a similar fashion, "Near Catalonia" is a measured lament for the woefully undersupplied loyalist forces:

We have the sweet noise of the sea at our back
and before us the bitter shouting of the gun;
and the brass wing of aeroplanes and the sun
that walks above us burning. Here we wound
our feet on metal fragments of the bomb,
the sword unburied and the poisoned ground.
Here we stand; here we lie; here we must see
what we can find potent and good to set
between the Fascist and the deep blue sea. (136)[27]

The poem then notes the things the loyalist soldiers lack: adequate defense against the bombs, airplanes, and poison gas of the well-supplied Fascist forces. All they have to offer in defense against the enemy is expressed in the moving conclusion:

26. Several years later, on August 2, 1944, Davidman married a veteran of the Spanish Civil War — the writer William Lindsay Gresham.

27. First published in *New Masses* 29 (October 18, 1938): 18.

> We have only the bodies of men to put together,
> the wincing flesh, the peeled white forking stick,
> easily broken, easily made sick,
> frightened of pain and spoiled by evil weather;
> we have only the most brittle of all things the man
> and the heart the most iron admirable thing of all,
> and putting these together we make a wall. (136)[28]

Whether pointed or poignant, Davidman's political poems in *Letter to a Comrade* reflect issues held dearly by the CPUSA, LAW, and fellow travelers holding a revolutionary ideology.[29]

That said, perhaps the key weakness of the political poems in *Letter to a Comrade* is that Davidman makes a serious artistic error: too often she tells rather than shows. Instead of following the dictates of her poetic conscience, she sells out to the CPUSA and writes propaganda rather than poetry. That is, while Davidman's political poems in *Letter to a Comrade* are genuine and deeply felt, in general they suffer from a propagandist's zeal. In "The Longest Way Round" she admits as much:

> [After joining the CPUSA] I learned too that my judgment of a book or movie must depend not on its artistic merit, but on its Marxist orthodoxy, or even on whether its author was a liberal contributor to the Party's needy treasury; and that, at the sight of a hero, a martyr, or a genius, I must say, not, "How wonderful!" but, "How can we *use* him?" I resisted all this somewhat, but mostly I gave in to it even before pressure was applied, and then persuaded myself that it wasn't there. By nature I am the sort of woman who nurses sick kittens and hates to spank her bad little boys; yet as a Marxist I would have been willing to shoot people without trial. In

28. See also "The Lately Dead" and "Poem for Liberation," *New Masses* 52 (September 12, 1944): 8; both in *Naked Tree*, 134, 229-30.

29. Davidman's revolutionary zeal was further evident later when she served as the editor for a volume of anti-Fascist poetry, *War Poems of the United Nations* (New York: Dial Press, 1943). For more on this, see Chapter 3. In addition to editing the book, Davidman published the following poems in the volume: "Fairytale" and "Trojan Women"; "For My Son" (under the name Megan Coombes-Dawson); "Four Years After Munich" and "Peccavimus" (both under the name Haydon Weir); "For Odessa" (by Boris Veselchakov, adapted by Joy Davidman); "The Young Pioneers" (by A. Bezmensky, adapted by Joy Davidman); and "Snow in Madrid" (reprinted from *Letter to a Comrade*); the first five are found in *Naked Tree*, 221-22, 202-3, 223, 224-26. I discuss these poems in Chapter 5.

practice I willingly gave my spare time, my spare cash, my love of truth, and my artistic conscience. (*Bone,* 91-92)

However, it should be noted that while written in the zealous tradition of proletarian literature, Davidman's political poems are not drivel; while a political agenda drives her selection of subject matter, the poems are more than simple set pieces.

Although the political poems are not the best poems in *Letter to a Comrade,* other poems in the book expose her profound understanding of the human condition — something I believe the most compelling, penetrating, and moving poetry does.[30] Whatever the merits of public, political poems, most readers find personal, private poems — ones that explore what it means to be human, ones that reveal artfully and truthfully the heart, the soul, the mind, and the spirit — to be more interesting. For instance, even though Davidman espoused atheism at this time in her life, several poems not only are concerned with religion, but also reveal Davidman's particular interest in Jesus Christ. Crucifixion is mentioned in "Spartacus 1938" and is the focus in "I the Philosopher": "It has befallen me to see a thief / With a lovely body crucified" (107). Yet it is in "Againrising" that Davidman offers her most compelling poem about Christ. She takes us through the critical hours on the day of his crucifixion:

> The stroke of six
> my soul betrayed;
> as the clock ticks
> I am unmade;
>
> the clock struck nine;
> my life ran down
> on gears of time
> with a sickened sound.
>
> The noonday struck
> a note of pride;

---

30. While some of Davidman's political poems expose profound understandings of the human condition, such as "Snow in Madrid" and "Near Catalonia," most are more intent on advancing her Communist agenda than on exploring the complexities of the human condition.

spread on the clock
I was crucified.

The clock struck one,
whose spear, whose dart
transfixed by bone
and narrow heart.

The sound of seven
filled me with bells;
I left great heaven
for little hells;

the midnight let
my blood run out
fierce and red
from my opened mouth.

Great chaos came
to murder me
when the clock named
the hour of three.

The dawn grew wide;
the clock struck five,
and all inside
I was alive. (148-49)

Written from the perspective of Christ, the poem portrays him with a simple and winsome voice, and it suggests something of the biblical notion of Christ's meekness: controlled power. This curious affirmation of Christ's resurrection — Davidman's ethnicity as a Jew might have militated against such a view — is fascinating and indicates someone capable of great empathy and longing for spiritual fulfillment. In "The Longest Way Round" she later writes: "If ever a human life was haunted, Christ haunted me" (*Bone,* 84).[31]

Another poem exploring the human condition is "Skeleton" (158). The poem imagines a body and its longing for physical, external beauty. In the

31. For more on Davidman's early interest in Christ see *Bone,* 86.

first stanza, the body is mesmerized by what it knows to be the danger of placing its hopes on external beauty: "Beauty came to me in the shape of a wolf / And stared at me with yellow eyes of a wolf / Desiring the good red heart to gnaw upon, / Coveting the heartstrings" (158). In addition, the body hears the direct threat to it spoken by beauty in the next two stanzas: "I will be fed with the bones of your hands / And the cords of your throat that ripple up and down / Playing at music . . . / I will devour the knowledge in your eyes / And the love on your lips shall fill my belly . . . / Give me your heart and body to feed upon / For I am lean." The final stanza intimates that the body has given in to the siren call of seeking external beauty: "Now the light wind lives whistling in my shell / In the heart's place and singing in the skull; / Beauty the wolf has eaten out my soul / And left me empty." Stripped bare, its bones open to the air, the body realizes that beauty not only took away its physical life but also stole its soul. All who have similarly erred can find in this poem an apt warning.

However, the most powerful poems in *Letter to a Comrade* exploring the human condition are the ones that concern romantic love. As a whole, these poems reveal a woman intent upon experiencing *eros* as comprehensibly as possible — its joys, its ecstasies, its sensual delights, its soaring passions. Moreover, these poems reveal a woman pursuing with single-minded intensity a lover who will completely satisfy her — and if once she finds this lover, she will never let him go. In some of the love poems Davidman offers a steely-eyed view of what it takes to survive as a woman. For example, her "To the Virgins" is nothing like Robert Herrick's "To the Virgins, to Make Much of Time." While the latter is a breezy entreaty for virgins to enjoy sexual activity as soon as possible in order to thwart time's effect on the body, the former is a hard-fisted warning to virgins to put themselves first and be wary of love: "Whatever arrow pierce the side / Or what confusion wring the mind, / Cherish the silver grin of pride / To stiffen your mouth in a whistling wind. / . . . Love yourself / And show the pleasant world your teeth" (97). Davidman counters Herrick's *carpe diem* with self-preservation. In like fashion, her "This Woman" rejects traditional ideas of femininity: "Now do not put a ribbon in your hair; / Abjure the spangled insult of design, / The filigree sterility, nor twine / A flower with your strength; go bare, go bare" (126). Instead, Davidman says a woman should take on the hardness of a tree: "Branching from the broad column of your flesh / Into the obdurate and fibrous mesh / Stubborn to break apart and stiff to hew; / Lost at your core a living skeleton / Like sharp roots pointing downward from the sun."

Notwithstanding this hardness, however, many poems celebrate passion and the ecstasy of physical love. Sometimes she is an enchantress weaving spells to bind her lover to her as in "Sorceress Eclogue": "I for my lover / cook magic over woodfires to call him home. / . . . This is magic made with a leaf and a leaf; / by this incantation his body drawn home" (129). Through her incantations she will pull him toward her so that "I shall kiss you with your mouth sticky with honey / your eyelids stuck together with sleep; / the summer shall enclose us in the heavy heat" (130). Highlighting both sensuous and sensual details, in the end she will have him: "I shall put my hands over your hands / and feel the blood beginning in your arm / and run my hands over the hair on your arm" (131). At other times she is helplessly driven to her lover as in "Little Verse":

> Do not speak of him
> Lest I leave you
> To flow like water
> About his doorstep
>
> Or like a moth
> Touch his eyelids
> With sleepy dust;
> Or like a lover
>
> Trouble his hearing
> With sweet lust;
> Or leave my body
> Upon his doorstep. (145)

And still at other times she is lonely, looking for her lover to quell her melancholy, always it seems through physical contact as she suggests in "Il Pleure dans Mon Coeur": "Only turn your lips to my lips and let your hair / lie in my hand or tangle in my hand, / and fall asleep, and let your body stand / between my sorrow and the weeping air" (123).

But most often she is a possessive, aggressive lover. In "Obsession" this aggression takes a dark turn: "I have not forgiven my enemy / The splendor of the eyes in his skull / Or that his mouth is good to see / Or that his thought is beautiful." Hatred becomes her sustaining force: "And I have kept me warm in the cold / Hating the valor of his mind" (128). Indeed, without hatred she would find it hard to go on: "This hate is honey to my tongue /

And rubies spread before my eye, / Sweet in the ear as any song; / What should I do, if he should die?" (129). In other poems she is possessive without being obsessive. For instance, in "Night-Piece" Davidman claims she will build protective rings around her lover:

> I shall make rings around you. Fortresses
> In a close architecture of wall upon wall,
> Rib, jointed rock, and hard surrounding steel
> Compel you into the narrow compass of my blood
> Where you may beat forever and be perfect,
> Keep warm. The blood will keep you warm, the body
> Will curl upon you not to let the air
> Sting you with ice. And you shall never be wounded
> By your bright hostile business of living, while
> I and my charitable flesh survive . . .
> . . . Nor shall you
> Suffer one touch of pain or recollection of evil
> While you are in my bed. (116)

Her zeal to protect, shelter, nurture, and cull out her lover is akin to that of John Donne in poems such as "The Good-Morrow," "The Sun Rising," and "Break of Day." However, Davidman is perhaps even more determined to guard her lover than Donne was; consider what she says about the multiple rings she will build around her lover:

> Now the first ring
> Is the devious course of my blood going all around you
> And you with a blind mouth growing in my flesh
> In the likeness of a child. You cannot break free,
> For I have locked a little of your life
> Into my life; and the second ring to enclose you
> My breast and arms; then a smooth round light
> And a wall winking with sleek and brittle windows
> With darkness cowering at them; the cold starry endless enemy
> Crowding you in, crushing my arms around you
> To keep off black terrors. (116-17)

Her blood, her breasts, her arms encircle and protect her lover, culminating in the poem's final lines: "Keep warm, / My lover. Lie down lover. If there is peace / Arrested in any memorable fragment of time / I have shut you in with it and drawn circle" (117). The energy, the passion, the aggressive desire to possess communicated by this poem certainly suggests something about Davidman's approach to romantic love; if she wanted a man, she would go for him.

A similar poem is "The Empress Changes Lovers," brilliantly written from the perspective of an empress's discarded lover.[32] Stung by her decision to throw him over, he warns her that she will not find it so easy to forget their passion:

> . . . You shall recall
> Forever the tingle and flash of my body embracing you,
> The way my strength came forth, the angles of my elbows,
> The placing of my ribs, long clasps of thighs
> And a flat back; you'll not obliterate
> Any of my tricks of touching you to give you pleasure,
> And worse for you you'll not forget your pleasure,
> As thus and thus you prickled up your skin
> And licked out with your rough dry catlike tongue
> To which I tasted salt. Kill what you like;
> You will not kill the antic of your own body
> That remembers me, nor the words, the physical attitudes
> And warm rooms, qualities of light, and secretive fabrics
> That mean my name; the very smell of my flesh in passion.
> But you'll remember, and you will regret
> As long as flesh likes pleasant things, and the tenderness
> By me created in you will absently come to haunt you
> Without a name, and faceless, dumb, and eyeless
> Ask for my body. (142)

Davidman's explicit description of and details about sexual love here suggest a frankness akin to D. H. Lawrence. While we never learn why the empress has decided to put him off, her former lover has the last word, mocking her future lovemaking sessions: "Never your special lust for me and its answers,

32. The point of view in this poem could be that of the empress, but the verbal cues in the poem argue for a male perspective. For instance, at one point the persona says: "Let no recollection / Of any time when you were a woman come / Grinning at you with mortality written on bare teeth." Also, the phrase "the way my strength came forth" almost certainly refers to ejaculation. *Naked Tree,* 142.

/ And the peculiar and lovely delight you had in me; never / The pleasure your senses got from me merely by wanting. / I'm saying you will not have me ever again" (143). In this poem love is reduced to animal passion — flesh, sweat, heat, climax, and a longing for more and more. There is no holding back in this kind of love; it wants what it wants when it wants it, and no amount of self-denial can thwart the driving passion of this kind of erotic love.

Yet in spite of poems expressing the full pleasure and excitement of passion, Davidman also suggests in other romantic poems that the core of the beloved — the essence of the person — cannot be touched by the lover. There is separateness, a distance that even passion cannot overcome. This is nowhere clearer than in "Division." It begins by celebrating a rich passion that knows sweet climax:

> Behold how sweetly we have come together;
> Rich night and air, the dark embracing air
> And union of the ceiling and the floor
> Enclosing passion; love, cool formal sheets,
> And secret wool of blankets. And so sweetly
> We come together; so the clasp, the spasm
> Answer each other, suitably invent
> Exhaustion sweeter than content. (145)

Recalling something of Maria's phrase "the earth moved" from Hemingway's *For Whom the Bell Tolls* to describe the ecstasy of love making, Davidman suggests the soaring nature of the lovers' passion with the phrase the "union of the ceiling and the floor." Still, passion alone is not enough: "Is there no more / To say? the body answering a body / In its own fashion perfect as a flower; / Is there no more to say?" (145). As she explores these questions and others she wonders why the consummation of physical passion is not enough to satisfy the deepest longings of her soul: "Shall I have of you / The lovely mud, unreasoning, the flesh / Beautifully and unimportantly nourished, / While the irrelevant brain stares off into space / At a blank wall; is there no more to say?" (146).

As close as physical passion brings them, it never satisfies the longing of her soul to meet another soul "face to face":

> I will not eat you; I desire of you
> Not to devour your separate nature; never

> Shall I suck out your soul. Let us keep lonely;
> But I would see the eyes of loneliness
> In your eyes meeting me; I would perceive
> In this queer universe, life and the spirit,
> And from the locked and isolated self
> Salute the world outside.

And here is the poem's greatest irony: passionate lovers are nonetheless lonely, unable to make deep soul connections:

> I clamorous, I the imperative,
> I the fond conqueror of your love, the lover,
> The lion crying in the wilderness,
> I conscious of your life, your thought, your soul
> (Call it) now hold your body quite as closely
> As one can meet another, and the body
> Asks and is satisfied, complete, made perfect,
> While the brain stares at nothing.

Indeed, the poem's opening ecstasy celebrating passion is undercut by Davidman's suggestion that her lover is just another object, another thing that has physical substance but no reality beyond that:

> You are not real.
> You are like wood and rock, like earth, like satin;
> You are a touch, a taste. You are the animal
> Gold rippling thighs of horses; or disturbing
> And twisting cats; you are the muscles of tigers,
> The objective eyes of owls. You are not life;
> I am life. I find your accidental body,
> I take you for my pleasure, and all's done;
> And I am sweetly fed. No more, no more? (146)

While passion brings her some solace, her lover remains separate, distant, and apart. Accordingly only her interior life has meaning for her; it is only there she will find fulfillment. Yes, she will continue to enjoy her lover's body, but as the final question hints, there is "no more" she can expect from him. In addition, she will never turn away from physical passion since she could "no more" bear isolation than he. Finally, "no more" may be a plaintive query to the universe, asking in effect: "Is there no more to life than sexual pleasure? Is there nothing beyond the physical, no transcendent reality that lovers can experience?" "Division" reflects at least to some degree Davidman's failed search for a long-term romantic relationship; the poem highlights that sexual consummation is no guarantee of emotional, psychological, and intellectual intimacy — a quest she repeated many times as a young adult and one that she continued to pursue until her marriage to C. S. Lewis.

The last two romantic poems to consider are "Prothalamion" and "Yet One More Spring." A prothalamion is a song or poem celebrating a marriage, and in Davidman's poem the focus is upon the male figure:

> Who is this who is coming;
> not less than the desire of wind
> shall the hungry heart desire the sound;
> not less than the rain walks
> shall he walk upon the barren ground;
> who is this who is coming:
> the shadow bearing light
> the awful spirit bearing brightness
> the shadow with the light about his feet
> ....
> who is this with shining in his hair
> who is come quietly as the dripping mist
> comes down upon the midnight and makes no sound;
> who is this who is coming:
> he is quiet as a river running underground. (133-34)[33]

These opening lines recount a breathless anticipation for the appearance of this lover; he is desirable, regal, brilliant, powerful, awe-inspiring, magnificent, and moving with silent but sure intention. In contrast to the frustrated sexual passion of "Division," "Prothalamion" ends with the promise not only of sexual consummation, but also of fruitful procreation:

---

33. Astute readers will see in this poem interesting parallels to the myth of Cupid and Psyche and note its uncanny foreshadowing of C. S. Lewis's retelling of this myth in his *Till We Have Faces* (1956), a book that Davidman and Lewis collaborated on together. For more on this, see Chapter 9.

> Open the door of the room to him that is come,
> that he may enter quietly and take possession;
> make soft the path upon the floor of the room;
> open the arms of the woman to him
> that he may take possession;
> open the body of the woman
> that his seed may be acceptable into her womb. (134)

The thrust of this prothalamion hints, perhaps, at Davidman's longing for a genuine and deeply fulfilling romance and bears witness to her intimation that there may be a lover for her in the future who will fulfill her.[34] Regardless, this poem celebrates a warm sexual love characterized by openness, selfless giving, virility, fertility, and fecundity.[35]

Immediately following "Prothalamion" is "Yet One More Spring." Ostensibly about the spring time, the poem actually focuses upon death: "What will come of me / After the fern has feathered from my brain / And the rosetree out of my blood; what will come of me / In the end, under the rainy locustblossom / Shaking its honey out on springtime air / Under the wind, under the stooping sky?" (134). Davidman wonders rhetorically if she will be "voiceless" and "unremembered." In answer she provides one of her most powerful poetic passages:

> Out of my heart the bloodroot,
> Out of my tongue the rose,
> Out of my bone the jointed corn,
> Out of my fiber trees.
> Out of my mouth a sunflower,
> And from my fingers vines,
> And the rank dandelion shall laugh from my loins
> Over million seeded earth; but out of my heart,
> Core of my heart, blood of my heart, the bloodroot
> Coming to lift a petal in peril of snow,

---

34. Although she was disappointed in this in her marriage to Gresham, I think she later found it with Lewis. For more on this, see Chapter 8.

35. Davidman's Renaissance literary studies brought to her attention Edmund Spenser's "Prothalamion" (Spenser is generally credited with having invented the term "prothalamion"). Interestingly, C. S. Lewis wrote an epithalamium (a post-nuptial song), "The Small Man Orders His Wedding" (*The Collected Poems of C. S. Lewis: A Critical Edition,* ed. Don W. King [Kent, OH: Kent State University, 2015], 346).

Coming to dribble from a broken stem
Bitterly the bright color of blood forever. (135)

She will be no "shrinking violet" in death. The rich, concrete imagery of these
lines suggests a vigorous resistance, a fierce sensibility, an all-consuming in-
tensity that indelibly mark Davidman's verse as uniquely hers. Every part of
her will rise again through the natural objects she will infuse.

If the poem were to stop here, it would be a great success. Yet Davidman
does not limit her legacy to mere reincarnation in nature. Where she will be
best remembered is in the heart of her lover:

But I would be more than a cold voice of flowers
And more than water, more than sprouting earth
Under the quiet passion of the spring;
I would leave you the trouble of my heart
To trouble you at evening; I would perplex you
With lightning coming and going about my head,
Outrageous signs, and wonders; I would leave you
The shape of my body filled with images,
The shape of my mind filled with imaginations,
The shape of myself. I would create myself
In a little fume of words and leave my words
After my death to kiss you forever and ever. (135)

Her promise to live on in the mind of her lover is striking, and anyone who
has read C. S. Lewis's *A Grief Observed* will be struck by how these lines
presage much of what he says about Davidman there.[36] Indeed, if it were

36. For instance:

> For a good wife contains so many persons in herself. What was H. not to me? She was my
> daughter and my mother, my pupil and my teacher, my subject and my sovereign; and al-
> ways, holding all these in solution, my trusty comrade, friend, shipmate, fellow-soldier. My
> mistress; but at the same time all that any man friend (and I have good ones) has ever been
> to me. Perhaps more. If we had never fallen in love we should have none the less been always
> together, and created scandal. That's what I meant when once I praised her for her "mas-
> culine virtues." But she soon put a stop to that by asking how I'd like to be praised for my
> feminine ones. It was a good *riposte,* dear. Yet there was something of the Amazon, some-
> thing of Penthesileia and Camilla. (*A Grief Observed* [London: Faber and Faber, 1961], 39)

The book was first published under the pseudonym N. W. Clerk. For Lewis to relate David-
man to Penthesileia (her name means "mourned by the people"), the Queen of Amazons

somehow possible, which I admit it is not, the final lines from this poem would be Joy Davidman's prothalamion and epithalamium to Lewis. If ever a poet foresaw how her memory would affect her lover, it was Davidman in this poem.[37] She could not have known, of course, that this lover would be Lewis, nor could he have had any inclination that he was being "pre-loved" by Davidman with such intensity, but later events suggest the inevitability of their coming together as friends, companions, and ultimately lovers.

It remains to offer a critical assessment of the poetry in *Letter to a Comrade*. The first characteristic of the poems is that we see a poet carefully practicing her craft; alliteration, anaphora, assonance, consonance, caesura, enjambment, and irony appear throughout. Also notable is her use of simile (as in "End of a Revolutionary": "When I am born again / I shall come like the grass-blade; / I shall be fertile and small / As the seed of grass" [156]) and metaphor (as in "Sorceress Eclogue": "I am the earth of which the corn is grown" [130]). Most noticeable is the prevalence of free verse. Perhaps her arresting voice needed the malleable nature of free verse — with its varying meter, lack of rhyme, and reliance on rhythm, cadence, and pace — for her to work at her best. Although on occasions she uses rhyming couplets ("Submarine," "Prayer against Indifference," "Four Elements," and "Waltzing Mouse"), lines of alternating rhyme ("To the Virgins," "Snow in Madrid," "The Alchemist," "Obsession," "In Praise of Fascists," "Againrising," "Tortoise"), stanzas of *abba* rhyme ("Il Pleure dans Mon Coeur," "Fly in Amber"), and the sonnet ("This Woman" and "An Absolution"), most of the forty-five poems in *Letter* are written in free verse. Davidman's free verse is best when she uses it to create concrete (and, at times, startling) images as in "Lament for Evolution":

> It is bitterness to know that I am alive;
> it is bitterness to find no reason for life, Apollo,

---

who led her troops in support of Priam during the battle of Troy, and Camilla, who in the *Aeneid* aids her ally King Turnus against Aeneas and the Trojans, suggests not only his deep love for her but also his admiration of her invincible spirit and courage as she battled the cancer that eventually took her life. Only a woman with an intellect the equal of Lewis's could have ever won his heart — something Davidman certainly did.

37. It is proper to connect here the discussion of "Obsession" above with "Yet One More Spring"; both poems show a lover consumed with possessing the beloved. However, while the speaker in "Obsession" comes across as a dark, aggressive lover driven at least in part by hate, the speaker in "Yet One More Spring" is less aggressive. She suggests it is not a destructive hatred fueling her desire to possess her lover; instead, she claims that his unforgettable memories of her will haunt, perplex, and possess him after she is gone.

except the subterfuge and apology of dying,
and to fear death, knowing the flesh will crawl,
nerves, bubbling glands, voracious guts, crawl screaming
away from dying. It is bitterness
in knowing life, anticipating death, playing softly with emotion,
to feel the blind slug brain recoil, turn inward,
and love its own contemplating lunatic eyes
sick with disgust; it is I, Apollo. (125)

In short, Davidman worked hard to craft poetry that was literate, provocative, accessible, and direct.

The second important aspect of *Letter to a Comrade* concerns the contemporary poets who may have most influenced her.[38] Obviously her penchant for free verse reflects the influence of Walt Whitman. Not surprisingly, another important influence was Stephen Vincent Benét; she wrote him on August 18, 1936: "You mention the influences which have affected my poetry (among which your own is not lacking); I am somewhat uneasily conscious of them nowadays, yet I feel they are fading rapidly from my more ambitious work" (*Bone,* 1-2).[39] In discussions with Benét about the final selections for *Letter to a Comrade,* Davidman revealed another influence: "You are right too about 'Artificers' [not included in *Letter to a Comrade*]; I think the Elinor Wylie poem was consciously in my mind as I wrote it" (July 26, 1938; *Bone,* 13).[40] Other influences were Edwin Arlington Robinson, W. H. Auden, Robert Frost, and Ridgely Torrence.[41] On the other hand, there are poets she resisted, including T. S. Eliot and Ezra Pound; she once referred to the latter as a "disgusting idiot" and "Mussolini's kept poet" (*Bone,* 23 and 37). Moreover, as poetry editor of *New Masses,* she published poets including Langston Hughes, Margaret Walker, and Aaron Kramer; that she favored these poets suggests they may have influenced her own work.[42]

---

38. For a comprehensive list of writers who influenced Davidman, see the reading syllabus she recommended to Aaron Kramer, "Education of a Poet," in her letter of January 26, 1948, in *Bone,* 68-71.

39. Benét's letter to Davidman in which he mentions influences upon her has not survived.

40. American poet and novelist Elinor Wylie (1885-1928) later married William Rose Benét, the brother of Stephen Vincent Benét. "Artificers" is published in *Bone,* 6.

41. Ridgely Torrence (1874-1950) was a poet and dramatist.

42. Margaret Walker (1915-1998) was an African American poet and educator. Her *For My People* (1942) won the Yale Younger Poet Prize. Aaron Kramer (1921-1997) was a poet,

However, perhaps the most outstanding characteristic of the poetry of *Letter to a Comrade* is Davidman's arresting voice — as many love poems mentioned above illustrate — one that is definite, sharp, and penetrating. When we read her verse, we find a voice that is focused, concentrated, hard, insisting to be heard, earnest, serious, determined, not suffering fools lightly, confrontational, zealot-like, insightful, and piercing. This arresting voice frequently employs the imperative. Many lines are orders: "Turn comrade," "Comrade, go," "Never let in the universe," "Love yourself," "Assault the door, break down the door, break open the door," "Let me have truth at my tongue's root," "Lie down lover," "Now with me / bow and set your mouth against America," "Only turn your lips to my lips," "Now do not put a ribbon in your hair," "Open the door of the room to him that is come," "Do not speak of him," "Let / The troubled fires of my body be / A thin light in an interstellar cave," "Sever the bone annihilate the sinew / stop up the nostril choke the mouth." This arresting, commanding voice dominates Davidman's poetry, suggesting someone eager to be in control, unbowed by challenges, and comfortable with exercising emotional power and persuasion. Another way to put this is that often her poems have a conversational and rhetorical edge — argumentative, persuasive, and insistent. She does not plea; she orders. She does not cajole; she commands. She does not entreat; she demands. Given her Communist sympathies and her tendency to use her verse at times in support of the CPUSA, and given her frank and openly sexually informed relationships, we should not be surprised at the arresting voice we find in so many of her poems in *Letter to a Comrade*. This arresting voice becomes even more pronounced as we turn to examine her work as an editor and a book, theater, and film reviewer for *New Masses*.

---

translator, and literary critic. His works include *The Poetry and Prose of Heinrich Heine* (1948), *The Prophetic Tradition in American Poetry* (1968), *Melville's Poetry: Toward the Enlarged Heart* (1972), and *Neglected Aspects of American Poetry* (1997).

CHAPTER 3

Communist Writer and Reviewer (1938-1945)

As Davidman was developing her skills in both fiction and verse, events conspired in the late 1930s to lead her to invest the lion's share of her creative energy in nonfiction — especially in the service of the CPUSA. Her service to the Party took many forms, but two involved her work as a writer. First, from April 1938 through July 1945 Davidman's poetry and book, theater, and film reviews appeared regularly in *New Masses,* the semi-official weekly magazine of the CPUSA.[1] Second, she edited a volume of World War II anti-Fascist war poems, *War Poetry of the United Nations* (1943); in addition, she edited and wrote the foreword for *They Look Like Men* (1944), a volume of poetry by Alexander F. Bergman, a young Communist poet who died of tuberculosis at twenty-eight. In what follows I briefly trace the history and literary/political agenda of *New Masses,* offer a critical evaluation of Davidman's nonfiction work as a reviewer for *New Masses,* and discuss her work as editor of the two volumes of anti-Fascist verse.

New Masses was the literary descendant of two radical periodicals.[2] The

---

1. In *And God Came In: The Extraordinary Story of Joy Davidman* (New York: Macmillan, 1983), 37-50, Dorsett briefly considers some of Davidman's publications in *New Masses.* See also Abigail Santamaria, *Joy: Poet, Seeker, and the Woman Who Captivated C. S. Lewis* (New York: Houghton Mifflin Harcourt, 2015), chs. 4 and 6.

2. For more on the history of the CPUSA and *New Masses,* see Daniel Aaron, *Writers on the Left* (New York: Harcourt, 1961); Michal R. Belknap, *Cold War Political Justice: The Smith Act, the Communist Party, and American Civil Liberties* (Westport, CT: Greenwood Press, 1977); Arthur C. Ferrari, "Proletarian Literature: A Case of Convergence of Political and Literary Radicalism," in *Cultural Politics: Radical Movements in Modern History,* ed. Jerold M. Starr (New York: Praeger, 1985); Barbara Foley, "Women and the Left in the

first, *Masses* (1911-1918), was, according to Daniel Aaron, a "spectacular organ of socialism, anarchism, paganism, and rebellion."[3] Such a critical judgment is not surprising, given the masthead statement that appeared in every issue during the early editorship of Max Eastman:

THIS MAGAZINE IS OWNED AND PUBLISHED COOPERATIVELY BY ITS EDITORS. IT HAS NO DIVIDENDS TO PAY, AND NOBODY IS TRYING TO MAKE MONEY OUT OF IT. A REVOLUTIONARY AND NOT A REFORM MAGAZINE; A MAGAZINE WITH A SENSE OF HUMOR AND NO RESPECT FOR THE RESPECTABLE; FRANK, AR-ROGANT, IMPERTINENT, SEARCHING FOR THE TRUE CAUSES; A MAGAZINE DIRECTED AGAINST RIGIDITY AND DOGMA WHEREVER IT IS FOUND; PRINTING WHAT IS TOO NAKED OR TRUE FOR A MONEY-MAKING PRESS; A MAGAZINE WHOSE FI-NAL POLICY IS TO DO AS IT PLEASES AND CONCILIATE NO-BODY, NOT EVEN ITS READERS — THERE IS A FIELD FOR THIS PUBLICATION IN AMERICA.[4]

Politically, *Masses* aggressively advanced a socialist agenda and for that caught the eye of the United States government; matters came to a head just prior to America's entry into World War I when *Masses* loudly opposed conscription. By April 1917 it was banned from the U.S. Postal Service, and

---

1930s," *American Literary History* 2 (Spring 1990): 150-69; Michael Folsom, ed., *Mike Gold: A Literary Anthology* (New York: International, 1972); Granville Hicks, *Granville Hicks in the* New Masses (Port Washington, NY: Kennikat Press, 1974); Irving Howe and Lewis Coser, *The American Communist Party: A Critical History* (New York: Praeger, 1957); Maurice Isserman, *Which Side Were You On? The American Communist Party during the Second World War* (Middletown, CT: Wesleyan University Press, 1982); Harvey Klehr, *The Heyday of American Communism: The Depression Decade* (New York: Basic Books, 1984); David Madden, ed., *Proletarian Writers of the Thirties* (Carbondale: Southern Illinois University Press, 1968); James E. Murphy, *The Proletarian Moment: The Controversy over Leftism in Literature* (Chicago: University of Illinois Press, 1991); Alfred North, ed., *New Masses: An Anthology of the Rebel Thirties* (New York: International Publishers, 1969); Fraser M. Otta-nelli, *The Communist Party of the United States: From the Depression to World War II* (New Brunswick, NJ: Rutgers University Press, 1991); Walter Rideout, *The Radical Novel in the United States, 1900-1954* (Cambridge: Harvard University Press, 1956); and Alan M. Wald, *Exiles from a Future Time: The Forging of the Mid-Twentieth-Century Literary Left* (Chapel Hill: University of North Carolina Press, 2002).

3. Aaron, *Writers on the Left*, 18.

4. Cited in Aaron, *Writers on the Left*, 22 (caps in original).

Eastman and his colleagues were indicted for conspiring to obstruct the draft.[5] Although the trial ended with a hung jury, *Masses* never recovered.

After the suppression of *Masses,* the second periodical, *The Liberator* (1918-1924), appeared, largely subsuming and intensifying the socialist agenda of *Masses.* With Eastman as editor and others on his editorial staff, including Floyd Dell and Joseph Freeman, *The Liberator* marched steadily toward enthusiastic support for the Bolsheviks in Russia. Mike Gold, who joined the editorial staff of *The Liberator* in 1921, soon began to urge an even more revolutionary agenda for the periodical than Eastman; in particular, Gold vigorously pushed what he called proletarian literature — poems and stories by and about workers and their plight. In 1922 *The Liberator,* with its philosophical base squarely set in Bolshevism, was turned over to the Workers' Party, a transparent organ of the CPUSA. Since it was no longer primarily a periodical directed by artists and writers, *The Liberator,* now with an entirely political agenda, lost the interest of most of its former writers and readers; it folded in 1924.

With the demise of *The Liberator,* Gold and others established *New Masses* (1926-1948), largely in an effort to recapture the spirit of *Masses;* that is, they wanted to combine literature and politics as had the earlier periodical. *New Masses* (hereafter *NM*) was published initially as a monthly beginning May 1926; as a result of financial difficulties and political infighting, Gold became the sole editor from 1928 to 1930. In a bellwether article published in January 1929, "Go Left, Young Writer," Gold pressed for the emergence of a proletarian writer, a "wild youth of about twenty-two, the son of working class parents, who himself works in the lumber camps, coal mines, and steel mills, harvest fields and mountain camps of America. . . . He is a Red but has few theories. It is all instinct with him. His writing is no conscious straining after proletarian art, but the natural flower of his environment."[6] Such writers could be effective only if they based their work upon personal experience: "Write. Your life in mine, mill, and farm is of deathless significance in the history of the world. Tell us about it in the same language you use in writing a letter. It may be literature — it often is. Write. Persist. Struggle."[7] In that same issue of *NM,* Martin Russak added: "A real proletarian writer must not only write about the working

5. Aaron, *Writers on the Left,* 36.

6. Mike Gold, "Go Left, Young Writer," *New Masses* 4 (January 1929): 3-4. Reprinted in Folsom, ed., *Mike Gold: A Literary Anthology,* 188.

7. Gold, "Go Left, Young Writer," in Folsom, ed., *Mike Gold: A Literary Anthology,* 189.

class, he must be read by the working class . . . [and he must embody] bitter hatred, absolute class solidarity, and revolutionary passion."[8] In September 1930 Gold offered more detail about the nature of what he called "proletarian realism" in his "Notes of the Month": such literature dealt "with *real conflicts* of men and women who work for a living. It has nothing to do with . . . sickly mental states nor mental anguish"; it "does not believe in literature for its own sake, but in literature that is useful, has a social function"; it would be written in "as few words as possible"; it would contain "swift action, clear form, the direct line, cinema in words"; and it would do "away with lies about human nature. We are scientists; we know what a man thinks and feels."[9]

Such a view of literature threatened to reduce it to thinly veiled propaganda; at the same time, such literature supported the revolutionary aims of the CPUSA in the 1930s. Given the tremendous social upheaval resulting from the stock market crash in 1929 and the subsequent Great Depression, the CPUSA found fertile ground in the thousands of unemployed, homeless, and displaced. Yet, ironically, readership of *NM* lagged so badly that it ceased publication in September 1933 with a circulation of only 6,000 copies a month. When it reappeared as a weekly in January 1934, with Granville Hicks as editor, it had, by necessity, broadened its revolutionary agenda; by December 1934 its circulation had increased to 25,000 weekly, and Gold had essentially stepped back from editorial involvement.[10]

By advocating and publishing proletarian literature, the reinvented *NM* carried forward the banner of the CPUSA in a highly public fashion. The short story "Quiet and Safe" by Len Zinberg is representative of one stream of proletarian realism that appeared in *NM*. Offered from the perspective of a strike breaker, the story purports to give us an inside view of his cowardly psychology. In recounting his tentative journey toward the picket lines, the strike breaker worries that there are no policemen around to protect him; he imagines being attacked by those on the picket line: "Those dirty bastards waiting to slug him, and there was no cops! Those saps, just hoping to smack

---

8. Cited in Arthur C. Ferrari, "Proletarian Literature: A Case of Convergence of Political and Literary Radicalism," in *Cultural Politics: Radical Movements in Modern History,* ed. Jerold M. Starr (New York: Praeger, 1985), 175.

9. Folsom, ed., *Mike Gold: A Literary Anthology,* 206-8. In fairness, Gold's view on the nature of proletarian literature softened and broadened over time. For more on this see Murphy, *The Proletarian Moment;* and Rideout, *The Radical Novel in the United States.*

10. Ferrari, "Proletarian Literature," 179; and Rideout, *The Radical Novel in the United States,* 149-50.

him one, and they would hit him. He could feel the dull smacking sound of a fist on a jaw, on a soft eye, on a nose, on a soft stomach; a lot of fists landing on his face." Whatever authorial distance Zinberg may have had as he began writing the story disappears in the next paragraph when we read: "As he wiped the sweat from his thin oval face, he saw the door of the building open and a cop come out. The scab thought, the sonofabitch must have been smoking in the hallway, not even looking out for me."[11]

Now that readers know for certain they are reading about a scab, they can be sure he will be paid in full by the end of the story. The little forced tension created in the story concerns how the scab manages to get past the picket line by attaching himself to a mailman; smirking to himself about how he has fooled the strikers, the scab takes an elevator up to his workplace only to find he is early and locked out. When he hears the elevator coming up again, he is in a panic, certain the strikers are coming to beat him up. However, when he sees it is the mailman, the denouement occurs and the story ends: "The mailman was passing him and the scab grinned and said 'Hello, *pal*. Kind of . . .' The postman swung from his knees as he turned, a heavy roundhouse blow that sent the scab crashing against the wall; then he slipped to the floor. . . . The scab lay there quietly, a slim trickle of blood running out of the side of his mouth and down over his broken jaw."[12] In spite of Zinberg's intention that we find irony in how the story ends, given its title, cartoon characters, facile understanding of human nature, and transparent hatred for the "scab," the story is more laughable than convincing.

The poetry appearing in *NM*, especially before Davidman became the poetry editor, was sometimes not much better. For instance, in the introduction to "Eight New Poets" we read the following:

> [These poems are] indicative of the extent to which the social crisis and the agitation for a literature with social emphasis and proletarian bias has permeated the general literary scene and influenced a new group of writers. A number of them have no connections with working-class organizations, but their sympathies are definitely with the proletariat. This symposium is presented with the hope it will stimulate a new interest in and encourage a social poetry.[13]

11. Len Zinberg, "Quiet and Safe," *New Masses* 28 (July 12, 1938): 152. A scab is the derogatory name for a strike breaker.

12. Zinberg, "Quiet and Safe," 153.

13. "Eight New Poets," *New Masses* 22 (February 16, 1937): 11.

"Winter Haven" describes the plight of "cold boys, loading gunnysacks with coke"; "Monday Morning" offers a snapshot view of a hobo jungle and sardonically notes that "strong coffee is almost as good as lysol is, to wash / the ache from the bones"; "Dirge for the Fearsome" mocks those who lack the courage to fight for labor; "Poem in the Pressroom," " 'Fired!,' " and "Phyllis and Corydon" lament the helplessness of workers against their bosses; "Meaning" considers a worker and his wife in their struggle to survive and find meaning in life; "Death of Barbusse" attempts to evoke the revolutionary spirit of W. B. Yeats; "Intellectual to Worker" is an ironic dramatic monologue in which a writer tries to convince a laborer that the work each does supports the revolution.[14]

Perhaps the key example in this collection of proletarian verse is "Sonnet":

The living soul is nailed upon a graph
and money bends the index toward despair
but, cushioned soft, our half-hog humans laugh
the child's way, ego's — their private joy sole care.
And still they throw as gypsies do a card,
staking the world come fortune lapse or thrive;
still pitch coins to a ghetto-ghost in the yard;
still yap "Stay yoked!" and still, "Be glad alive!"
here's paradox, puffed to your size: reject your class,
parcel your pity off for a fool's iota,
fatten yourself like a pet bug under glass,
live for yourself and lo! death's sure your quota!
But death damned more, to end as fascist meat,
hung like a butchered rabbit by your feet.[15]

Whatever the merits this has in advancing proletarian realism — and I am not convinced there are any — has there ever been an uglier poem?[16]

Not everything appearing in *NM* was as crude as these examples; indeed, another stream appeared containing writings by many luminaries of contemporary American literature, including William Carlos Williams, Robinson Jeffers, Theodore Dreiser, Sherwood Anderson, John Dos Passos,

14. "Eight New Poets," 12-13.
15. "Eight New Poets," 13.
16. For an example of the kind of nonfiction "proletarian realism" appearing in *NM*, see Milton Blau's "I Never Found a Job," *New Masses* 35 (April 16, 1940): 17-18.

Edmund Wilson, Erskine Caldwell, Langston Hughes, Richard Wright, and Ernest Hemingway. Lesser lights included Granville Hicks, Horace Gregory, James Farrell, Margaret Walker, Muriel Rukeyser, and, of course, Joy Davidman. These writers, largely uncomfortable with the propagandist stream, subtly helped transformed the meaning of proletarian literature. A case in point was the active support of *NM* for the loyalists during the Spanish Civil War. In his June 22, 1937, essay "Fascism Is a Lie," Hemingway writes: "Really good writers are always rewarded under almost any existing system of government that they can tolerate. There is only one form of government that cannot produce good writers, and that system is fascism. For fascism is a lie told by bullies. A writer who will not lie cannot live or work under fascism."[17] Had Hemingway known of the similar bullying of Communism in the Soviet Union, he might have changed the title of his essay to "Totalitarianism Is a Lie"; be that as it may, his essay suggests how interest in proletarian literature flourished in the pages of *NM* throughout the 1930s.

With the literary success of *Letter to a Comrade* and her zealous support of LAW, and eager to use her talents as a writer, Davidman considered herself a potentially useful tool of the CPUSA. She looked for a way to help the cause. Since she had been reading *NM* for some time, particularly the poetry, she eventually made her way to the offices of *NM* and offered her services. Almost immediately she was brought on board as a poetry editor. No lover of proletarian literature herself, and convinced that many of the poems previously published in *NM* were simply bad poems despite their proletarian rhetoric, she set about to raise the quality of verse appearing in *NM*.[18] For instance, she wrote to one correspondent: "The best thing about

17. Ernest Hemingway, "Fascism Is a Lie," *New Masses* 23 (June 22, 1937): 4. See also William Rollins, "What Is a Proletarian Writer?" *New Masses* 15 (January 29, 1935): 22-23; Alan Calmer, "The Proletarian Short Story," *New Masses* 16 (July 2, 1935): 17-19; Calmer, "Portrait of the Artist as a Proletarian," *Saturday Review of Literature* (July 1937): 3-4, 17; and Philip Rahv, "Proletarian Literature: A Political Autopsy," *Southern Review* (Spring 1939): 616-28.

18. In another instance of her efforts to improve the writing of poetry, records show that for the fall 1943 term, on Wednesday evenings from 7:00 to 8:30 p.m., she taught "Poetry Workshop" for the School of Democracy, an anti-Fascist, pro-Communist institution in New York City. The course description reads: "This course will cover the origin, function, and basic technique of all verse-forms, with practice in writing them; a study of the historical development of poetry in its relation to society; an analysis of the tasks, opportunities, and subject matter of modern poets; and thorough analysis and criticism of the student's work. Special attention will be devoted to technical problems, to the various types of verse forms, and to the subject matter best suited to reflect current issues and experiences" (School for

Aaron Kramer's work is that it unites proletarian themes with proletarian language. You have no idea how rarely one finds a so-called Workers' Poet who writes in language the workers can understand. . . . And that's what I like about the Kramer boy's work; it achieves poetry with ordinary words and conversational diction, the best and the hardest way of achieving it" (April 28, 1939; *Bone*, 23-24).[19]

In another case she wrote Communist poet Harold Harwell Lewis a lengthy letter in which she offers a generous but trenchant critique of his poetry:

> Poetry must appeal to the imagination and the emotions; correct political statement is not enough. Otherwise, why not write an editorial and the hell with verse? And to appeal to imagination and emotion, the poet must use both himself; he must work through the five senses, not through the power of argument. It is no good to talk about a million dead men in general terms; it presents no image. But take just one of those men — describe his eyes and his voice and the way he brushed his hair back with a grin, tell what he had in his pockets, mention his private jokes and his favorite amusement and his first love affair — and you have created a person. Now, when you kill him, the reader will feel that someone real has died. Or, if you want a mass approach, really *see* a battlefield with a million corpses on it. Take a good look at each one, touch it, examine its wounds, smell it, figure how it died, scare away the flies and the crows and try to arrange the corpses decently, gather up the shattered pieces and bury them in a great trench. When you have done all that in your mind you will be able to write about it and make it real. . . . Poetry is the people's art and must talk their language. And it must not scream; violent punctuation and italics, like dirty words, just make poetry silly by over-emphasis. What the words do not contain, you cannot add with punctuation. And poetry must not argue; once you argue with your reader you have thrown away the chance of rousing his sympathetic emotions. . . . Just stop reining in your imagination; let it go and take a look at the real lives and sufferings of real people on this earth. Then come back and tell simply what you

---

Democracy [Handbook], 13 Astor Place, New York, "Course Listings, Fall Term: September-December 1943," 22).

19. Selections of Kramer's poems appeared along with Davidman's in *Seven Poets in Search of an Answer*, ed. Thomas Yoseloff (New York: Bernard Ackerman, 1944). Later letters to Kramer himself were less complimentary.

have seen. I'm pretty sure you can do it; and that will be poetry. (June 7, 1943; *Bone,* 38-39)[20]

In a later letter to Kramer, Davidman is quite pointed in her critique of the weaknesses of his poetry:

If your real desire is not to do the best possible work but only to get personal self-satisfaction out of whatever work you do, then you had better not read past this paragraph. . . . Brace yourself, boy; here it comes. The trouble with your poetry is [your] sheer unwillingness to get an education. . . . You seem to have little power of self-criticism. There are some fine things . . . but they are side by side with work which no one should be willing to have printed.

Worse yet, you have not developed your powers of observation. You seem to regard the visible world merely as a means of making a political point. . . . All you seem able to appreciate in *any* experience is its possible political implication. This is all very well, and it is possible to be a good human being on this basis; but it is not possible to be a good poet. . . . The . . . most serious general point I want to make is that you simply do not know the English language well enough.

It is not that you can't write grammatically; you can. But grammar is only the bare bones of a language. Its flesh and blood are generations of association of ideas, so that a word has not only its dictionary meaning but a whole range of emotional values, from the comic to the tragic, the grotesque to the exquisite. Words also have *class* associations; a given word or idiom may stamp you at once as proletarian, middle class, or gentleman — as literate or illiterate; as city-bred or rural, modern-minded or old-fashioned. No doubt you know this in theory. What you have not realized is that your own use of words stamps you, to the eye, say, of an intelligent college senior with a turn for literature — stamps you as a boy trying to make bluff serve instead of education.

It is not because you write simply. You don't write simply. You write

20. Harold Harwell Lewis (1901-1985) wrote for a number of Communist publications, including *New Masses* and the *Daily Worker.* In addition, for a time he published his own magazine, *The Outlander.* His volumes of poetry include *Red Renaissance* (Holt, MN: B. C. Hagglund Publisher, 1930), and *Road to Utterly* (Holt, MN: B. C. Hagglund Publisher, 1935). For more on H. H. Lewis see Douglas Wixson, "In Search of the Low-Down Americano: H. H. Lewis, William Carlos Williams, and the Politics of Literary Reception, 1930-1950," *William Carlos Williams Review* 26, no. 1 (2006): 75-100.

with an appalling variety of out-of-date bourgeois affectation; words that not even a college professor would use in speech, let alone a worker, come tumbling off your typewriter in all their mid-Victorian lushness. You are wearing the cast-off rags of bourgeois language, and you don't even know it. (January 26, 1948; *Bone,* 55, 59-61)[21]

However, her work as poetry editor was not the primary literary contribution Davidman made to *NM;* instead it was her facility as a book, theater, and movie reviewer — especially the latter — that best portrays her contribution to the cause.[22] Indeed, during her most active period as a writer and editor for *NM,* March 1941 through July 1943, she was publishing a book or movie review in almost every issue.[23] Her initial reviews, published from December 1938 through May 1939, were book reviews. An early book review — that of Kenneth Porter's volume of poetry, *The High Plains,* on February 7, 1939 — illustrates again her arresting voice, but now in the form of a poison pen. Davidman begins kindly enough: "In an age when so much verse is verbally profuse and emotionally costive, technically dazzling and stale with the pedantry of an Ezra Pound, it is sometimes refreshing to come upon a book wherein purpose and passion somewhat outrun technique." However, her pen turns sharp later on when she dismisses some of Porter's religious poems; in particular, she says "The Lord's Supper" rises "to singular heights of silliness . . . with its comparison of a mountain to a sliced cake."[24] In correspondence with Porter on February 19, 1939, she tries to ameliorate her criticism:

21. Specifically, Davidman was offering comments about Kramer's *The Thunder of the Grass* (New York: International Publishers, 1948).

22. She also published a number of her own poems in *NM;* these are discussed in Chapter 5.

23. There are two notable gaps in Davidman's publications in *NM* that should be explained here. The first one occurred from June 1939 through December 1940, in part because she was putting the finishing touches to her novel *Anya* (1940); in addition, from spring 1939 until December 1939 she moved to Hollywood for six months in an abortive attempt to write movie screenplays. For more on this, see Chapter 4; see also Oliver Pilat, "Girl Communist [Joy Davidman]: An Intimate Story of Eight Years in the Party," *The New York Post,* November 5, 1949, and Dorsett's *And God Came In,* 38-39. The second gap occurred from November 1943 through August 1944; the cause for this gap was her pregnancy and the eventual birth of her first son, David Lindsay Gresham, on March 27, 1944. Douglas Howard Gresham was born November 10, 1945.

24. "Kansas Poet" (book review of *The High Plains* by Kenneth Porter), *New Masses* 30 (February 7, 1939): 26-27.

I was rather hasty in calling "The Lord's Supper" silly, I'm afraid. Looking at it now, I see it was the whole sacramental idea which annoyed me; I'm inclined by nature to call anything sacramental sentimental, being an iron materialist. As for the imagery, I've seen the mountains you speak of and I know the symbolism, but the whole philosophy of the poem is so unlike mine, and so unlike, indeed, that of your own later work, that I could wish you had followed your first impulse in not printing it. (*Bone*, 16-17)

In the letter Davidman goes on to admit her tendency toward sharp criticism: "I must tell you something about that review; it's probably the most favorable I've ever written, for the cat in me comes out in reviewing; and it was originally half of a longer review, the other part of which was devoted to a book which I boiled in oil by way of contrast. But I cut that out, attacked by an uneasy conscience because I knew the book's author" (*Bone*, 18).

Davidman's candid admission of her aggressive tendency to unsheathe her pen is borne out in many later film reviews. She did not suffer fools lightly. For example, she begins one review: "When all the hack ideas in Hollywood are laid end to end, you get something like the package labeled *Come Live with Me.*" Then she adds: "The laughs are spaced as widely as a seven-year-old's teeth . . . and Jimmy Stewart's attempt to get into his wife's arms is nothing you ought to see after a heavy meal."[25] About Barbara Stanwick's acting in one film, Davidman writes: "[Her] girl reporter is a soggy stain on the film. She does her emotional scenes as a series of impassioned squawks."[26] In one of her most blistering reviews she savages the World War II movie *I Wanted Wings:*

This reviewer has always considered herself fairly articulate, yet, face to face with *I Wanted Wings,* she feels the poverty of her vocabulary. All the words that describe it adequately are unprintable. . . . [The film] makes no bones about its intentions. It is a recruiting poster in style, sentiment, and static quality. If you imagine yourself compelled to stare at such a poster for two solid hours, you will have some idea of the entertainment value of this juicy offering. . . . Using the crudest of appeals, *I Wanted Wings* alternates uplifting pep talks with uplifted blondes. A more flaccid script would

25. "Humdrum Cinema" (movie reviews of *Come Live with Me* and *So Ends Our Night*), *New Masses* 38 (March 18, 1941): 29-30.

26. "Huey Hooey" (movie reviews of *Meet John Doe* and *Rage in Heaven*), *New Masses* 39 (April 1, 1941): 31.

be hard to imagine. . . . It is astonishing, indeed, how many women there are in the Air Corps (Hollywood version). They attend court-martials, they stroll across the field cheerfully snapping pictures of bombers, they stow away in airplanes. And they never wear any underwear, or much overwear for that matter. . . . [It] is a limping affair; you find yourself looking closely at the screen to make sure the projector hasn't stopped. There are, of course, some extremely beautiful and intelligent airplanes, that contrast favorably with the human performers. . . . If Miss Veronica Lake ever puts on a brassiere, her acting ability will disappear.[27]

She is equally severe with *That Uncertain Feeling*, a film that "is a soufflé that has been left standing too long. . . . Its final consistency is such that you could sell it as an old rubber tire, and not even a goat would notice the difference in taste."[28] About *Penny Serenade* she remarks: "All that you can get from [this film] can be obtained more economically by slicing an onion. Besides, an onion doesn't smell that bad."[29] Concerning "a repulsive young [actor] named Victor Mature, who is being served up as a skinful of sex appeal," she opines: "Having appeared in several bad movies, Mr. Mature is within the province of this reviewer, who would trade her rights in him for enough fertilizer to nourish the snapdragons in her windowbox."[30] Perhaps her most terse dismissal of a film is the following: "There is only one thing wrong with *Young Mr. Pitt;* it is a lie."[31]

Although Davidman often sharply criticizes the films coming out of Hollywood — which I explore in the next chapter — she consistently praises one genre of films it produced: "This reviewer has said nasty things about Hollywood. Yet today she wishes to make partial amends. There is at least one branch of the film art in which Hollywood remains supreme. I refer, of course, to the screwball comedy. When they want to fill a picture with lunatics, boy, do they fill it with lunatics."[32] For instance, her first movie

27. "Rover Boys on Wings" (movie reviews of *I Wanted Wings* and *Topper Returns*), *New Masses* 39 (April 8, 1941): 28-29.

28. "Three Films" (movie reviews of *That Uncertain Feeling, The Flame of New Orleans,* and *Penny Serenade*), *New Masses* 39 (May 20, 1941): 30.

29. "Three Films," 31.

30. "Neptune's Pets" (movie reviews of *Washington Murderdrama, Power Dive,* and *Border Vigilantes*), *New Masses* 39 (June 10, 1941): 28-29.

31. "False History" (movie review of *Young Mr. Pitt*), *New Masses* 46 (March 23, 1943): 30.

32. "Shining Screwballs" (movie reviews of *Love Crazy* and *Shining Victory*), *New Masses* 39 (June 17, 1941): 28.

review in *NM,* "Marxist Mania," has nothing to do with the father of Communism. Instead, she lavishes praise on the Marx brothers' film *Go West:* "For slapstick as it ought to be, thank God, there are still the Marx brothers."[33] Davidman also gives high marks to many Disney films: "*Dumbo* is the most delightful Disney so far . . . [with] a circus full of animals, all with personality, all of remarkable and interesting shape." She compliments the color and draftsmanship of the illustrators, the lively music, and "the general atmosphere of affectionate gaiety." Davidman especially praises the parade of pink elephants: "So you think *you've* seen pink elephants? Hah. Precision requires me to add that they are not all strictly pink; how about the neat little number in a rather surprising plaid?"[34] She also enjoyed well-done musicals; regarding *Louisiana Purchase* she uncharacteristically coos: "[It] is enchantingly carried out all through; its wit is gay and natural, its plotting extraordinarily cogent, and its bright and light and fantastic technicolor is admirably suited to the unreal world of the musical film. . . . *Louisiana Purchase* is a darling picture. As this reviewer is beginning to melt slightly at the edges, we had better stop here."[35]

Another genre of films she consistently reviewed was, not surprisingly, the war movie. Although she could be savage, as her evaluation of *I Wanted Wings* has already shown, Davidman actually wanted there to be better movies about the realities of the war — in part because she was an American and in part because she was a Communist intent on exposing Fascism at every turn. In time there were better-produced war movies. Among many she singled out for commendation were *Target for Tonight, Mrs. Miniver, Ring of Steel, One of Our Aircraft Is Missing, Wake Island, Commandos Strike at Dawn, Air Force, Hangmen Also Die, Action in the North Atlantic,* and *Bataan.* She commends *Mrs. Miniver* as "an American war film to be proud of . . . [for] its adult dignity, the restrained power of its tragedy, and its foursquare approach to the fact of the people's war."[36] In *One of Our Aircraft Is Missing* Davidman is thrilled to find "that the [story of] trapped airmen can make a first-rate, sober, and genuinely heroic film." Of the film's portrayal of Nazis, she says: "They are always there, a lurking terror: never quite seen, hence all

33. "Marxist Mania" (movie review of *Go West*), *New Masses* 38 (March 4, 1941): 27.

34. "Other Movies" (movie reviews of *Dumbo, All That Money Can Buy,* and *Target for Tonight*), *New Masses* 41 (November 4, 1941): 27.

35. "Dinner Knives" (movie reviews of *The Man Who Came to Dinner* and *Louisiana Purchase*), *New Masses* 42 (January 20, 1942): 29-30.

36. "Under the Bombs" (movie reviews of *Mrs. Miniver, Nazi Agent,* and *Ring of Steel*), *New Masses* 43 (June 30, 1942): 29.

the more horrible. They snarl orders outside a church full of praying people; they growl at each other round the corner where the Englishmen are hiding. . . . The movie as effectively portrays our enemy as it presents the heroism of our allies."[37] *Commandos Strike at Dawn* draws high praise because "this film of the fighting Norwegian people says, at last, exactly the right things about an occupied nation, about quislings, and about Nazis."[38] She singles out *Hangmen Also Die* as so great a film "that the critic's task becomes humble study of [its] methods. . . . [It] may well be America's finest artistic comment on the war."[39]

Davidman also had the good fortune to be writing movie reviews for *NM* during a period in which appeared some of the finest movies ever made, including *Citizen Kane, The Maltese Falcon, How Green Was My Valley, Casablanca, Keeper of the Flame,* and *The Ox-Bow Incident.* She says *The Maltese Falcon* makes "the movie detective story completely adult. . . . Sam Spade, the amorous but grim detective, is more effective than Sherlock Holmes ever was, proving in Humphrey Bogart's adroit hands that a detective can be human and doesn't have to wear a funny hat." Characterization, she argues, is the particular strength of the film: "The detective, the villains, the sweet little liar of a heroine, are all memorable people. Even the widow in the background, weeping, is an incisive study of one kind of fraud."[40] *Keeper of the Flame,* which ignited a firestorm of critical controversy for implying there existed a secret conspiracy to promote American Fascism, is a critically important film according to Davidman because "now as never before American fascism must be stamped out, before it loses the war for us; and *Keeper of the Flame* is a bright weapon to kill it with." She also heaps praise on an unlikely place: Hollywood: "The producers of MGM who backed the picture are to be congratulated." And while she also has compliments for the director, George Cukor, and the key actors, Spencer Tracy and Katharine Hepburn, it is the anti-Fascism message she most endorses: "The driving force of the film . . . transcends individual contributions, uniting them into

---

37. "Dutch Underground" (movie reviews of *One of Our Aircraft Is Missing, George Washington Slept Here, A Yank at Eton,* and *Iceland*), *New Masses* 45 (November 17, 1942): 29-30.

38. "Commandos Strike at Dawn" (movie reviews of *Commandos Strike at Dawn* and *China Girl*), *New Masses* 46 (February 9, 1943): 27.

39. "But the People Live" (movie review of *Hangmen Also Die*), *New Masses* 47 (May 4, 1943): 28.

40. "The Maltese Falcon" (movie reviews of *The Maltese Falcon, It Started with Eve,* and *The Man Who Seeks the Truth*), *New Masses* 41 (October 21, 1941): 28.

a single clear statement: the enemies of the people are moving among us under cover of darkness. They must be exposed."[41]

Another important group of films that Davidman reviewed for *NM* were the dozens coming out of the Soviet Union. Predictably, Davidman only found praise for these films; while it is certainly true that some of them deserved her commendation, it is also true that she did not exercise the same critical eye with them that she did with the American, British, and French films she reviewed. In other words, she followed the Party line in reviewing the Soviet films; they were essentially all good films — no matter the weaknesses and flaws — because they came out of the Soviet Union and implicitly illustrated how Communism was a superior form of government than either capitalism or Fascism. Examples are legion. In her first review of a Soviet film, *The New Teacher,* she inadvertently reveals her bias: "*The New Teacher* . . . is rather a lovely thing. . . . It is hard to put into words just why. . . . All one can say is that the picture dances and leaps with the joy of life."[42] Regarding the Soviet documentary *Soviet Frontiers on the Danube,* she says: "You can see what happy people really look like. When the Red Army marched into Bessarabia, years of misery and persecution were wiped out. . . . The Soviets need no guards between themselves and the people; throughout the villages, the entire population swarms out, clambers over the tanks, brings little bunches of wild flowers and presses them into soldiers' hands." While an impartial reviewer would at least suggest the possibility that such scenes are perhaps part of a propaganda campaign, Davidman never entertains the thought. Instead, she sings the film's praises: "One could go on forever without conveying a tenth of the emotional power of *Soviet Frontiers.* This reviewer does not, ordinarily, label films 'must'; but *Soviet Frontiers* is a 'must' picture. You have to go and see it; you can't afford not to."[43] The editors at *NM* and their CPUSA comrades must have been pleased at this endorsement.

Other glowing reviews include *Wings of Victory* ("It has remained for the Soviets to produce the first great film on flying, because only the Soviet, only a socialist state, could understand that the man is more important than the

41. "Keeper of the Flame" (movie reviews of *Keeper of the Flame, Chetniks,* and *Hitler's Children*), *New Masses* 46 (March 30, 1943): 28-29.

42. "Soviet Love Story" (movie reviews of *The New Teacher* and *That Hamilton Woman*), *New Masses* 39 (April 22, 1941): 28.

43. "Soviet Frontiers" (movie reviews of *Soviet Frontiers on the Danube* and *Underground*), *New Masses* 40 (July 15, 1941): 27.

plane"),[44] *The Girl from Leningrad* (its fighting scenes "are perhaps the best of all shots of modern war"),[45] *Guerrilla Brigade* ("Never was a Soviet film a more magnificent tribute to the common man — his suffering, his heroism, his triumphs. Indeed, it is hard to think of *Guerrilla Brigade* as a film at all, or of its men and women as actors; the thing is a piece of living history"),[46] *This Is the Enemy* (the film "has brilliantly solved the problem besetting all our novelists, playwrights, and screen writers; the problem of integrating a struggle of individuals against Nazis with the great struggle of humanity"),[47] and *In the Rear of the Enemy* ("It happens to be a rather tremendous film; but it is still more tremendous as a statement of the brotherhood of peoples").[48] About the musical *Volga-Volga,* she positively gushes: "Do the Soviets *have* to come out on top in everything? They already have the best diplomats, the best kindergartens, the best economic system, the best life — but is that enough for them? No; they go and get the best musical comedies too. I turn green. I gnash my teeth with envy."[49]

It remains to consider her work as a movie reviewer. In general she is a very good film critic, drawing in large part from her experiences in Hollywood. First, she is conscientious and regular in her reviews; even if she dislikes a film, she explains why. Second, she is not always caustic and can be quite generous; for example, about *Out of the Fog* she says: "[It] is so good as to leave this reviewer without a chance to exercise her poison pen. A tale of decent, ordinary human beings threatened by a gangster, the film has obvious symbolism, and its final rallying of the gentle people to destroy the gangster is the rallying of the oppressed the world over."[50] Third, she often writes about the technical excellences or failures of a film, including writing, lighting, camera angles, editing, musical scores, and direction; another way to put this is that she takes her craft as a movie reviewer seriously, relying

44. "Perfect Landing" (movie reviews of *Wings of Victory* and *The Land Is Bright*), *New Masses* 41 (November 25, 1941): 26.

45. "The Girl from Leningrad" (movie review of *The Girl from Leningrad*), *New Masses* 42 (January 6, 1942): 26.

46. "Guerrilla Brigade" (movie reviews of *Guerrilla Brigade* and *The Ghost of Frankenstein*), *New Masses* 43 (April 21, 1942): 28.

47. "This Is the Enemy" (movie reviews of *This Is the Enemy* and *Laugh, Town, Laugh*), *New Masses* 44 (July 7, 1942): 30.

48. "Heroes Are Human Beings" (movie reviews of *In the Rear of the Enemy, Desperate Journey, Manila Calling,* and *Tales of Manhattan*), *New Masses* 45 (October 13, 1942): 30.

49. "Volga-Volga" (movie review of *Volga-Volga*), *New Masses* 39 (May 27, 1941): 25.

50. "The Face of China" (movie reviews of *Ku Kan* and *Out of the Fog*), *New Masses* 40 (July 8, 1941): 27.

upon her Hollywood experience for the technical insights she makes on a film under review.[51] For instance, she is almost gracious in her comments about *Rage in Heaven:* "[This film] has passed through many hands since James Hilton [who wrote the novel upon which the screenplay was based] let it fall with a dull thud. This reviewer had a crack at writing it, too, in her Metro-Goldwyn-Mayer days, and it is with great magnanimity that she admits the film is much better than she or James Hilton left it."[52]

Fourth, although she turns a blind eye to the critical defects of films coming out of the Soviet Union, in other regards she is an honest reviewer. When films fail to deliver, for example, she rarely minces words:

> Writing a film script is much like writing anything else; you get a bright idea, you put it on paper quickly in the first flush of inspiration, and then the hard work starts. The bright idea will not carry you through the intricate business of developing a coherent plot and creditable motivation. For some Hollywood offerings, however, that first fine careless rapture seems to be enough. Behold such a job as *Million Dollar Baby,* which is terribly clever as long as the sap is still rising, but, in its latter two-thirds, as juiceless as last year's pine needles.[53]

Fifth, she uses language effectively; she never wastes words, opines thoughtlessly, prattles for effect, or panders to the lowest common denominator. Finally, she treats film as art; accordingly, she tries to write movie reviews that respect film for its potential to move viewers toward a greater understanding of the human condition.

As has been shown, Davidman's keen desire to advance a Communist agenda found expression in her work as a poetry editor and reviewer for *NM.* In addition, she served as the editor of *War Poems of the United Nations: The Songs and Battle Cries of a World at War,* a book sponsored by LAW.[54] In

51. See, for example, "Cameras as Weapons," *New Masses* 45 (December 8, 1942): 28-29; "The Camera as Narrator," *New Masses* 46 (February 2, 1943): 29-31; and "Script and Screen" (commentary by screenwriter Lester Cole disagreeing with Davidman's earlier article "Camera as Narrator"; Davidman answers), *New Masses* 47 (April 20, 1943): 28-30.

52. "Huey Hooey," 31. The writer she is complimenting for the screenplay is Christopher Isherwood.

53. "Fantasy and Fun," *New Masses* 40 (August 19, 1941): 30.

54. Joy Davidman, ed., *War Poems of the United Nations* (New York: Dial Press, 1943). For more on the development of *War Poems* see Dorsett, *And God Came In,* 40-43, and Santamaria, *Joy,* ch. 7.

compiling the poems for the volume, Davidman solicited help from various writers, particularly those she knew from her work with *NM*. For example, in a letter to Ruth Lechlitner on October 28, 1942, she writes:

> As a symbol of America's solidarity with the other anti-Axis forces, we are asking leading American poets to undertake the translation into English verse of original material in other languages. Literal prose translations will be supplied with the originals. May we invite you to submit for consideration war poems you have written? May we also count on you to undertake some of the translations? If so, please let us know which foreign languages you prefer to work from, if any, and how many poems you will translate. The sooner this volume appears in print, the more valuable it will be as a morale builder. A prompt reply will, therefore, be very much appreciated. (*Bone,* 31-32)[55]

In her foreword she outlines the reason for the volume: "Poems are an integral part of the underground movements in the occupied countries of Europe, but few of them have reached us. Nevertheless the war has already stimulated poets everywhere so much that an anthology like this one can provide a fair sample of the poetry of the anti-Fascist struggle."[56] She notes that poems are included that reflect "the tragic battle of Republican Spain against Fascism, and the lonely struggles of German and Austrian anti-Fascists." French poems "printed under Vichy . . . [gain] a peculiar interest through the ingenuity with which [the] authors express anti-Fascist sentiment in veiled language." In a comment revealing a less than unbiased perspective, she says "the section from the British Empire has been deliberately limited by us in order to exclude certain defeatist and appeaser elements which are fortunately losing their quondam influence on renascent British poetry."[57] American poets included herself, Stephen Vincent Benét, William Rose Benét, Langston Hughes, Norman Rosten, Ridgely Torrence, Carl Sandburg, and Mark Van Doren. Other well-known poets are also represented, including Bertolt Brecht, C. Day Lewis, Federico Garcia Lorca, Pablo Neruda, Boris

---

55. Ruth N. Lechlitner (1901-1989) was a poet and journalist whose work appeared in *New Masses.*

56. The dedication of *War Poems* reads: "In memory of Alexander F. Bergman and S[ol]. Funaroff: Poets of the American People." Poems by Bergman and Funaroff appear in the volume. Also appearing are poems by William Lindsay Gresham (a veteran of the Spanish Civil War and by this time Davidman's husband), Aaron Kramer, and Ruth Lechlitner.

57. *War Poems,* vii; subsequent references are given in the text.

Pasternak, and Octavio Paz.[58] Davidman often translated portions or all of the foreign language poems, and if she could not always find a poem supporting a particular anti-Fascist perspective, she was not above writing a poem to that effect and inventing the author; this was the case with "For My Son" written under the name Megan Coombes-Dawson and "Four Years After Munich" and "Peccavimus" written under the name Haydon Weir.

For the most part the poems in *War Poems* are grist for LAW's and Davidman's anti-Fascist mill. For instance, the opening lines of "Stigmata" by Fritz Glueckselig offer a snapshot of a stereotypical portrait of a Nazi SS member: "The little fellow with the pale face, / at whom the storm trooper shouted: Hey, kid, / you with the face like a girl! I like your looks! / Come over here a minute! I'm-going-to-hit-you!" (10). Predictably a beating follows, and the poem concludes: "[He] sobbed out loud / as if the bruises on his cheeks were only / the symbols of a greater and deeper pain." Czechoslovakian Karel Toman's "Cemetery 1938" ends with: "I shall not slaver upon the new master; / I shall hide in your heavy earth. / I shall mingle with my ancestors; / I shall mingle with Czech earth" (73). "To the International Brigades" by Spaniard Rafael Alberti pleads: "Stay with us! — are crying the trees, the plains, the small / particles of light, living again in the thought / of the one word, Brothers! that shakes the sea and sky. / At the sound of your name Madrid grows vast and bright" (173). It is difficult to find exceptions to such pathos — that is, poems that are genuinely conceived and artistically executed. Certainly there are no poems in *War Poems* that could be compared to the work of World War I poets such as Edward Thomas, Rupert Brooke, Siegfried Sassoon, Wilfred Owen, Isaac Rosenberg, Charles Sorley, Edmund Blunden, Ivor Gurney, or David Jones.[59]

In writing the foreword for and editing the poems in Alexander F. Bergman's *They Look Like Men*, Davidman was both advancing a Communist agenda and placating a soft spot in her heart for Bergman.[60] Several years before the publication of *They Look Like Men*, her compassion for the young

58. I discuss Davidman's own poems appearing in *War Poems* in Chapter 5.

59. In fairness to Davidman, by default she ended up doing most of the work on the anthology, writing later: "As for [*War Poems*], *that* was a rush job and shows it — originally planned as a League of American Writers production, it was left on my shoulders when the League folded up. I did the whole thing — collection, translation, and what-not — in four months, and am not particularly proud of the result" (May 29, 1951; *Bone*, 119).

60. *They Look Like Men* (New York: Bernard Ackerman, 1944). In a jacket blurb we read: "The Collected Work of an Anti-Fascist Poet Whose Death at the age of 28 Frustrated the Fulfillment of a Brilliant Talent."

poet had been created when *NM* assigned her to write a piece on Bergman, who "went on fighting for socialism as long as he could breathe . . . , [his death being that] of a gifted proletarian writer."[61] In her article on Bergman, Davidman tells the story of her visits to him in the hospitals where he spent over five years dying of tuberculosis. Although she admires his courage as he faces the grim finality of his advancing disease, she is most impressed by his commitment to the cause, noting that "he went on breathing longer than his lungs warranted because he still had something to say . . . breathing desperately with the rags that were left of his lungs, [because] he saw the new life of socialism shining outside his bedroom window." In the article Davidman only touches upon the strength of Bergman's poetry: "He wrote an extraordinarily direct and flexible kind of free verse; he approached social problems with a passion of bitterness and a passion of tenderness." The hard edge of Davidman's arresting voice sums up the cause of Bergman's death: "He could have been saved . . . by decent doctors, proper working conditions, and above all by a social system in which tuberculosis is not an occupational disease of the working class. He was a worker and he died because he was a worker, as surely as if he had been clubbed by company police or smothered in a mine." Such a damning of the existing social order is both reductionist and disingenuous, but Davidman knew it well suited the ideology of *NM*.

In her foreword to *They Look Like Men*, written several years later, she continues this strident tone. The opening paragraph states unflinchingly: "For Alexander Bergman was not only a fine poet but a fighting poet. His lyrics are so many victories over his own impending death and the great death of Fascism" (7). Her comments throughout the foreword rarely discuss the aesthetics of Bergman's verse — he "was no verbal trickster seeking a juggler's applause"; instead, she praises him for writing "out of a profound emotional honesty . . . [with] phrases [that] stab you with that sudden knife-thrust without which poetry is mere words, words, words. . . . All this, and anti-fascism too" (7-8). Perhaps conscious that she should say something about Bergman's artistry, Davidman does point out that "Bergman was never the mere mother of slogans . . . [since he] never tried to substitute the bare bones of political argument for the living and breathing body of verse" (8-9). Yet her foreword fails to explore this argument with any depth, focusing instead on what she sees as the power of his verse to evoke emotional responses — more often than not responses in support of principles sacred to the CPUSA. One example from the volume will suffice as an illustration.

61. "Poet of the Poor," *New Masses* 39 (June 10, 1941): 12.

In "Letter from a Sick Comrade" Bergman explains why he is so vigorously fending off his approaching death, concluding:

> But as things are
> and being what I am, a communist,
> I hold death off, an enemy,
> and in the guerrilla war
> the hours seized from death
> are weapons used
> against death's own regiments,
> bringing closer to me that day
> in which I want to be remembered. (36)

That Davidman befriended the mortally ill Bergman is surely praiseworthy and suggests her capacity for deeply felt compassion; that she could only see his poetry through a lens magnified by LAW and CPUSA reveals the extent to which she was bound to their ideology.

One concluding example of Davidman's zeal to support the Party in the pages of *NM* should be noted: one of her several attacks on racism. In her book review of Margaret Walker's *For My People,* Davidman points out that Walker was the "first Negro poet to win the annual Yale Series of Younger Poets award . . . [speaking] for the Negro in poetry as Richard Wright has spoken for him in prose. . . . When she directs her poems most explicitly to the disinherited Negroes of our country, she speaks with the universality of [Walt] Whitman."[62] Unlike her lack of analysis regarding Bergman's poetry, Davidman is quick to note Walker's merits as a poet: "Her idiom is our familiar spoken language; her ballads of Negroes in the southern slums are part of the folklore of all America." She also refers to Stephen Vincent Benét's foreword where he lists Walker's other strengths, including the use of free verse, blues rhythms, and the sonnet. To these attributes Davidman adds what she calls Walker's "extraordinary vividness of observation." Yet Davidman always has in view the use to which such poetry can support the Party and advance the agenda of *NM:*

> The contribution of the Negro in our culture has rarely shone more impressively than in this book. It is not only Miss Walker's individual con-

---

62. "Margaret Walker: Negro Poet," *New Masses* 46 (February 23, 1943): 24-25; Margaret Walker, *For My People* (New Haven: Yale University Press, 1942).

tribution, magnificent as it is, that strikes us, but the extent to which the longings of generations of Americans have been given voice by the Negro. . . . The South emerges as a live land with living people in it, beautiful and vital as every land can be, however misused. We understand that there is something to love as well as something to hate in the South. For Northerners, at any rate, that understanding cannot emerge from Faulkner studies of degeneration or from Gone-With-The Wind mythology. It takes the complete vision of a poet like Miss Walker to make us see the potentialities behind the misery.

Davidman celebrates how in Walker's verse "felicity of expression" is bolstered by "the intensity of her social comment," creating poems that "are signposts pointing the future's road." A road, no doubt, engineered by the CPUSA and mapped by *NM*.

Davidman was an effective tool of the Party via her work for *NM*, in total publishing over ninety movie or play reviews (covering more than 190 works), fifteen book reviews, more than a dozen poems, and a dozen or so opinion pieces.[63] Although she later recognized that she often turned a blind eye to the artistic failures of the book or film she was reviewing, in her early zeal to right the wrongs of the world through her support of the CPUSA — "the world was out of joint, and, goody, goody, who so fit as I to set it right?" (*Bone*, 90) — she willingly used her literary gifts as a faithful soldier of the cause.[64] Moreover, as this chapter has suggested, Davidman's work as a screenwriter in Hollywood influenced her film critiques. In the next chapter we explore the particulars of what became in effect a pointed and scathing attack on the Hollywood that first invited her in and then tossed her out.

---

63. Davidman's last publication in *NM* was the poem "Quisling at Twilight," *New Masses* 56 (July 31, 1945): 4. The last time her name appears on the *NM* masthead as a contributing editor was 59 (April 16, 1946): 1.

64. In other examples of her loyalty to Communist ideology, Franklin Folsom lists her as being elected to the National Board of LAW during the Fourth American Writers Congress, June 5-8, 1941. See Folsom, *Days of Anger, Days of Hope: A Memoir of the League of American Writers, 1937-1942* (Boulder: University Press of Colorado, 1994), 333. During this same Congress, Folsom notes, Isidor Schneider and Davidman "spoke for poets by reading verses by Meridel Le Sueur and 'America's Young Black Joe,' by Langston Hughes" (206).

CHAPTER 4

Into the Lion's Den: Joy Davidman and Metro-Goldwyn-Mayer (1939)

As noted in the previous chapter, from June 1939 through December 1940 there was a significant gap in Davidman's appearance in *NM*, in large part because she moved to Hollywood from July 1939 through December 1939. She was lured by the $50 a week salary offered her by Metro-Goldwyn-Mayer (MGM) as a part of its Junior Writer Project, an effort intended to develop young screenwriters.[1] In what follows, I explore why Davidman's tenure at MGM was unsuccessful, including her personal unhappiness and rejection of the Hollywood ethos as well as her later acerbic writings about the film industry, focusing particularly upon its political conservatism, its racism, and its sexism.

Given Davidman's Communist fervor and what we might expect to be a corresponding disregard for capitalism, it might appear hypocritical that in the spring of 1939 she turned away from *NM* and LAW for Hollywood and for making money. Yet Larry Ceplair and Steven Englund in their book *The Inquisition in Hollywood: Politics in the Film Community, 1939-1960* summarize the draw:

> There is no mystery or complexity in the motivations that brought these people to Hollywood: money was the biggest, if by no means the only

---

1. For more on this, see Oliver Pilat, "Girl Communist [Joy Davidman]: An Intimate Story of Eight Years in the Party," *The New York Post,* November 6, 1949; Lyle W. Dorsett, *And God Came In: The Extraordinary Story of Joy Davidman* (New York: Macmillan, 1983), 38-39; and Abigail Santamaria, *Joy: Poet, Seeker, and the Woman Who Captivated C. S. Lewis* (New York: Houghton Mifflin Harcourt, 2015), ch. 5.

lure. Some of the most serious writers in America — Robert Sherwood, Elmer Rice, William Faulkner — went to Hollywood when they needed money. Lesser-known screenwriter hopefuls came to Hollywood in many instances with families to support and debts to pay. All, famous and non-famous alike, were frequently bowled over by the amounts of money handed out in weekly salaries — up to (and occasionally over) $1,200 per week at a time when the income tax was almost nil and the dollar worth four or five times its current value.[2]

Once there, however, Davidman was quickly disillusioned by the "creative model" that essentially turned screenwriters into the pawns of the producers. Ceplair and Englund point out that " 'excessive' artistic innovations or experimentations outside of timeworn genres invariably bowed before the remorseless inquisition of the producer: where's the action? who gets the girl? where are the laughs? where's the menace? . . . The writer had to learn early that it was the producer's idea of a good screenplay which mattered, not his own." They also note that "the writers who lasted in Hollywood learned how to do their best with whatever was thrown at them while at the same time removing (as much as possible) their ego investment in the script itself. That sort of effort is foreign to the creative process in general, but the writer's survival in the motion picture process demanded this ability."[3]

Such conditions were hardly congenial to the opinionated, arrogant, and headstrong young woman from New York City. In addition, she despised the amoral atmosphere surrounding her. Specific insights into why she was so unhappy in the Junior Writer Project come from several letters written during this time. On July 18, 1939, after less than two months in Hollywood, she writes her friend James Still admitting her unhappiness.[4] She begins by contrasting the physical environment of Hollywood and New York City: "Look at where I am![5] It's horrible. I'm a New Yorker, used to crowds, strang-

---

2. Larry Ceplair and Steven Englund, *The Inquisition in Hollywood: Politics in the Film Community, 1939-1960* (Garden City, NY: Anchor, 1980), 3.

3. Ceplair and Englund, *The Inquisition in Hollywood*, 6, 8.

4. James B. Still (1906-2001) was a poet, short story writer, and novelist who lived most of his life in Knott County, Kentucky. He and Davidman met in the summer of 1938 while both were in residence at the MacDowell Colony.

5. The letterhead features a picture of a lion's head within a circle. Above the circle is "Loew's Incorporated: Ars-Gratia-Artis." Below the circle is: "Metro-Goldwyn-Mayer Pictures, Culver City, California."

ers, loud noises and sudden explosions — but not to this" (*Bone, 25*). More problematic, however, is the unsavory ethos she finds in Hollywood:

> All you have ever heard about Hollywood is true; not only are the people mad, dishonest, conscienceless, and money-grubbing, but they are all these things at the top of their voices. There is a continuous rapid-fire rattle of talk at a Hollywood party, louder than any machine-gun. Perfect strangers rush over, wave their drinks in your face, tell you discreditable stories about their best friends (who are always famous stars), remark that Joan Crawford Is Slipping,[6] and announce how much they paid for their clothes, manicure, and cigarette holders. Intelligence is measured by the raucousness of the laugh and the speed of the wisecrack. Genius is measured by the expensiveness of the automobile and the number of screen credits. (Screen credits are an invention for giving each of one hundred writers a share of the responsibility in a bad picture.) (*Bone, 25*)[7]

She envies Still's life in rural Kentucky and contrasts it with hers: "I am entangled in a nest of cement. I am writing this from a studio; there are thirty sound stages all around me with films flowering on each. I don't like it."[8] Yet at this early point she was willing to stay, in spite of her dissatisfaction with her work: "But it pays for my food and drink — reasonably well too. I never got money before for doing nothing; but although I've tried to work here, it's impossible. I get the work done, and nobody cares. As for finding someone to read it, [it is impossible]" (*Bone, 25*).

It is also obvious that Davidman missed Still personally, suggesting that they may have been romantically involved before she left New York:

6. Joan Crawford (1908-1977) was a very popular MGM film star in the 1930s and 1940s.

7. Ceplair and Englund write: "Few screenwriters enjoyed the over-populated, dog-eat-dog world engendered by the lure of film (and film salaries) and the producers' manipulation of the ensuing labor supply. Screenwriters competed for the available assignments and credits, but only one third of them received even a shared credit during any one year. . . . With 'teams of writers' being 'thrown into the breach,' the problem of allocating credits was an endless and sticky one" (*The Inquisition in Hollywood*, 8-9).

8. Ceplair and Englund report that screenwriters such as Davidman would have been assigned to "MGM's sterile cubicles" (*The Inquisition in Hollywood*, 5) where they "were expected to abide by a strict set of studio rules governing their output and attendance. . . . Writers were told to report to their offices at nine or ten in the morning, take no more than an hour or an hour and a half for lunch, and not depart for home until five or six in the evening. They also worked half a day on Saturdays. This constituted the minimum" (9).

I wish you'd write me more. I'm homesick for the peace and quiet of the subway in this terrible flat city full of pink and green stucco and frowsy palms. I wish I could be in New York to see you. I can't leave here for six months — not then, unless they throw me out (which they probably will). I expected you North in April; was looking forward to it. Why on earth did they ever want me here anyhow? (*Bone, 26*)

In the letter she further confides to Still how much she longs to be doing her own writing rather than serving as a film writer: "How I would like a log house deep in the hills just now, and a chance to work at my own work. I've finished a new book of poems though; to be called *Red Primer*."[9] Her final comment in the letter is a wistful allusion to a Scottish love song made famous by Robert Burns: "Green grow the rashes, O. Do they still? Write me" (*Bone, 26*). Is she punning on Still's last name in the last line of her letter? Although it is impossible to confirm that Davidman and Still were romantically involved at this time, her letter surely suggests there was more than a casual relationship between them; moreover, her unhappiness in Hollywood would be even more understandable if we could attribute it not only to homesickness but also to romantic longing.

In another letter, Davidman writes a friend and laces her letter with scathing satire and sarcasm about Hollywood:

As you will see from the sunburst lion overhead, I am a slave of the films now, degraded past all recognition.[10] Every day at lunch I have to strain Robert Taylor out of my soup.[11]

Every horror you have ever heard about Hollywood seems to be true. God knows there's plenty of heartlessness in the writing game and plenty of fakes; but out here they're the rule. Most of us in New York were decent people living lives that made sense; but something seems to happen even to human beings here. Of course most of those here aren't human beings; they're bright boys whose poppas are down to the last yacht, so they're making a bit of extra cash to redeem the old palace from the mortgage.[12] But there are a

9. This book has not survived. For more on this see Chapter 5.
10. The letterhead is the same as the letter to Still.
11. Robert Taylor (1911-1969) was a popular male film star in many MGM films of the 1930s and early 1940s.
12. Elsewhere she says: "Apparently if you flunk Harvard Business School there is only one place father can put you — and that is Hollywood" (Pilat, "Girl Communist," November 6, 1949).

few who were once Marxists, and who have turned into collectors of swanky houses, expensive phonographs, beautiful automobiles, and who announce the price they paid for everything the minute you meet them. O I do not like this place. (July 19, 1939; *Bone*, 26-27)[13]

Her disdain for the people she works with does not extend to the actors, most of whom she says "aren't really so bad though; the ones I have met around here are hardworking and seem normal" (*Bone*, 27). Instead, she despises most of the writers, directors, and producers; the one exception "is my immediate boss [who] is a swell person, and I enjoy working with him; but none of the writing I do is very likely to be looked at by a producer." Presumably part of her loathing was self-directed since she herself was one of the writers, and this explains the self-fulfilling prophecy that concludes her letter: "In six months the company can kick me out of here if it wants to. I am looking forward to it. God, I'm homesick" (*Bone*, 27).

Bored and buried in the miasma of Hollywood, Davidman became cynical and proposed a script in which a girl scientist who was also a hot air balloonist falls in love with a skywriting pilot.[14] Her superiors were not amused: "They called me in on the carpet and said severely 'Miss Davidman, *You are*

13. Although there was a small but vocal Communist presence in Hollywood during this time period and although she joined the leftist leaning Screen Writers Guild, Davidman never seems to have warmed to her comrades there.

14. In a poem that was probably written while she was in Hollywood, "Ballade of a Roll in the Hays," Davidman combines farce with sarcasm — and at least some of the latter directed at herself:

> We are the writers of Hollywood!
> Hear us gurgle and gulp and gush;
> Watch our heroes wade through blood,
> Lookit our heroines wallow in plush!
> We are masters of moony mush,
> Creative artists, and how it pays!
> Take those clothes off Crawford . . . hush,
> Remember it's got to get past Will Hays!
>
> All our wives are misunderstood,
> All our cuties are oh, so lush;
> If we wrote Little Red Riding Hood
> We'd have her meet with wolf with a rush;
> A wolf in the bed is worth two in the bush!
> Be subtle, boys, there are ways and ways . . .
> Frinstance, Hedy in "Ecstasy" — shushh,
> Remember it's got to get past Will Hays!

kidding MGM.' I knew my days were numbered."[15] In fact, by January 1940 she was back in New York, and in another letter to Still we find an additional insight into her dissatisfaction with Hollywood: she could not bear for her film scripts to be critiqued:[16]

> New York is a foot deep under snow this morning and I love it. The film business fired me with many compliments two months ago; the consensus of opinion was that I didn't take kindly to "consultation." Once, in a moment of emotion, I said No to a producer, so they were right. I'm too much of an egoist to listen to anyone tell me how to write; I wouldn't take it from [John] Steinbeck,[17] let alone some degenerate illiterate of a producer whose knowledge of America is gleaned from glimpses he gets from an airliner. (February 15, 1940; *Bone,* 27)

Davidman's self-confessed pride was arrogance verging on self-righteousness. For example, she goes on in the same letter to lambaste almost everything associated with her MGM experience: "Have you ever spent any time with the

---

> How it hurts that we've got to be good,
> Dealers in lukewarm slime and slush!
> We've got hair on our chests, we could . . .
> (Censored to spare the goils a blush) . . .
> In our apelike arms we'd crush
> Oomph girls like heroes of Hemingway's;
> Great Garbo, ve loff you so mosh!
> Remember it's got to get past Will Hays!
>
> *L'Envoi*
> Prince, while we write for a baritone thrush,
> An infant canary, our art decays!
> We are organizing a *Putsch*!!!
> Remember it's got to get past Will Hays! (*Naked Tree,* 183-84)

William H. Hays (1879-1954) was elected the first president of the Motion Picture Producers and Distributors of America (MPPDA) in 1922, and his main task was to establish moral rules and guidelines for the films coming out of Hollywood — this in an effort to prevent states from setting their own individual censorship rules. Hays's own form of censorship eventually came to be known variously as the Hays Code, the Production Code, or simply "The Code."

15. Pilat, "Girl Communist," November 6, 1949.

16. For more on this, see Pilat, "Girl Communist," November 6, 1949; Dorsett, *And God Came In,* 38-39; and Santamaria, *Joy,* ch. 6.

17. Novelist and short story writer John Steinbeck (1902-1968) wrote mostly about simple people confronting insurmountable problems. His best-known works include *Of Mice and Men* (1937), *The Grapes of Wrath* (1939), and *East of Eden* (1952).

disgusting rich? I used to think there was no sort of human being I couldn't understand and get along with. But I've learned otherwise; I can't even talk to café society without losing my temper" (*Bone*, 27-28).[18]

With her six-month sojourn to Hollywood behind her, Davidman returned to New York City and eventually threw herself into writing for *NM*, with a particularly sharp pen when it came to Hollywood. In most of her movie reviews when she refers to the film industry her tone is hypercritical, attacking the ethos of Hollywood, including its political conservatism (read: its failure to support a Communist agenda), its racism, and its sexism.

Davidman frequently castigates filmmakers for making movies that support the political status quo or that fail to attack the ills of the late 1930s and early 1940s. A case in point is her critique of Frank Capra's *Meet John Doe*. She criticizes the movie "that presumes to speak for the common man, the John Doe who is unemployed, confused, bedeviled by a sick economy. Yet, all through, the picture slyly sabotages the common man."[19] Davidman's Communist convictions slant her summary of the movie, noting that "John Doe's program for saving the world consists of staying out of politics and preaching a few homilies. No better opium could be devised for the people, as the Moral Rearmament boys know. On top of this, [a] fascist millionaire decides to use the movement to get himself elected President." Furthermore, she excoriates Capra for betraying his own convictions:

> In the past Capra has refused to soft-pedal his slashing assaults on the little tin gods running the country. Here, however, he seems eager to be as inoffensive as possible. The millionaires keep the power and the poor stay poor and are more contented about it. And a really nasty touch in the film is a leering caricature of a labor leader, complete with eyebrows. As an approach to the genuine problems of working people, the film seems a deliberate attempt to obscure the issues; to conceal war, starvation, and homelessness in a tangle of spun sugar.

18. In addition, Ceplair and Englund note: "The story department, not the screenwriters, bore the responsibility of supplying production with filmable properties. . . . [Screen] writers were encouraged to submit original ideas, but the fixed notions of producers were so rigid that it was unusual for a writer to write and sell five or six originals in the course of a career. In general, the job of the screenwriter was to adapt and transform: he took the material handed him by the story department and made it over into the schematic, concentrated, formalized geometry of a screenplay" (*The Inquisition in Hollywood*, 5-6).

19. "Huey Hooey," *New Masses* 39 (April 1, 1941): 30-31.

Her final comment is deft and damning: "All the picture needs to make it complete is to have F. D. Roosevelt lean from the clouds in the finale, a god from the Democratic machine, and make Capital and Labor kiss each other."

In her *NM* pieces Davidman also consistently attacks the financial leverage the eight major Hollywood studios — MGM, Paramount, Twentieth Century-Fox, Warner Brothers, Radio-Keith-Orpheum (RKO), Columbia, Universal, and United Artists — use to create and maintain a monopoly.[20] In one review essay she details the abuses of the monopoly and then offers a blistering conclusion:

> Put in plain words, the function of capitalist films is to lie to the people. [Americans] are to be lulled, by soft music and high-grade [female] legs, into accepting every horror that the monopolists have in store for them. At the moment the horror on the menu is war; so your evening's "entertainment" is a compact dose of war propaganda. Comedians adjure you to buy defense bonds; romantic heroes, fluttering their eyelashes, urge you to die for the British empire. The movie industry, with its brothers in monopoly, has its own program for solving industrial problems; a program that will brush [governmental oversight committees'] good intentions aside like straw.[21]

In another review essay, this time of Leo C. Rosten's *Hollywood: The Movie Colony — The Movie Makers*,[22] Davidman observes that in Rosten's book "what should have been objective research disintegrates into a hash of gossip, generality, and prejudice," especially because Rosten "slanders the Hollywood Anti-Nazi League and the Motion Picture Democratic Committee. . . . This book is not a survey of Hollywood; it is an appeasement of Hollywood — the Hollywood of reaction, labor-baiting and Red-baiting, and cheap escapism."[23]

---

20. Ceplair and Englund write that these eight Hollywood studios "dominated the film industry and markets not only in America, but throughout the world for the next quarter century. Among them, the majors controlled 80 per cent of the total capital investment in the movie business; they produced 65 per cent of all feature films and 100 per cent of all newsreels in the United States; they controlled 80 per cent of the nation's first-run movie theaters, and received about 95 per cent of all film rentals" (*The Inquisition in Hollywood*, 1).

21. "Monopoly Takes a Screen Test," *New Masses* 39 (June 24, 1941): 29-30.

22. Leo C. Rosten, *Hollywood: The Movie Colony — The Movie Makers* (New York: Harcourt, Brace, 1941).

23. "Quack, Quack," *New Masses* 42 (February 10, 1942): 24.

A second focus of attack by Davidman is Hollywood's racist portrayals of African Americans. At times, she admits, Hollywood appears to mean well in its presentation of African Americans. For instance, she argues that *Tales of Manhattan* has

> quite genuine good intentions. The trouble with it is its ineptitude; it wants to do right by the Negro, but doesn't know how. The Hollywood cliché of the Negro as clown has been with us too long a time, and, like all people who use clichés to save the trouble of thinking, the Hollywood producers have come to believe in their own creation. Many of them are constitutionally incapable of seeing the Negro as anything but uneducated, superstitious, yet happy-go-lucky. Thus it comes about that while Negroes of *Tales of Manhattan* are voicing the ideas of sober and responsible adults, they are simultaneously cavorting like . . . like café society.[24]

About MGM's re-release of *Gone with the Wind* in 1942, Davidman writes that "no one needs to be told that this four-hour explosion of technicolor is an offensive racist and fascist plea for disunion; no one, apparently, but its makers. The attenuated graces of Vivien Leigh will hardly compensate Americans for being told to hate each other on geographical, racial, political, or any other grounds."[25] It is not that Davidman is blind to sincere efforts by Hollywood to critique racism; she has high praise for *Native Land* and its gritty portrayal of violations of civil liberties: "A church in Arkansas, where white and Negro meet; the ambush, the cries of deputy sheriffs blending with the voices of bloodhounds, the white man and the Negro hunted into the swamp. In an unforgettable sequence they cower among the lush reeds and the glittering summer bushes. The white man supporting the wounded Negro, they emerge cautiously on the road, while [Paul] Robeson's voice sings a magnificent lament; and they are shot down there."[26]

But, according to Davidman, films such as *Native Land* are the exception. Too often stereotypical racist views dominate Hollywood films. Her ire reaches a boiling point when she learns about the planned release of *Captive Wild Woman* by Universal Studios. In an open letter to the readers of *NM* on March 23, 1943, entitled "Goebbels's Missing Link," she unloads her full fury:

24. "Heroes Are Human Beings," *New Masses* 45 (October 13, 1942): 31.
25. "Fourth Down," *New Masses* 43 (April 14, 1942): 30.
26. "Native Land," *New Masses* 43 (May 19, 1942): 28.

No idea of Herr Doktor Goebbels has ever been too grotesque for our American fascists to ape.[27] Two words from the wizened little monkey in Berlin, and Martin Dies starts cutting monkeyshines in Congress.[28] It would appear that Dr. Goebbels has imitators in Hollywood as well; for his racist propaganda, in its filthiest form, is expressed in a picture planned by Universal Studios.

Hollywood's treatment of the Negro has usually been ill-informed and ill-natured to an outrageous extent. *Captive Wild Woman,* however, out-Herods Herod. Among the more brutal and unprincipled exponents of southern lynch law there used to be a theory that the Negroes were the mythical Missing Link. Possible only to minds of the ultimate degree of illiteracy, this idea was used as a sort of warped justification of the bestialities inflicted upon helpless Negroes. But it was too grotesque to survive long except among the most virulent poll taxers.

It is a shock, therefore, to discover that Universal Studios is planning to resurrect the Missing Link idea, in conformance with Nazi racial theories by which only that non-existent animal, the Aryan, is quite human. In *Captive Wild Woman,* apparently a horror quickie of even more incoherence than usual, the inevitable Mad Doctor decides to turn a female gorilla into a human being. By itself this would be merely silly; but someone had the idea of making that human being into a Negro girl! Lest you should conceivably miss Dr. Goebbels' point, the final script leads the girl up to a mirror while she is giving way to her "lower emotions" — namely jealousy. As the emotions get lower, her skin grows darker, until she relapses through stages of subhumanity into the gorilla again!

Sheer illiteracy, though it explains some Hollywood phenomena, can hardly be the sole cause of this piece of fascist propaganda. It is tempting to suggest that the gentlemen responsible, in trying to reduce human beings to the ape level, were looking for company in their own misery; but it is more to the point to ask who gave them their orders? And it is still more to the point to see that those orders are countermanded by the American people. This film has not yet been released, has not even been publicized; its makers no doubt intend to slip it over quietly as a routine horror melodrama. They can be stopped.

27. Joseph Goebbels (1897-1945) was the German propaganda minister under Adolf Hitler and the Nazis.
28. Martin Dies (1900-1972) was a congressman from Texas who was fiercely anti-Communist. In May 1938 his congressional resolution created the House Special Committee on Un-American Activities.

Protest to the OWI [Office of War Information] as well as to Universal Studios should be effective in throttling Dr. Goebbels' apes. Meanwhile, one might suggest to the gentlemen responsible for *Captive Wild Woman* that, if they must hunt for a Missing Link, they might try to find one between themselves and decent humanity.[29]

In a not so subtle way, she accuses Universal Studios of being the stooge and toady of the Nazi propaganda machine — Universal Studios, according to Davidman, is little more than a puppet of the master Nazi propagandist, Goebbels. This letter is not the critique of an objective film reviewer; instead, it is the jeremiad of a zealot. It is more like the outraged rant of a fire-and-brimstone preacher than a critical debunking and dismantling of a seriously flawed film.

The tone of this open letter, moreover, suggests that underneath Davidman's controlled veneer of informed critical judgment, an Old Testament prophet lurks, ever ready to call down the wrath of an angry God upon those in Hollywood who perpetuate racist stereotypes. This air of self-righteousness carries over into Davidman's greatest negative judgment against Hollywood: its condescending, manipulative, and degrading portrayal of women. In many film reviews she attacks what she sees as Hollywood's sexism. For example, in her review of *She Knew All the Answers,* Davidman says the film becomes "downright offensive . . . in the presentation of an office spinster of the old school, who lifts eyebrows constantly, simpers over her imaginary beauty, and faints at the mention of passion. If this lady ever really existed, she has gone to an unwept grave long ago. Cannot Hollywood give us a rest from the comic old maid?"[30] Davidman is capable of seeing satire in some of the portrayals of women; in fact, she delights in *The Feminine Touch* because Rosalind Russell's "combination of cavewoman and dumb bunny is enough to carry any story. This reviewer, indeed, inclines to the belief that no picture is bad if Miss Russell's in it."[31] Russell also comes in for praise for her role in *Take a Letter, Darling;* Davidman writes about her that "an independent woman who earns her own money is not only more honorable but also more desirable than a clinging female who proposes to

29. *New Masses* 46 (March 23, 1943): 29; *Bone,* 32-33. The movie was released on June 4, 1943. For Davidman's less critical evaluations of the movie studios, see "The Will and the Way," *New Masses* 45 (October 27, 1942): 28, 30-31; and "The War Film: An Examination," *New Masses* 45 (November 24, 1942): 29-30.

30. "Tripe and Taylor," *New Masses* 40 (July 1, 1941): 31.

31. "New Movies," *New Masses* 41 (December 23, 1941): 28.

marry it. . . . [Russell] is explicitly and sincerely complimented for standing on her own two feet like a self-respecting adult instead of hunting a millionaire like . . . well, the average Hollywood heroine."[32]

Hollywood's sexism bears the full weight of Davidman's scorn in the longest review essay she published in *NM.* "Women: Hollywood Style" is a careful, thorough, well-supported, and articulate piece of rhetoric intended to expose and eviscerate the sexist ethos of Hollywood's major film studios.[33] Her damning indictment of Hollywood for its screen portrayals of women may also be a delayed response to her own lack of success there. "Women: Hollywood Style" is essentially a charge that the men running Hollywood are male chauvinists. She begins by citing a line from the movie *Tom, Dick, and Harry,* where the female lead, Ginger Rogers, says: "It's as natural for a girl to want to make a good marriage as for a man to want to get ahead in business." Davidman then argues that the male producers of the movie would be surprised that such a line might open them to a charge of misogyny:

> They sincerely believed themselves to be glorifying the American girl. . . . *Tom, Dick, and Harry* accepted as natural and right and healthy the doctrine that the American girl should sell her sex in the most profitable market. Nor does the market end with marriage. Once caught, the husband must be held; and woman's life work, hundreds of films imply, is holding her man with the aid of the beauty parlor and judicious fits of the sulks. The movies dress this doctrine prettily; they adorn it with revealing negligees, demure maidservants, and incredible kitchens that are paradises of labor-saving gadgets.

Long before feminism was a cultural given, Davidman argued several of its principal tenets:

> In the United States, the emancipation of women is part and parcel of the democracy we are fighting for. Increasingly, women succeed along lines once reserved for men; as in the Soviet Union and Britain, women replace men whenever possible in the war effort. Nor are their homes worse run, their children worse cared for. On the contrary, as any psychologist knows, women who have realized their potentialities as creative human beings make better mothers than frustrated women who must take all

32. "Exciting Soviet Film," *New Masses* 43 (June 16, 1942): 29.
33. "Women: Hollywood Style," *New Masses* 44 (July 14, 1942): 28-31.

their ambitions out on their children. Thus the films are lagging behind the country. Their half-unconscious war against the emancipation of women certainly gives unintended support to one of the tenets of fascism — the deliberate debasement of womanhood.

Although Davidman does note the legitimate strength of *Tom, Dick, and Harry* — it did not mock "the historic fight of women for independence" — in the end the heroine opted for marriage with a man who would take care of her: "*Tom, Dick, and Harry* never made any suggestion that the heroine might have something to offer the world as an individual; she was merely, to put it nakedly, something to be marketed. The salient feature of the film, indeed, was a series of dreams forecasting the girl's probable future with each man. In each case, her life was entirely what the man chose to make it."

Davidman then analyzes a group of films dealing with unhappy wives who, rather than acting as independent agents, become briefly infatuated with another man; however, once these "romances" prove equally unsatisfying, the wives crawl back to their husbands, "chastened among the dolls." As a result, Davidman argues, most Hollywood movies suggest that women can only be happy, not when they exercise their own desires and aspirations, but rather when they "know their place" and settle for being good wives, mothers, and home-makers. "The cardinal point of woman's emancipation — the admission that she can have a successful career and a successful marriage — is almost never made" in popular Hollywood films. Instead, films are filled with caricatures of women: the crotchety schoolteacher, the frustrated and unglamorous professional woman, or the office sourpuss.

Davidman then contends that Hollywood glorifies female beauty and objectifies women into sex objects:

In forcing women into the harem, the important thing is to make the women like it; they must be induced to accept their unhealthy fate as highly moral and emotionally desirable. Consequently we have [a whole school] of films, glorifying a morbidly passive and self-effacing female type; the great range of movies, superficially quite inoffensive, which never say a word derogatory to women yet present them in a dependent and inferior position as a matter of course. . . . The routine film heroine has no integrity, no sense, no reliability. She is always breaking off her engagement when a more enticing prospect comes along; yielding spinelessly to the blandishment of the brash youth whom she began by resenting; falling among thieves and Nazi spies; dancing helplessly in the background while the villain conks the hero; slapping faces at insults to her imbecile "dignity"; making an idiot of herself at baseball games. But ah, she has beauty! She has S[ex] A[ppeal], and has It, she has Oomph; she has a wonderful apparatus for getting men excited. . . . That is all she knows on earth, and all she needs to know.

Davidman claims the reason for this sexual exploitation is simple: money. In addition, "this nakedly financial motive" shows "the plain fact that filmmakers write as they think. If they regard woman as a commercial article, that is because pretty girls come to Hollywood from all over the country to trade in their beauty. Beauty is a drug on the market in southern California."

In "Success Story," a poem written in February 1940, only a month or so after she left Hollywood, Davidman offers a bitter parody of how "pretty girls come to Hollywood . . . to trade in their beauty":

girlie girlie girlie said the producer
in this business you gotta gotta gotta
give give give if you want to be a star
shine in the sky and own a private bar

so the blonde let down her hair
stepped shrinking out of her underwear
and in due course of time all sorts of honor
not to mention gelt was heaped upon her,
and when she went swimming in her private pool
her long hair floated on the water behind her
like dreams, like seaweed, like mist,
only much more often kissed:

for ten years she Rapunzel Melusina[34]
the water fairy waggled her breasts in front of
American men from seven to seventy-seven
and what was left of the European market,
marrying and being given in marriage
four times to what the studio could scrape up to cover her shame
with the aid of the fashionable abortionist.

34. Melusina appears as a beautiful, supernatural female in a number of folktale motifs; she is often portrayed as a mermaid, the sense in which Davidman uses her in this poem.

Nevertheless and in spite of precautions taken
other younger breasts enraptured the attentive eyes of
the bald-headed perspiring man who took it out in fan letters
and Rapunzel with her hair a little specious
started doing mother parts
        and who cared
then or when they fished her from the water,
Melusina with her hair all curly
and the tongues clucking girlie girlie girlie? (*Naked Tree,* 187-88)

In the final section of "Women: Hollywood Style" she moves to a discussion reminiscent of her jaundiced experience in MGM's Junior Writer Project. In spite of the many good people working in the film industry in southern California, Davidman notes that the film culture "concentrates in articulate people most of the prevailing attitudes of our civilization, good and bad . . . [so that] in Hollywood may . . . be found some of the most degenerate and parasitic elements of our society — the swamis, the astrologers, the debutantes, the fifth columnists, the reactionaries of every size and shape." It follows, then,

in presenting woman as they do, the films present in intensified form an attitude that exists wherever reaction may be found; an attitude based at least in part on facts. For there is no denying that thousands of young girls do think of themselves as articles for the marriage market; do track down a husband as the sole end of existence; and do feel cheated when they discover that glamorized Love is not a sufficient full-time occupation. Neither, let it be admitted, is having a baby.[35] How great a part the movies play in forming girls according to this pattern is not easily measured. Perhaps the greatest single cause of harm is in the compensatory mechanism which women develop, and which the movies encourage, to overcome the unhappiness of their frustration and disappointment — a mechanism which has made the neurotic, attention-getting woman so frighteningly familiar in our society. Taught to value herself only by her reflection in a man's admiring eyes, many a woman spends her whole time in desperate scheming for attention, in frenzied resentment of people or ideas that

35. Here Davidman is not speaking from experience with regard to marriage and having children. That would come later; less than three weeks after the publication of this article, she married William Lindsay Gresham on August 2, 1942.

"come between her and her family"; many a woman clings pathetically to girlishness well into her fifties. These cases are not intrinsically inferior people but poisoned people; the film is not the major source of poison, but an important contributory cause of what amounts to an undermining of the family.

Although she affirms that movies are not the sole cause of a woman's lack of genuine self-esteem, she does see a vicious cycle: "The movies, out of carelessness or miseducation or corruption, imitate and prettify some of the worst features of daily life; and life promptly imitates the movies." In her conclusion, she offers a possible solution: "Meanwhile young women are miseducated out of respect for themselves as human beings, and — equally deadly — their menfolk are warned not to respect them. . . . The true corrective is in the education of the American people. When the people at last repudiate completely all expressions of male chauvinism, the movies will hastily follow suit."

The importance of "Women: Hollywood Style" is threefold. First, it illustrates Davidman's willingness to take on an entire industry — one from her perspective that had essentially chewed her up and spat her out — with energy, insight, and candor. Many of her arguments against the way in which movies trivialize women and glorify sex are still valid, even though much has changed in Hollywood's portrayal of women during the last seventy years. Second, it shows her expressing radical positions that she never bothers to document — for instance, the claim that "any psychologist" knows working women make better mothers "than frustrated women who must take all their ambitions out on their children" is never linked to an expert study. This is the zeal of the revolutionary, the argument of one who knows she is right, the righteous (and sometimes arrogant) word of one whose authority is her own sense of moral superiority. Finally, "Women: Hollywood Style" reveals a passionate personality intent on righting the wrongs perpetuated by a system she finds repellant, exploitive, and manipulative.

Davidman's early success — she was only twenty-three when *Letter to a Comrade* was published and twenty-four when she first went to Hollywood — may in part explain her scorn for what she found in Hollywood — that and its rejection of her. She did not suffer fools lightly, and in her view she encountered many fools at MGM and the other film studios. A piqued self-image and bruised ego are not easily assimilated into the psychology of someone like Davidman — brilliant, opinionated, confrontational, perceptive, and vain.[36] Marriage to William Lindsay Gresham and having two children later softened some of her views, but she still evidenced disdain for stereotypical views of women five years after her Hollywood experience, writing her friends Jerry and Alice Jerome on January 19, 1945: "I'm feeling very cheerful these days . . . except for the limited opportunities for writing. In the grimmer moments of floor scrubbing I meditate between my teeth articles on male chauvinism. Why, why, why, is it always the Joys and Alices that stop writing to mind infants, and never the Bills and Jerrys? Men is WORMS" (*Bone,* 40).[37]

As the last two chapters have illustrated, Davidman's nonfiction writing for *NM* consumed a good deal of her time from 1938 to 1945. While her frequent appearance in the pages of *NM* as a reviewer and essayist gives the impression that she had turned her back on writing fiction and poetry, such an impression is inaccurate. In fact, she published over thirty poems during these years in *NM* and elsewhere; moreover, she wrote but did not publish at least 125 more poems. In addition, in 1940 she published *Anya* — a thoughtful, compelling, and intensely powerful novel. It is to these works that we now turn our attention.

36. She wrote to Still on February 15, 1940: "I've sold my novel [*Anya*] to Macmillan — it happened when I was still in California, and I gloated over my writer-colleagues, none of whom were capable of producing more than a ten-page screen story" (*Bone,* 26).

37. V. J. Jerome (1896-1965) emigrated from Poland in 1915, and joined the CPUSA in 1924. In 1935 he became editor of *The Communist,* publishing many essays in support of Communism and related causes. Alice Hamburger was his third wife.

CHAPTER 5

Other Published Poems (1938-1945)

Before we examine the poems of this period, one important contextual matter needs to be noted. On August 23, 1939 — less than two weeks before the opening of World War II — German Foreign Minister Joachim Ribbentrop and Soviet Union Foreign Minister Vyacheslav Molotov signed the Nazi-Soviet Non-Aggression Pact (also referred to as the German-Soviet Non-Aggression Pact and the Ribbentrop-Molotov Pact). Thousands of erstwhile devoted members and supporters of LAW and CPUSA read this agreement as a direct betrayal of the core principles of Communism. That the great enemy of the CPUSA, Fascism, was now a co-conspirator with Communism was more than many American Communists could stomach. For Stalin and Hitler to get in bed together effectively dealt a body blow to LAW and CPUSA. While Davidman's letters and writings of this period do not reveal her own feelings of betrayal, the seeds of her later rejection of Communism were certainly sown at this time.

Although Davidman's work for *NM* was her primary literary occupation after the appearance of *Letter to a Comrade,* she continued writing poems; in fact, between April 5, 1938, and July 31, 1945, Davidman published twenty-eight additional poems that had not already appeared in *Letter to a Comrade.* Moreover, we know she completed two other manuscripts of poetry; together, these two manuscripts contained the bulk of these twenty-eight published poems. On July 18, 1939, she wrote James Still about the first of these two manuscripts: "I've finished a new book of poems . . . to be called *Red Primer.* You won't see it for a while, however" (*Bone,* 26). Seven months later she told Still the title of the volume had changed: "As for the poetry, it's called *Rise and Shine* now, and I'm waiting for the Yale Press opinion on it"

(February 15, 1940; *Bone,* 28). Three months subsequent to this she sent the manuscript to her mentor, Stephen Vincent Benét, and asked for his advice:

> Here is my new book as it stands today, stripped of everything except *what* I really like; but a good deal may happen to it in the next few months. I'd have sent it along much earlier, but it was in a state of flux and I was busy correcting proofs on my novel and wishing I could afford to rewrite it.[1]
>
> Do you think it's good enough to print as it stands, or ought I to wait a while? If there are any changes you can suggest, I wish you'd tell me. (May 20, 1940; *Bone,* 29)

We do not have Benét's response, but perhaps he suggested the poems were not "good enough to print as it stands." In any case, *Rise and Shine* was never published, so we are left to speculate about its contents.[2] The initial title, *Red Primer,* is certainly suggestive; that is, this volume may have tilted toward poetry similar to her political poems in *Letter to a Comrade* and in *NM.* However, without definitive evidence one way or the other, we are left to supposition. In what follows I discuss eleven published poems that might have been intended for *Rise and Shine.*[3] In addition, because she planned, compiled a table of contents for, and wrote the poems for a third volume of poetry that she may have intended to entitle *Courage,*[4] I discuss the seventeen published poems designed to be included in that volume.

Rise and Shine

One of the poems perhaps meant to be included in *Rise and Shine* was her first published poem in *NM,* "Strength through Joy." Published in the April 5, 1938, issue of *NM,* the poem is a satiric attack on Fascism. For instance, she neatly parodies the satanic pride of Hitler:

---

1. She is referring to her novel, *Anya* (1940).

2. As of now, no manuscript version has come to light.

3. These published poems appeared between April 5, 1938, and December 19, 1944, in journals or books including *Fantasy: A Literary Quarterly with an Emphasis on Poetry; New Masses;* and *Seven Poets in Search of an Answer.* I also include in this discussion a twelfth poem, "Ten Dead Workers," that was written during this time but not published until it appeared in *Bone,* 23-24; see more below.

4. I surmise the title of this volume since the poems are found inside DP Box 1, Series 4, Folders 20-25 entitled "Courage."

                        For I am he
the maker of honor, the hand bestowing judgment
seen in a cloud, the jaws of desolation,
begetter of dead men, eater of my sons,
and when any man is gnawed by the mouth of a cannon
I grow new teeth. I am filled with iron,
with fire and exhalations; I am magnificent,
honor the nails of my feet and the parings thereof
each being capable of killing. I am precious
and a treasure to women; honor then my knees
and the clasp of my thighs. And I will give you,
you, my dear children, my loving children, you
wearing my symbol on the fat of your arm
the beautiful moment, the moment of beautiful pain
with which you burst into flames; the high, the radiant
and honorable death. (*Naked Tree*, 48)[5]

Hitler, or perhaps more broadly the National Socialist German Workers Party, is portrayed as inexorable, irresistible, and insatiable; human beings are only so much fodder in its determined pursuit of power. In addition, perhaps with tongue in cheek, Davidman suggests that women swoon at its powerful charm and that its followers — its "children" — proudly bear the swastika, eager and willing to die for the fatherland. Events of the next seven years would reveal that "Strength through Joy" was less parody than prophecy.

Another poem that might have appeared in *Rise and Shine* can be dated with some certainty since it appears in Davidman's letter of April 28, 1939. In the letter, she offers an extended critique of the poetry of Aaron Kramer.[6] One strength of his poetry, she writes, is that "it unites proletarian themes with proletarian language. You have no idea how rarely one finds a so-called Workers' Poet who writes in language the workers can understand." She confesses her own verse was once too rarified ("I was once a sinner in that direction myself"), but then adds that she has "recently succeeded in stating my verse in direct terms." As an example, she encloses "a poem I wrote last

---

5. Davidman dates this poem as March 1938.
6. The book she was critiquing in her letter was Kramer's *The Alarm Clock* (sponsored by Branches 25 and 134 of the International Workers Order and the Young Communist League of Bensonhurst: privately printed, 1938).

night to show you what I mean" (*Bone,* 23).[7] The poem, "Ten Dead Workers,"
is typical of her political poems:

> Over this blood
> Stretch the blank shroud,
> Modestly cover it;
> Lest it offend
> Comfortable men,
> Put flowers over it;
> Use for its sheath
> The funeral wreath.
>
> Lest your blood cry
> Loud to the listening sky,
> Lest it breed riot,
> Their money spent
> On careful print
> Will keep it quiet,
> Disguise its flavor
> For their breakfast paper.
>
> Lie still, you dead,
> Wrapped in the heavy bed;
> Lie cold and meek.
> Your graves possess
> In decent humbleness;
> They will not hear you speak.
> The living speak your word
> And will be heard.[8]

Davidman's assessment of the poem in the letter where it appears — "I think anyone can understand what I say here, and I think too it is worth saying" (*Bone,* 24) — is both immodest and accurate; while not a great poem, there is no missing its political point. In spirit it is akin to the best of her political poems in *Letter to a Comrade,* including "Letter to a Comrade," "Spartacus

---

7. According to Davidman, then, the poem was written April 27, 1939.
8. Published for the first time in *Bone,* 23-24.

1938," "Survey Mankind," and "Prayer against Indifference." Almost certainly it appeared in the *Rise and Shine* manuscript.

Another possible inclusion in *Rise and Shine* is a group of three poems published collectively under the title "Amateur Night in Harlem."[9] The first of these, "High Yellow," marvels at the beauty of an African American female dancer:

> What tree are you grown from,
> what flower from your mother's nipple come;
>
> what leaf is your tight hair dancer?
> How are you cut and carved and set in motion, satinwood,
> your knees turned on the lathe, your belly smoothed,
> your round eyelids and your neck polished smooth? (*Naked Tree,* 84-85)

Davidman "would like to touch your flesh," "get pleasure from your touch," and "possess the muscles of your thighs." In this dancer there is fascinating allure: "We have known / no body so beautiful and brown, / no laughter so entirely meant, / no dance so fine, no lust so innocent" (*Naked Tree,* 85).

The second poem in this sequence, "New Spiritual," sees in energized jazz dancing the seeds of revolution. Davidman underscores this by invoking the name of John Brown:

> Shout like bells across the nation,
> Shake your hips and go to town,
> Swing a song of revolution,
> Do the shag in the name of John Brown.
> Hear the jazzband how it sings
> John Brown's body muted on the strings.
>
> Whisper revolution on the drum;
> John Brown marching with an army of banners
> Shaking red on the stormy air.[10]

9. The three were published in *Fantasy: A Literary Quarterly with an Emphasis on Poetry* 7, no. 1 (1941): 21-22. Davidman dates the first as November 1938 and the second and third as April 1939.

10. John Brown (1800-1859) was an ardent foe of American slavery and planned a scheme to arm slaves and lead them in a revolt against their masters. On October 16, 1859, he led twenty-one men on a raid of the federal arsenal at Harpers Ferry, Virginia. The revolt was

The powerful rhythms, the pulsating beat, and the shouts of the dancers suggest that radical change is coming:

> Listen to John Brown shouting in the cold,
> Shouting in the night with the trumpet note,
> Marching with an army in the narrow street
> With the drum, with the horn, with a million pairs of feet.

Davidman believes what she is witnessing presages a new day:

> Take the hands away from the muted throat,
> Let it open and sing in the name of John Brown,
> Making music shine around the town,
> Ringing freedom all around the town. (*Naked Tree,* 165)

The third poem in this sequence, "So We Can Forget Our Troubles," is a retreat from the furious activity of the first two. Now the female dancer of "High Yellow" is emotionally dispassionate as she performs on stage, intuitively longing to escape, perhaps to a place more beautiful than the stage screen depicting an alluring landscape, "being the place we all would go, / Set about with trees and curtained with distance, / The fabulous flowers, the legendary snow." Her yearning for this place of beauty is highlighted by the poem's final lines: "We leave our eyes and go to sleep / Deep out of trouble, deep in limbo, deep" (*Naked Tree,* 166).

In contrast to this sequence are two poems appearing in *NM* at about the same time that might also have been intended for *Rise and Shine.* Although "For the Gentlemen" and "Prophet without Honor" were not designed to appear as a sequence, they are linked by being a return to poems reflecting the political agenda of the CPUSA. "For the Gentlemen" is a blunt warning to the leaders of capitalism — the captains of industry:

> When you see red
> it will be too late;
> the night will be dead,
> the sun will not wait.

---

quickly put down, with most of Brown's followers killed or captured. Brown was convicted of treason and hanged on December 2, 1859.

She also mocks their imagined influence and power:

> When you command
> the sea to stand still
> at the safe edge of sand,
> do you think that it will?

Once the revolution comes, she intimates, their real impotence will be apparent:

> You're up a tree now;
> say, while you rave,
> say, can you see now
> the depth of your grave?[11]

"Prophet without Honor" alludes to Mark 6:4 where Jesus notes, upon his return to Nazareth, those there who belittled his message and his miracle working: "Jesus said to them, 'A prophet is not without honor except in his own country, among his own relatives, and in his own house.'" In her poem Davidman suggests that the overwhelming majority of American society is happy with a prophet who, unlike Jesus, does not challenge the status quo:

> If you come down to us and say
> there's nothing more than everyday
> over the hills and far away,
>
> nothing to think we have not thought,
> no novelties in tears and laughter,
> no fight that we have never fought,
> nothing before and nothing after;
>
> if you come down and tell us this
> you'll buy our love, you'll buy our kiss.[12]

11. "For the Gentlemen," *New Masses* 38 (December 31, 1940): 23; *Naked Tree*, 180. Davidman dates this poem as December 1939. Davidman later published this poem under the title "For the Nazis" in *Seven Poets in Search of an Answer*, ed. Thomas Yoseloff (New York: Bernard Ackerman, 1944).

12. "Prophet without Honor," *New Masses* 38 (January 14, 1941): 14; *Naked Tree*, 192. Davidman dates this poem as March 1940.

However, if a prophet, like Jesus, offers a vision of the future — one that challenges the established order of things — then beware: "But if not, if you stand and stare / over the sky to bluer air, / we'll crucify you standing there." Her message is subtle but transparent: early 1940s American society is frightened by the suggestion of significant social restructuring as advocated by the CPUSA and is willing to murder its Communist saviors.[13]

"Pacific Shore," written during Davidman's brief sojourn to Hollywood as a movie screen writer, tenderly explores a family's quiet despair at having been evicted from their farm, apparently for failure to meet their mortgage:

> What do we do now?
> What do we do now?
> Slice the seabeach open with the plough,
> salt our tears with the seawater,
> seed with our bodies the unpregnant sea?
> What do we do now?
> Plant our bodies in the ebb and flow?
> Harvestless man, wife and son and daughter,
> bury ourselves in the nice cheap water?[14]

What should they do? "Shoved off the earth, where do we go from here, / to what clean homestead in what heavenly sphere?" Should they simply accept the way capitalism has driven them off their land? Davidman concludes the poem with a not-so-veiled call to revolution: "Turn around and take it back again, / turn again and take the country back / that the bank nibbled in the honest man's track / . . . Turn back, turn back our faces to the sun." The political edge to "Pacific Shore" suggests that it, too, may have been intended for *Rise and Shine.*

Several poems probably intended for *Rise and Shine* explore the direct impact of World War II on a personal, intimate level. "Prayer for Every Voyage" is a woman's plea that the ocean release her drowned lover so that he can "slash his way through the sea once more / and carry the guns to the fighting men."[15] In another war poem, "The Dead Partisan," Davidman portrays the execution of a brave member of the resistance: "The man they were shooting /

13. This is another poem that indicates Davidman's deep-seated interest in Christ, and it has connections to "Resurrection" and "Againrising."

14. "Pacific Shore," *New Masses* 39 (March 25, 1941): 24; *Naked Tree,* 172. Davidman dates this poem as June 1939.

15. "Prayer for Every Voyage," *New Masses* 47 (April 27, 1943): 16; *Naked Tree,* 221.

came walking out singing / with a smile on his mouth / and his face to the sun."
As he is executed, however, his eyes urge on the remaining freedom fighters:

> He said: fear nothing but fear.
> Fear the rat and your heart
> sick on poisoned bread;
>
> fear the snake in your belly
> rubbing along the ground;
> fear the worm in your head
> crawling without a sound;
>
> he said; be afraid
> of no bullet, of no pain.
>
> This man who was dead
> Looked at us and said:
> only be afraid
> not to be men.[16]

"Dialogue for D-Day" is a counterpoint between the voice of despair and the
voice of hope regarding the future of a newly born child. Despair says, "the
world will bite too hard for this small hand; / its teeth are sharp and poisonous
with lies. / It is a skull with swastikas for eyes." Hope replies: *"It is the brainpan
of a living man / singing with the future. It will speak / in promises of honey sum-
mertime. / Give it to your child."* When Despair wants to know how Hope can
be so certain of the future, it says: *"We go / across the hungry sea to make it so."*[17]
"Sonnet to Various Republicans" scorns those who are afraid and unwilling to
risk all for freedom; such cowards, Davidman says, can only exclaim: "'There
is nothing there, / Nothing but ruin and the death of kings.'"[18]

Before leaving this discussion of the published poems Davidman may have
intended for *Rise and Shine,* we look at three related poems that appear in the
anti-war volume Davidman edited, *War Poems of the United Nations.* Written
under the pseudonym Megan Coombes-Dawson, Davidman's "For My Son"

---

16. "The Dead Partisan," *Seven Poets in Search of an Answer,* 30-31; *Naked Tree,* 227-28.
17. "Dialogue for D-Day," *New Masses* 51 (June 20, 1944): 15; *Naked Tree,* 228-29.
18. "Sonnet to Various Republicans," *New Masses* 53 (December 19, 1944): 10; *Naked Tree,* 232.

is a moving affirmation by a mother who has lost her son to war. Because of his brave example to her, she is courageously facing an aerial bombardment:

> Knife in my belt against a thief,
> tune on my lips against a fear,
> I waited for their planes to fill
> the vacant moonlight on the hill,
> trying to be as brave in life
> as you were in your death, my dear. (*Naked Tree,* 223)

Employing another pseudonym, Haydon Weir, in "Four Years after Munich" Davidman considers those living in the English countryside under the threat of German aerial bombardment.[19] They long for the days before war and the threat of death from the sky; yet they face their fears bravely: "We part [the tree branches] with armed hands and stare at the sky; / see the enemy and truth in the green lane; / unafraid, unafraid, see sunlight and the planes" (*Naked Tree,* 225). "Peccavimus," also written under Weir's name, plays off the Latin meaning of the poem's title, "we have sinned." In the poem those who have not offered resistance to the forces of Fascism sweeping over Europe confess their many failings: "Now we are ashamed / of what we have been and have not been" (*Naked Tree,* 225). They are ashamed of having lived safe, comfortable lives while members of the resistance have risked all.

Courage

Although I have been speculating a great deal about which poems Davidman may have intended to appear in *Rise and Shine,* there is no need to speculate about which poems Davidman intended to include in her third volume of poetry, *Courage.* The Joy Davidman Papers contain the projected table of contents for this volume as well as all but eight of the sixty-five poems she intended to include.[20] Moreover, we find in Davidman's correspondence a

19. In the case of Weir she extended the fiction, noting at the end of "Four Years after Munich" that "Haydon Weir was killed in action in 1942."

20. See DP, Box 1, Series 4, Folders 20-25. I should note here that any number of the poems Davidman intended to publish in *Courage* could have initially been intended for publication in *Rise and Shine;* however, I have no way of substantiating such an argument since in the DP there is no record of a table of contents for *Rise and Shine.* Davidman's projected table of contents for *Courage* appears in the appendix at the end of this volume.

reference to this third volume of poetry. Writing to Aaron Kramer on September 9, 1946, Davidman says: "If my agent can sell it, I'll have another book of verse" (*Bone*, 47). While this could be a reference to *Rise and Shine*, I think it unlikely; six years had passed since her last reference to *Rise and Shine* in her letters. *Courage* would have been a fascinating volume, probably conceived, as the letter to Kramer suggests, sometime in early to mid-1946.[21]

Of the sixty-five poems Davidman planned to include in *Courage*, only seventeen had been previously published.[22] "The Devil Will Come" sees in mid-1930s America an obsession with materialism and consumption; since the Great Depression was still fresh in everyone's memory, this lends both an irony to and an impetus for consumer excess. Davidman brings this idea into relief against the World's Fair that opened on April 30, 1939, in New York City.

> The World's Fair opens and the golden key
> Unlocks the gates of heaven for the crowd;
> The rickshaws run, the subway trains are loud,
> And Faustus flowers in photography;
> Between the air and the electric light
> See Faustus painted on the astonished sight;
> Between the neon light of joy and sorrow
> Now showing: Faustus in the World Tomorrow.[23]

Drawing in part from her knowledge of Elizabethan literature, Davidman alludes to Christopher Marlowe's *The Tragical History of the Life and Death*

---

21. Davidman's table of contents for *Courage* appears to be inspired by a quote from *The Honourable History of Friar Bacon and Friar Bungay*, an Elizabethan-era stage comedy by Robert Greene (1558-1592). In scene 9 of the play a brazen head — an artificial head made of brass and under demonic control — speaks three times, saying "Time Is," "Time Was," and "Time Past." The table of contents for *Courage* is divided into three sections. The first, "Time Is," contains twenty poems. The second, "Time Was," contains twenty-two poems. The third, "Time Past," contains twenty-three poems. This tripartite division is repeated in the poem "Brazen Head," which appears as the final poem in "Time Was" (*Naked Tree*, 159-60; an earlier version of this poem under the title "Love Poem" is dated by Davidman as January 1939). That Davidman's table of contents was influenced by the Elizabethan writer Greene is not surprising since she would have been familiar with his work as a result of her master's study and thesis at Columbia University.

22. In my discussion of these poems I follow their order of publication rather than where Davidman placed them in the table of contents.

23. "The Devil Will Come," *New Masses* 32 (June 27, 1939): 6; *Naked Tree*, 162. Davidman dates this poem as February 1939.

of Doctor Faustus (1604), a retelling of the Faust legend — the story of a man who sells his soul to the devil in exchange for worldly pleasures. Davidman's Everyman Faustus, however, seems unaware of the soul-damning deal he has fallen victim to:

> He sets his feet upon the iron towers,
> A palace and a pylon on each hand;
> His shadow purples the imported sand,
> The murmurs of his mouth are hothouse flowers.
> Replete in fattened leather and in chrome,
> His car at evening ferries Faustus home
> Musing the gate-receipts, the dancer's knees —
> And yet, at midnight, Mephistopheles.

That is, returning home and delighting in his economic and financial success, her Faustus will be surprised to find that there is the devil (Mephistopheles) to pay. Davidman's Faustus is a happy, contented capitalist — little knowing that in his pursuit of money, possessions, and status he will eventually face an uncomfortable reckoning — one in keeping with the agenda of the CPUSA.

Another poem intended for *Courage* is "Jews of No Man's Land," first published in the *New Republic* on July 5, 1939.[24] Davidman, who most often resists writing about her ethnicity, is compelled in this poem to write openly about the atrocities being visited upon Jews as the Nazis swept across Europe. In 1935 the Nuremberg Laws on Citizenship and Race had denied Jews German citizenship, and the persecution of Jews accelerated quickly from that point. By 1938 many European Jews were effectively homeless, while brutal, wholesale killings and mass imprisonments of Jews in concentration camps were the norm. Even though "Jews of No Man's Land" has a political edge, it is primarily a poem attempting to capture the despondency and despair that displaced Jews were experiencing. The poem opens with a bleak immediacy:

> We, stripped in this unmerciful year,
> naked to the front and end of it, to the blast
> two ways from the future and the past,
> we despoiled of our houses; sold to the sky; here

---

24. "Jews of No Man's Land," *New Republic* 99 (July 5, 1939): 248; *Naked Tree*, 86-88. Davidman dates this poem as November 1938.

Poland to the right and to the left
Sudetenland; snarled at by two frontiers.[25]

Once comfortable "Jew / Jewess and Jew baby" now are "gnawed by the wind's mouth; / bearing our children in the dry ditch, between the winter's / slide of ice upon us and the autumn's rain." More alarming, however, they are "given to the hunter's / shot and bullet, fair game in a dry meadow, / foodless, without bread, without body, we Jews / houseless, tongueless, without value, without use." The poem then shifts to pointed rhetoric:

You who pity us, you who are troubled by our names,
you who lie awake with your skin full of meat and
comfort held closely inside your hand,
you who look at us out of the warm rooms;

hold hard to your good thing that you may not lose.
Thus and thus it was with us; the same bread,
white and smelling warm; the bed
such as you have it and the ceiling above it.

The poem concludes with a sober warning: "Learn how we were brought to this desolation, / how we were betrayed by our sleep and our / pleasant customs and peace and by the striking hour / lest it be done to each of you in your nation!" In this poem Davidman evokes a powerful sympathy for the plight of persecuted European Jews and issues a dark warning that a similar fate may await others unless the specter of Fascism is faced and destroyed. The tender emotion of the poem echoes "Snow in Madrid" and "Near Catalonia" from *Letter to a Comrade.*

Also planned for inclusion in *Courage* is "Office Window," a poem that

25. In the early twentieth century, Sudetenland was the name given to the northern, southwest, and western regions of Czechoslovakia that were inhabited by a majority of ethnic Germans. Hitler, seeing himself as the protector of these ethnic Germans, set into motion a series of events that led Czechoslovakia to arm its borders in 1936. Matters came to a head in March 1938 when Hitler's supporters in Sudetenland began to push for independence. In an effort to appease Hitler, British Prime Minister Neville Chamberlain agreed to cede Sudetenland to Hitler on September 15, 1938. Hitler's actions were a transparent foreshadowing of his military aspirations culminating on September 1, 1939, when Germany invaded Poland and triggered the start of World War II.

puts a different twist on the themes of "The Devil Will Come."[26] While the earlier poem was a study in consumer excess, "Office Window" focuses upon the anonymity of big city life. Ironically, even though one is surrounded by millions of others in New York City, the poem suggests that there is staggering loneliness and a sense of disconnect among the human beings who hurry to and fro from home to office to home again: "This is about a thing you are about; / this poem is about the business of living / which you have set about." Presented as an internal dialogue one city dweller has with herself wondering about someone she sees each day during her commute to work — "This is about your body under the overcoat / jammed in the rush hour with the shoulder against my back; / this is about your elbows and your neat eyelids, / the finicking contrivances of flesh and the universe / with which I am made familiar for an hour in the subway" — the poem imagines a day in the life of her familiar yet nameless and unspoken to fellow commuter:

> O my brother
> with our eyes we perceive the same squares of advertising;
> the light and dark goes past the subway window;
> so swiftly flicker the lights of day upon day
> flash and the sun comes down bang and the moon rearisen
> we ride in darkness flash and the sun rearisen
> red light green light and riding in the subway
> we have seen our lives chase each other past the subway windows.

She even wonders about his life after work, speculating about his walks in the country, his evenings spent lying in the grass in Central Park, and his night life:

> And when you are done writing your name in beer or water
> with your fingertip upon the restaurant table
> when you have heard the music come round again
> and the horns perishing where they were born;
> when you have seen the film come round again
> the necessity of sleep is come upon you.

---

26. "Office Windows," *Fantasy: A Literary Quarterly with an Emphasis on Poetry* 6, no. 3 (1939): 5-7; *Naked Tree,* 68-71. Davidman dates this poem as August 1938.

Do you dream
that you are falling down an endless flight of air
set without steps in the mockery of stars?

The poem ends with a decided tone of uncertainty about the meaningfulness of such an existence: "But whether you dream this or another thing / you will be called back and with pain remake your morning face; / brother tell me why / sharer of weekly salary tell me why / fellow sufferer of the compulsions of humanity tell me why?" Davidman's musings and reflections in "Office Window" sharply contrast with her poems driven by a political purpose; here she ponders over a most basic question confronting each human being: In the end, does my life — does anyone's life — have meaning and purpose beyond the everyday scramble to eat, sleep, work, and begin the routine over again the next day? A serious concern with such issues links this poem to ones in *Letter to a Comrade,* including "Skeleton."

"In All Humility," also intended for *Courage,* recalls poems in *Letter to a Comrade* concerning romantic love such as "Il Pleure dans Mon Coeur," "Sorceress Eclogue," and "Obsession."[27] The speaker — apparently a woman — contrasts the physicality of her love in contradistinction to divine love, particularly through explicit allusions to Christ. For instance, the poem begins:

Now I rejoice that I am made of common earth;
I celebrate this double handful of the dust;
I would not have it anywhere forgotten
That I am child of no miraculous birth
And by no fabulous fathering begotten,
But by a man on woman in his lust.

Although she admits human love is imperfect, passion — especially sexual intercourse — sustains and empowers human beings: "See now; my hands are broken by your love, / My body is good bread / Made and broken that you may taste thereof; /My breast is good to put beneath your head." Her arguments climax as the poem concludes:

You shall rise afresh
From my embrace to fight anew your ancient wars,

---

27. "In All Humility," *Fantasy: A Literary Quarterly with an Emphasis on Poetry* 6, no. 4 (1940): 27; *Naked Tree,* 76-77. Davidman dates this poem as September 1938.

And by my arms made brave
Conquer for a little time the assaults of the grave
Before the returning sun shall see you dead.
Subdue your ambitious spirit to find in me
Reviving nourishment; accept my bed
As a perishable pleasure of mortality,
And love my earth, perceiving in my face
The natural comfort of the commonplace.

This return to writing about romantic love illustrates that Davidman's concern with passion and sexual fulfillment is never far from the surface of her experience, and it suggests that her inner life was one ever longing for sexual intimacy.

Like "Office Windows," "Though Transitory" is another poem dealing with fundamental issues of the human condition.[28] It concerns the joys of being young:

This is a good thing to be young;
having the brightness laid along my skin
gold and the gold hair slightly
stirring with the lift of my arm; a good thing
having the clear brave whites of my eyes shining
and the eyes moving lightly.

Even language is empowered by youth: "In the time of youth there is a sweet taste in speaking." The speaker celebrates being strong and virile: "Being young / it is a good thing to feel the joints of my body / swing upon each other with pure delight." There is a resiliency, a fervor, a bounce-back quality of the young that must be enjoyed:

And when I am hurt
youth is a shield to turn the blow and a good medicine
like a green leaf laid over aching eyes;

for I am never so bruised upon the mouth,
so betrayed into sickness that I cannot rise

---

28. "Though Transitory," *Fantasy: A Literary Quarterly with an Emphasis on Poetry* 6, no. 4 (1940): 26-27; *Naked Tree,* 81-82. Davidman dates the poem as October 1938.

tasting the morning; take the wind in my teeth
remade by the dear miracle of youth.

This almost light-hearted poem is rare for Davidman, and it suggests a wry acknowledgment that even though youth is transitory — ever at the beck of time's movement — it is to be enjoyed and treasured. One is reminded of the end of Joseph Conrad's "Youth" when an older Marlow reflects back on his earliest adventure at sea:

> I remember my youth and the feeling that will never come back any more — the feeling that I could last for ever, outlast the sea, the earth, and all men; the deceitful feeling that lures us on to joys, to perils, to love, to vain effort — to death; the triumphant conviction of strength, the heat of life in the handful of dust, the glow in the heart that with every year grows dim, grows cold, grows small, and expires — and expires, too soon, too soon — before life itself.[29]

Marlow's reverie about youth is slanted by his having now lived to be an older man, while the persona of Davidman's poem lacks such perspective; youth, while admittedly transitory, engages openly with all life throws its way, confident in its capacity to rebound and move forward.

"For the Happy Man," recalling the theme of both "For the Gentlemen" and "Prophet without Honor," portrays how those enjoying the fruits of capitalism neglect to remember those suffering from its darker consequences: "Do you remember how good it is / kissing the water's lip, / afterward diving into sleep / sheets and blankets, warmth and peace?"[30] Unlike "For the Gentlemen" and "Prophet without Honor," however, there is no implied warning or threat; instead, the poem ends with a soft appeal: "You remember all the evenings, you / remember the games and the singing and the love; / they are good things for any man to have. / Give them to us all, we want them too."

Like "Pacific Shore," another political poem from *Courage,* "Dayspring," catalogs the sufferings of the poor and ends with a metaphor suggesting change is coming:

---

29. Joseph Conrad, *Youth* (Baltimore: Penguin, 1975), 34-35.

30. "For the Happy Man," *New Masses* 38 (February 18, 1941): 36; *Naked Tree,* 190. Davidman dates this poem as February 1940.

What of the night?
Nothing very much.
The rich hold tight
with a nervous clutch.
The poor let life go
by inches; death
does a good business
sucking up breath
and exploiting heartbreaks.
The sound you hear
is the noise that pain makes.
Nothing very much
to report of the night.
Only, eastward,
Notice the light.[31]

Still another political poem meant to be included in *Courage,* "Here in the City," details the life of a poor family — particularly a young child — enduring excruciating summertime heat in a city tenement building:

At nine o'clock the child asked for a drink of water.
At ten o'clock the child, its hair flat with sweat,
whimpered, woke, and asked for a drink of water.
The mother saw prickly heat on its arms and legs,
pushed the bed a little nearer the window.

But there is little relief for the child since "all night the flies / sizzled upward from the garbage pails / ranked along the alley to salute the dawn."[32]

"Coldwater Canyon," written just as Davidman was leaving Hollywood, is very much in the tradition of a valediction — it is her resigned goodbye to all that she disliked about and all that thwarted her during her stay in Hollywood: "The bird that sang to us some time ago, / blue, seawater blue, kingfisher blue, / has got so draggled in the heavy snow / the glory has gone out of him."[33] She

31. "Dayspring," *New Masses* 39 (June 17, 1941): 17; *Naked Tree,* 187. Davidman dates this poem as February 1940.

32. "Here in the City," *New Masses* 40 (July 8, 1941): 20; *Naked Tree,* 168. Davidman dates this poem as June 1939.

33. "Coldwater Canyon," *Accent: A Quarterly of New Literature* 2 (Summer 1941): 200; *Naked Tree,* 178-79. Davidman dates this poem as December 1939.

says, "nor has life got any use for us; / we are not good servants in our stained clothing." Although Davidman went to Hollywood with great expectations and not a little arrogance, in this poem she says she leaves with no anger or venom:

> Only let nothing cry us up again,
> no bird, no honor, no awakening drum;
> let us go peaceably among the dead men,
> safe into darkness out of the abyss of sun.

"Game with Children," written seven months later, gives voice to a more robust Davidman, brimming with anticipation at what the future might hold:

> Come now, let us be tigers,
> let us be tigers walking in the jungle
> under the leaves where the green dew lingers
> quietly, where nothing comes with guns.
> Nothing is strong enough to hurt tigers;
> see how they walk, shaking the dew from the leaves;
> let us be proud tigers in the cool evening
> stepping as softly as a man breathes.[34]

Like a tiger, she will fear nothing: "Tigers eat big dinners every day, / after which they always go to sleep / sweetly underneath the shining palm trees." Her future, she avers, is filled with potential: "Let us go away and be tigers."

"Trojan Women" transposes elements of the retreat from Troy by Aeneas and his family at the end of Book II of the *Aeneid* to a day's sojourn at Coney Island: "In the smoke and screaming air / they got across the bridges with their children, / carrying their household gods and silverware . . . / Coney Island / was the first place they landed."[35] What might have been parody — "It was a sweet place to love a man in, / the city with the lights and movie houses, / two rooms and kitchenette and frigidaire" — rises to something much grander: "And just then / the empire state building made a perfect candle / of explosion and illumination / and burst

---

34. "Game with Children," *Accent: A Quarterly of New Literature* 2 (Summer 1941): 200-201; *Naked Tree,* 196. Davidman dates this poem as July 1940.

35. "Trojan Women," *Accent: A Quarterly of New Literature* 2 (Summer 1941): 201; *Naked Tree,* 202-3. Davidman dates this poem as November 1940.

all the way up." This vision in the midst of banality is thrown into relief by the poem's conclusion: "And Troy town / reverberated as the walls came down."

After "Trojan Women" more than a year went by before Davidman published another poem. In fact from the summer of 1941 through April of 1943 — a period just short of two years — Davidman published only one poem, "Peter the Plowman," in *NM* on September 15, 1942.[36] It begins with apocalyptic images and dire warnings that people should face the truth about the evils of capitalism rather than hurrying "to get back to the shady nook in hell / where they lie down with arms around their worry / in decent privacy." This is Davidman the Communist, advancing the agenda of the CPUSA. But then, unexpectedly, the poem turns and focuses upon the prophetic role of the poet:

> I the songmaker, the sun's conscious lover,
> had my vision, not in dreamy weather,
> nor in lightning nor the burning bush,
> but soberly in winter while the sun
> lit up the loneliness of everyone;
> saw myself and all the songmakers
> as hollow bugles to the people's mouth
> speaking the Judgment word. I heard
> the tombs explode; I saw the dead arise.[37]

Divorcing the poet's prophetic insight from any religious origin ("nor the burning bush"), Davidman suggests instead it comes from the cold light of day. Poets find that through them, seemingly inexplicably, "rolled the everlasting sound / dragging sleepers up from underground." The poem then ends with Davidman's most explicit statement of how she sees herself as a poet:

> Poet, poet, you are the people's trumpet;
> golden and clean put yourself to their lips,

36. Yet we know she was incredibly productive during this time period, publishing seventy-three reviews and essays for *NM*. While this does not mean she stopped writing poetry, her attention had shifted to her prose work for *NM*.

37. "Peter the Plowman," *New Masses* 44 (September 15, 1942): 15; *Naked Tree,* 219-20. Davidman nowhere dates this poem, but I believe it may have been first composed in the winter of 1942.

tear yourself apart to shout their word
so that no gun is louder, no fear is louder,
no frightening bell is louder in its steeple;
till all the sunlight shines on all the people.

If this ending is Davidman's poetic manifest in brief, and I believe it is, it explains why much of her political poetry is outward looking — that is, it is poetry concerned with showing the moral and economic bankruptcy of the two worldviews she most despised at the time: Fascism and capitalism. The central problem with "Peter the Plowman" and others like it is their outward focus on social issues; that is, like the political poems in *Rise and Shine* and *Letter to a Comrade,* these are public poems revealing little about her personal experience; she paints on a very broad canvas her perceived understanding of the plight of her proletarian subjects.[38]

Perhaps the most unusual poem in *Courage* is "Fairytale." It is certainly unlike any other poem she published, with its focus upon another world, a world beyond the everyday, and it is at great variance with her political poems. In the poem Davidman imagines a castle to which she can retreat and be immune to the world's hurts, dangers, and perils:

Always, if you knew,
if you knew how to go,
you could walk down a street
(the daylight street)
that twisted about
and ended in grass;
there it was
always, the castle.[39]

Yet the poem's ending militates against its promise of solace: "Hate and heartbreak / all were forgot there; / we always woke, / we never got there." This longing for a place beyond the mundane may have been the start of Davidman's disaffection with the CPUSA and the beginning of a search that

38. I realize that in criticizing her political poems in this way I am open to the charge of having a bourgeois poetical sensibility — exactly the kind of sensibility Mike Gold and other proletarian critics of the 1930s would have both abhorred and vigorously attacked.

39. "Fairytale," in *War Poems of the United Nations,* ed. Joy Davidman (New York: Dial Press, 1943), 299-300; *Naked Tree,* 221-22. Davidman later included the poem in "The Longest Way Round" (see *Bone,* 89), and I quote it in Chapter 9.

would lead her to reject the materialism of Communism. Commenting on the poem later in her essay "The Longest Way Round," Davidman says as much:

> As a child I had a recurring dream: I would walk down a familiar street which suddenly grew unfamiliar and opened onto a strange, golden, immeasurable plain, where far away there rose the towers of Fairyland. If I remembered the way carefully, the dream told me, I should be able to find it when I woke up. To conventional psychologists, I know, such visions are merely "wishful thinking." But why should all human beings be born wanting something like that, unless it exists? . . . ["Fairytale" is] proof of the hope of heaven, making itself known even to one so willfully blind as I. (*Bone*, 88)

She finishes her comments on the poem by saying it is "a rather odd poem, perhaps, for the convinced atheist and communist who wrote it in 1940!" (*Bone*, 90).

"Dirge for the Suicides (In Memory of Ernst Toller)" commemorates Toller (1893-1939), a Polish Jew, who was a poet, playwright, socialist revolutionary, and political activist.[40] Haunted by his nightmarish experiences fighting in the trenches during World War I, he came to believe it was his duty as a human being to write political poetry, primarily in protest against the machinations of repressive governments. He became active in left-wing politics in Germany during the 1920s and early 1930s. After Hitler and the Nazis came to power, he fled to London in 1933. He eventually came to America; depressed and disillusioned, he hanged himself in a New York hotel room on May 22, 1939. The poem opens with a sardonic tone that is maintained throughout:

> Be kind to them, love them and give them praise,
> forgive them. It was not their fingers
> knotted the rope. Forgive them;
> it was not their hearts bred the heartsickness
> scattered the poison in the concentration camp.

---

40. "Dirge for the Suicides," in *Seven Poets in Search of an Answer*, 32-33; *Naked Tree*, 170-72. Davidman dates this poem as June 1939. Davidman was not the only writer to memorialize Toller. W. H. Auden published "In Memory of Ernst Toller" in his *Another Time* (1940).

Davidman identifies herself as one of the "living fighters" who, urged on by the example of Toller, continue to "get clubbed in the strike, faint in the demonstration, / manage to exist under the airplane bombs, / only do not die in our black moment / between the bang of three and four o'clock at night / knotting our own defeat about our throats." Her sympathy is with Toller, noting that his suicide was due in part to the sense of betrayal he felt from those who once had been his fellow protesters: "Forgive the martyr for his martyrdom, / the narrow bones, the brittle heart strings snapped / by some mere centuries of intolerable pain; / forgive the man who let himself be murdered / by forty thieves." As for Toller's betrayers — the forty thieves — she says:

> But kill the thieves;
> pile up the bodies of the murderers;
> beat no retreat from the interminable battlefield;
> suffer the spitting and the leather belts, but live;
> wash your hands in pain, but live, but live.

A related poem published at the same time is "Elegy for Garcia Lorca." Lorca (1896-1936) was a Spanish poet and playwright who was shot by a firing squad of Fascist soldiers during the early days of the Spanish Civil War. Davidman links his death to his bold stand against Fascism: "There was a man [who said] . . . / I perceive the dawn / walking upon the tops of the mountains, / setting its feet upon rooftops, / putting its fingers upon windowpanes to make their dust sparkle. / He said: I perceive the dawn arising in the heart of man."[41] In Toller's suicide and Lorca's execution Davidman finds new urgency for those supporting the agenda of the CPUSA.[42]

Another political poem intended for *Courage* is "Roncesvalles," published as "Poem for Liberation" in *NM*.[43] In this poem Davidman recalls an important incident from *La Chanson de Roland,* the well-known French poem that celebrates the Battle of Roncesvalles in 778. At the end of *Chanson,* Roland, headstrong but brave, whose forces are surrounded by the enemy, foolishly rejects advice to blow his horn in order to summon assistance from Charlemagne. The hopeless battle commences and Roland decides too

---

41. "Elegy for Garcia Lorca," in *Seven Poets in Search of an Answer,* 34-35; *Naked Tree,* 67. Davidman dates this poem as August 1938.

42. Davidman published Lorca's poem "Ballad of the Spanish Civil Guard" in her *War Poems of the United Nations,* 175-79.

43. "Poem for Liberation," *New Masses* 52 (September 12, 1944): 8; *Naked Tree,* 229-30. This poem was originally titled "Roncesvalles" and dated July 9, 1944.

late to blow his horn. Davidman shifts forward the setting of her poem to the French and Spanish countrysides of World War II, and attempts to invoke the spirit of courage and bravery of Roland for the modern day fighters defending their countries:

> The dead lie still, but something is not still;
> The battle talk is whispered to the horn
> by the chittering mouse, by the wind's rising roar,
> by the seething bush, by the great shout of trees,
> and thunder, thunder, over the Pyrenees . . .
> > Comrade Roland,
> > *Cumpaing Rollanz, car sunez vostre cor!*

In a footnote to the poem, Davidman herself offers a gloss on the last line: "Last line is from the *Chanson de Roland,* the national epic of France: Comrade Roland, sound your horn now." The call here is for those who oppose Fascism to rise up and assist the over-matched French and Spanish forces in their struggle against overwhelming odds. In its tone, "Poem for Liberation" has affinities with "Near Catalonia" from *Letter to a Comrade.*

Her most damning political poem in *Courage* is the last of the published poems that she intended to include, "Quisling at Twilight."[44] It focuses upon the interior life of a quisling — the World War II term the Allies used for one who collaborated with the enemy.[45] The poem is set in the quiet — perhaps too quiet — of an evening while a lonely betrayer of his friends and country wanders aimlessly about his deserted house, with all the lights switched on. Despite his need for light, he shuns any objects that might show him his face:

> > Sit in the armchair,
> not the one facing the mirror but the one
> next to the friendly fire but no not there
> where the fire makes pictures out of memory; there
> next the window but no not that the glimmering pane

---

44. "Quisling at Twilight," *New Masses* 56 (July 31, 1945), 4; *Naked Tree,* 240-41. Davidman nowhere dates this poem, but I believe it may have been first composed in the winter of 1945.

45. Dorsett believes this poem may contain veiled reference to Davidman's unhappiness regarding the breakdown of her marriage to Bill Gresham, a view I do not believe the poem supports. See Dorsett, *And God Came In: The Extraordinary Story of Joy Davidman* (New York: Macmillan, 1983), 55-56.

shows you your eyes; here here by the desk
but you see your face in the polish of the desk.

So much fine furniture but it costs too much
at evening with the sad colors and the voices
you know it costs too much.

The not-so-subtle point is that the quisling cannot bear to look at his own face because he is filled with shame and guilt regarding his moral compromises. Yet his shame and guilt are not enough to stop his internal rationalizations:

(but you meant no harm did you and there was nothing
else you could do was there and they promised order
a new order and you thought they would win
and there was a standard of living to maintain and a blonde
and you were afraid
and somebody had to keep the mob in its place
and you were afraid
and after all you were never the one who did the killing)

Expediency, self-interest, and internal justifications bring the quisling the only solace he can find; yet he remains haunted: "The desk and the mirror and the windowpane. / Nowhere to go where you cannot see your face. / The dead hands fumble for the latch."

One final poem intended for *Courage,* "Genetrix," was only published recently in *Bone.* It returns to the love poetry of *Letter to a Comrade,* and it is particularly akin to "Sorceress Eclogue," "Night-Piece," and "Obsession."[46] As in these earlier poems, the female persona is a possessive lover: "I shall have the making of you in my hands, / I shall make you over again; / I shall breed your body out of the pain of my womb / and put my flesh with it to make it wise."[47] This notion that she is the creator of her lover is both sensuous and sensual:

I shall put your bones together, one by one,
and set your heart beating in the midst of all

---

46. That "Genetrix" is similar in tone to the love poems in *Letter to a Comrade* is not surprising; it was originally intended to be included in that volume. For more, see *Bone,* 3-14.

47. Published in *Bone,* 10-11; *Naked Tree,* 55. Davidman dates this poem as June 1938.

and the mouth shall be you that plucks at my breast;
you will live in the eyesockets, and you shall be
a laughter, a small noise, a wordless happiness
closed in my arm, loving my breast and me.

The woman's mastery over her lover is completed in the poem's conclusion: "Man, you are a new creature, dear and wild / with your new thoughts and your familiar hair, / and being my lover, you shall be my child."

In assessing Davidman's published poems of 1938-1945, many of which were intended to appear in either *Rise and Shine* or *Courage*, we see that most are political poems similar to those in *Letter to a Comrade*, and, predictably, a number of them originally appeared in *NM*. Davidman took advantage of her editorial position at *NM*, creating something of a bully pulpit so that in her poetry she could aggressively advance issues important to LAW and the CPUSA. Yet she had not abandoned fiction, as her novel *Anya* (1940) proves; it merits our attention in the next chapter as it gives evidence of her sustained and largely effective work in prose fiction.

CHAPTER 6

Anya (1940)

The last several chapters have focused upon Davidman's poetry and prose nonfiction, inadvertently suggesting that she had abandoned writing fiction after the appearance of her short story "Apostate" in November 1934. However, a review of DP reveals that she remained actively writing fiction through the 1930s, including a number of short stories; at the same time, there is no evidence she tried to publish any of the stories.[1] In addition, we cannot with certainty establish when Davidman first began working on the novel that eventually resulted in the finished novel *Anya* since no manuscript version, dated or undated, appears in DP. However, if we turn to her letters, we find hints that she was probably working on the manuscript during her first residency at the MacDowell Colony in the summer of 1938.[2] On September 1, 1938, she writes James Still, noting that while she is happy to be back in New York, being there "doesn't keep me yet from missing the Colony"; in addition, she lavishes high praise on a short story Still has just published in the *Saturday Evening Post:*

> I want to tell you how much I liked your story. . . . Somehow I expected you to write like that, with that admirable trick of understatement and quiet strength and precision of detail. I understand now what you meant

1. See DP, Box 1, Series 5, Folders 41-73.
2. Dorsett suggests that Davidman "spent the summer of 1938 finishing . . . [the novel] started over a year before." Dorsett, *And God Came In: The Extraordinary Story of Joy Davidman* (New York: Macmillan, 1983), 29-30. See also Abigail Santamaria, *Joy: Poet, Seeker, and the Woman Who Captivated C. S. Lewis* (New York: Houghton Mifflin Harcourt, 2015), chs. 5 and 6.

when you described the time you spent over each sentence. There wasn't a bit of casual description in the story you hadn't thought about and made a part of the whole. I wish I could do so much with so few words; I'm apt to splash colors about like an impressionist painter. (*Bone,* 14)[3]

Having spent so much of her literary efforts on her poetry (she was at this time also putting the finishing touches on *Letter to a Comrade*), Davidman indicates here that her prose fiction may have been halting and sporadic in comparison.[4]

The first direct reference to her writing of *Anya* comes in another letter to Still, this time subsequent to her failed attempt to write screenplays. After leaving Hollywood and returning to New York, on February 15, 1940, she writes Still: "I've sold my novel to Macmillan — it happened when I was still in California. . . . It's going to come out next August or September" (*Bone,* 28). What these two letters and the historical evidence point to is that Davidman began working on *Anya* at least as early as the summer of 1938 during her first visit to the MacDowell Colony and that perhaps she finished a draft of the novel during the summer of 1939 while living in Hollywood. We also know she was still working on the novel as late as the following spring since in her May 20, 1940, letter to Stephen Vincent Benét she reveals that she "was busy correcting proofs on my novel and wishing I could afford to rewrite" (*Bone,* 29). *Anya* was published by Macmillan in early July 1940.[5]

When it appeared, critical opinion was mixed. The reviewer in the *Christian Century* said the "novel of Jewish life in Russia seventy years ago" was "merely the setting for the personality of Anya — tingling with sensory awareness of the world and of herself."[6] Regarding the cover blurb that claims the novel is written in a vein suggesting D. H. Lawrence, the reviewer said, "the resemblance is recognizable, but apparently superficial." Alfred Kazin began his review by noting that "*Anya* is one of those bitter-sweet comedies of sex out of European folklore whose modest importance lies in their attempt to recapture the memories of a particular race, a particu-

---

3. Still's story was "Bat Flight," *Saturday Evening Post* 211, no. 10 (September 3, 1938): 12-13, 50-51.

4. Later in the letter she adds: "Those last two weeks or so, after you left, I didn't do much work except for finishing my play and two or three poems" (*Bone,* 14). This play has not survived.

5. The original title of the novel was *Cookeh's Wife;* see a copy of the contract dated January 25, 1940, with Macmillan in DP Box 1, Series 3, Folder 17.

6. *Christian Century* 57 (July 10, 1940): 879.

lar time, a particular way of life."[7] Although he commended Davidman for having "written her book as a comedy [that is] fresh and gay," he criticized her narrative technique: "Her most zealous poetic images, her most labored concentration, result in sentences rather than scenes of genuine beauty and taste."

In a more positive review N. L. Rothman contradicted Kazin, writing that the novel is a "full-blown, beautifully written work of a keen intelligence. Miss Davidman has a natural flair for fresh and immediate seeing, and a sure knowledge of the swells and starts of emotion."[8] He went on to commend Davidman for her character development, particularly Anya: "It is in the sheer poetry of Anya's thought and speech that Miss Davidman gives us the best of her writing, and that best is something to read." Similarly, John Cournos called *Anya* "a powerful, well-written novel" that celebrates "the development of Anya from girlhood to womanhood and of the trouble she caused in the community by letting her passions over-ride its conventions and moral code."[9] Cournos was smitten with Anya, arguing that she "is something of a wanton, but she is real and thoroughly alive."[10] Dorothy Frye made a similar observation: "Anya is thoroughly alive and understandable, although not always lovable."[11] Frye agreed with Rothman that Davidman did well with character development, noting her "deft handling of minor characters." The reviewer in the *New Republic* was also positive, calling the novel "a careful portrait of a sensitive woman and also a first-rate reproduction of the [Russian] Orthodox folklore that helped the Tsar keep walls around the Ghetto."[12]

Davidman suggested the folktale quality of the story in her dedication: "To my mother who told me the story of Anya."[13] In brief, *Anya* is a novel about a young Jewish girl's sexual awakening set in a tiny Russian village between 1860 and 1887. When the novel opens, Anya is twelve years old; when it ends, she is forty-one, having broken almost every social taboo of the

---

7. "A Bitter-Sweet Comedy of Sex: Adventures of a Village Coquette in Russian Jewry," *New York Herald Tribune Books* (July 14, 1940): 2.

8. "Honest and Passionate," *Saturday Review of Literature* 22 (July 13, 1940): 10.

9. "A Sinner in Israel," *New York Times,* July 14, 1940, p. 7.

10. "A Sinner in Israel," 18.

11. Review of Joy Davidman's *Anya, Boston Transcript,* August 10, 1940, p. 2.

12. Review of Joy Davidman's *Anya, New Republic* 103 (August 12, 1940): 222. In addition, see Dorsett's brief discussion of the novel, *And God Came In,* 29-33.

13. This folktale basis explains, in part, the novel's lack of fully developed and psychologically complex characters, including most notably Anya.

Jewish community in the town of Tulchin. In fact, before her marriage she has several sexual encounters and after her marriage she has several more. She gives birth to six children — a son and three daughters by her husband, Cookeh (one girl dies in infancy, in part because of being deserted by Anya, and the two others are stillborn); a stillborn daughter by the Russian Colonel Muralov with whom she runs off to Odessa for a wild month of sex and pleasure; and a son by the only man she truly loves, Shimka, her first love who re-enters her life when she is forty. In addition to her sexual promiscuity, an obvious violation and flouting of her community's expectations, Anya despises the Jewish community — especially the prying and self-righteous women — that judges and condemns any action she takes contrary to communal expectations. Davidman's disregard for the Jewish community as portrayed in the novel leads one critic to write: "There are many moments in the novel when Anya appears to be a Jewish anti-Semite, hating her own people whose customs and laws she rejects . . . [and] while we cannot equate the author with [Anya] . . . we can say . . . that Davidman understands Anya's restlessness, her refusal to be like other Jewish wives and mothers, [and] her willingness to incur the wrath of her people to follow her own interests."[14]

In judging the artistic merits of *Anya,* I begin with several general observations. First, *Anya* is essentially a comedy. While there are many literary definitions of comedy, a very apt one for a discussion of *Anya* is found in Northrop Frye's *A Natural Perspective,* one of his several books on Shakespeare. "Comedy," writes Frye, "like all forms of art that are presented in time, is primarily an impetus to completing a certain kind of movement." For Frye the comic impetus is "a drive toward identity."[15] Anya's story, even with its folklore elements, is certainly one in which she tries to discover her identity. Her quest for identity is given to us in the context of the society in which she lives. Another way to put this is that *Anya* is a novel emphasizing the *social* life of a young woman in an isolated Jewish backwater in nineteenth-century Russia; it has little or no interest in the development of Anya's *moral* or *ethical* life. This latter point is particularly important since at no point in the novel does Anya feel any guilt or remorse for her actions, including her sexual infidelities, her repeated desertions of her family, and her shirking of her responsibilities as wife, mother, and community member.

14. Jeffrey Berman, *Companionship in Grief: Love and Loss in the Memoirs of C. S. Lewis, John Bayley, Donald Hall, Joan Didion, and Calvin Trillin* (Amherst, MA: University of Massachusetts Press, 2010), 27.

15. Frye, *A Natural Perspective* (New York: Columbia University Press, 1965), 118.

Other comedic elements include the following: Anya (perhaps to a lesser degree) and the other characters are flat, showing little psychological development; there is little concern with careful plotting — one episode could easily precede another with little damage to the narrative; there is no real tragedy in the novel, in spite of the death of Anya's parents and three of her children (in addition, we do not see the Jews endure either persecution or a pogrom); and with only a few exceptions, sex is portrayed as life giving and life affirming. Another literary understanding of comedy is that it is a story that has a happy ending, something that can be easily observed in *Anya* in spite of the trials, sufferings, and pain Anya experiences throughout her search for identity.

A second general observation about *Anya* is related to the first: it is a social novel in which the primary emphasis is upon how society impacts, controls, influences, and directs human behavior, including societal expectations, mores, and judgments. Because social criticism and the outer view of the central characters are all important, social novels offer a relatively shallow understanding of the inner workings of the human mind, emotions, and spirit. Characters appear to be in the power of social forces they cannot fathom or control, and insights into the destructive power of society take precedence over self-knowledge. What little self-knowledge there is comes about not through a character's reflections upon his or her inner world, but instead through social interaction and pressure. Social novels frequently employ the satiric mode, focusing upon important social problems, controversies, and questions, and looking for inspiration, answers, and solutions in environmental and cultural sources. In the social novel there is emphasis upon *what;* that is, the principal attention is upon place, setting, and action. And, as I have already suggested regarding *Anya,* there is a preponderance of flat characters. After we first meet them, they are predictable, psychologically simple, and naïve. As social pressures beat down these characters, readers feel sympathy for them, yet often they are uninteresting because we cannot really understand them. They often appear as passive pawns in the grip of forces they cannot control or comprehend. *Anya* falls in line with other comic and social novels such as Henry Fielding's *Tom Jones,* Charles Dickens's *David Copperfield,* and William Thackeray's *Vanity Fair.*

A final general observation concerns the question of whether *Anya* might be viewed as a *bildungsroman* — that is, a novel that recounts the youth and young manhood or womanhood of a sensitive protagonist who is attempting to learn the nature of the world, discover its meaning and pattern, acquire a philosophy of life, and become a mature adult. As we move through *Anya* — following the development of her life from the age of twelve to forty-one — we certainly might expect it to follow the trajectory of the typical *bildungsroman* familiar in works such as Charlotte Bronte's *Jane Eyre,* Dickens's *Great Expectations,* James Joyce's *A Portrait of the Artist as a Young Man,* and D. H. Lawrence's *Sons and Lovers.* In my judgment *Anya* — in spite of having all the trappings of a *bildungsroman* — is not a novel of development since Davidman, in the end, neglects to give enough of the inside view of Anya's thoughts, longings, psychological musings and reflections, and conscious mind for us to draw an informed judgment about her maturation. Although I risk overstatement, I suggest that Anya is first presented to us as a willful child; then we move through the novel witnessing occasion after occasion of her adult willfulness; and then the novel ends with a final example — perhaps egregiously so — of her continued willfulness. In short, I do not believe Anya's character undergoes much change in the novel, in spite of the many things that happen to her — both good and bad.

With these three general observations in mind, we turn to a more careful exploration of the novel. The first six chapters, in contrast to the argument I have just made, suggest that *Anya* might have become a *bildungsroman,* since they offer readers partial access to an inside view of Anya's developing character from the ages of twelve to eighteen while she is living in the small village of Shpikov. Two focusing leitmotifs are introduced in these early chapters. First, in chapter one, appropriately entitled "Young Animal," we see Anya's sensuous apprehension of nature and her sexual awakening. For instance, after her father, Taube, brings home a large piece of velvet, Anya's reaction is visceral:

> Anya's thin body quivered, because the girl wanted to feel the velvet on her naked flesh. . . . Touching the cloth lightly, the child felt her nails tingle with a desire to scratch it, and the intolerable slight sound of tearing threads made her shiver as it came into her mind. At this her stomach tightened, while her whole body waited intensely for the moment of perfect release relaxation, satisfaction which always arrived, at such shiverings, seemed imminent, yet never arrived, . . . Anya's strong teeth wanted to bite the velvet.[16]

Although this passage ostensibly reveals something of the twelve-year-old's delight in sensuous experience, it also foreshadows in a not-so-subtle man-

16. *Anya* (New York: Macmillan, 1940), 7; subsequent references in the text.

ner her soon to be awakened sexual consciousness. In fact, by the end of chapter one, Anya is sixteen and no longer a girl.[17] We read that "she liked to feel her hard body sway and return under her hand" (9), and when Russian soldiers riding through the town stare at her striking beauty, "such a gaze made her a little dizzy. Sudden things are terrifying or exciting: they make the breath tingle in one's throat, and the flick of eyes in passing comes swiftly. Yet she never gasped for breath at the glance of the shy Jewish boys, with their brown eyes of a poet or a dog" (12).

Anya's early sexual precociousness is highlighted in chapter two when, on a hot summer day, she is unconsciously looking for sexual release: "Unknown to her, the crowd of egotistic and sensual little animals that lived together, making her body, brewed and drank intoxicating juices, so that she trembled" (13). When a childhood friend, Yankov Raffsky, walks by, Anya invites him to sit down by her; instead Yankov runs away, frightened yet fascinated by his former childhood playmate who soon becomes the object of his own awakening sexual fantasies. Also introduced in this chapter is Shimka, a disreputable drifter who becomes the only man Anya genuinely loves. Even though her father warns Anya about Shimka, she schemes and connives ways in which she can accidentally run into him. She delights in the flirtation: "It amused Anya to observe how one day the back of his hand would brush against her wrist in walking, or he would touch her with his whole arm, while on the day after, with seeming naturalness, his thigh would press against the thin stuff of her dress. Before long she was herself devising pleasant accidents of this kind, and anticipating with expectant shiverings of her skin the new approaches which would occur to him" (19). By autumn she is completely besotted with Shimka: "She had, she wanted, no other than Shimka: reliable property, yet a hard bearded creature alien to her in many ways, and by that hot mystery nursing disorder in the veins. Life is sometimes a bubbling in hidden blood at the touch of what is queer. . . . This Shimka created for Anya that tingling in the veins, easily named desire" (23). Anya longs for Shimka on an animal level, and finds it increasingly hard to resist him. Anya's heightened sensuous and sensual nature is explored in great detail throughout the remainder of the novel.

A second critical leitmotif introduced in the first six chapters is Anya's reaction against how the Jewish community of Shpikov evaluates, appraises, judges, and condemns her. Anya is stiff-necked and willful in her response

---

17. That so much time passes in the first chapter and that so little is given of Anya's inner world during these four years argues against designating *Anya* a *bildungsroman*.

to what she sees as the community's rigid, self-righteous, suffocating, and controlling judgment. When she begins to flirt with Shimka, for example, her father scolds her, telling her "it is not nice . . . it is not Jewish" (17). In addition, when the Jewish community begins to whisper about her behavior, Anya is not ashamed; instead, it is "a sauce to her of pleasure" (20). Time and again she enjoys piquing the community's curiosity about her bad behavior until her father believes the only way to control her is to get her married. She angrily rejects his proposal: "Her own throat was full of a bitter taste, her pride invaded. Feeling herself slapped by the inquisitive stubby fingers of the Jews, the girl struck viciously at anyone soft enough to be hurt. Let them stay out of her clean mind, her private mind" (28). Anya's fierce independence, her inviolable sense of self, and her reckless disregard for the opinions of others surface regularly in the novel. When she does finally agree to marry, it is on her own terms: "Yes, [I'll shove my scorn] down their throats. . . . Heads of good girls, walking averted, take mud on your pursed lips; old women, mud on your shawls and dreadful tongues. . . . Gurgle and choke in your filth I throw back at you" (30). She decides to marry Yankov, essentially as a way to spite her community and as an act of revenge against him; ever since their first awkward encounter Yankov has lingered in the background, sexually stimulated by Anya's beauty and bold independence, yet wary of her flouting of the expectations of the Jewish community.

Although outwardly she throws herself into the marriage preparations, internally she resents what is coming, and she fantasizes about Shimka: "The sweet passion Anya had for Shimka, her friend, beat softly and vainly against these female intensities of bitter and lusting revenge" (34). When news of her engagement is heard, Anya's reputation is rehabilitated, and she is welcomed into the coteries of the other young women of the town; moreover, the wagging tongues of the older gossips are silenced. Two months go by during which Yankov clumsily tries to kiss Anya — thus fueling even more her determination to spite him by marrying him — and Shimka, hearing of the impending marriage, leaves town. Desperate for news of Shimka, Anya visits their old haunts; this only gives her greater pain: "And her obstinate spirit twisted itself, curved and recurved upon the thought of Shimka; her fingers ached with pain at the thought of him" (48). As the agony of losing him overwhelms her, she constantly fantasizes about him, even inventing possible scenarios concerning his whereabouts and his certain return to her. Finally, realizing he is gone and will not return, Anya instinctively sabotages her wedding: when Vorontsov, a handsome Russian general, comes riding by, she accepts his invitation to mount his horse and ride through her town in order to create a public spectacle. Anya's willful independence and her heightened sexual appetite are nicely combined in this act: "When the horse moved, Anya gripped its ribs with her legs, which felt warmer, and the beast's muscles rippled mellowly under her thighs. The splendor of this man and beast was like a rough medicine that she gulped down to purge her body of Shimka" (55). She takes full advantage of the scene she is creating: "They will say that I slept with him. . . . And she arched her back against him . . . [as] they were entering the village. . . . At her door Vorontsov kissed her again as he set her on her feet, feeling satisfied with himself. . . . And though the lane appeared to be deserted Anya knew better, watching him salute and ride off, with her back to those accusing blinds that were drawn just not all the way" (56-57).

Just as she knew it would, her behavior scandalizes the Jewish community, her wedding is cancelled, and she is free to set herself even more fiercely against societal expectations. Still fantasizing about Shimka, she has it out with Yankov, who somewhat understandably curses and despises her. For Anya, however, his seething rage is a satisfying salve: "The black curse rattled over her lightly, where she sat arching her throat and smiling at him. In some way, Anya knew that she was doing to him that which she had always wanted to do. She did not understand, but she triumphed. Her smiling eyes burned his eyes, as obscurely she had meant it to" (66). She further tortures Yankov by lying about her sexual exploits: "'Shimka has touched me with his hands . . . Shimka took me into his house with him. I have befouled my body with many men, Yankov. A Russian has lifted my skirt with his hand'" (66-67). Driven mad by Anya's taunting, Yankov ravishes her: "For a moment what he did was incomprehensible, since not thus had Anya encountered lust, then she strained half experimentally against the grip of his arm" (67). Yet Anya's independence, indeed her manipulation of this entire event, is suggested in her reaction to her first experience of coitus: "She had just time to feel strangely elated because he was so strong, and to understand that this, a necessary, an inevitable, a preordained thing, could not be stopped, before her hatred ebbed and melted away, leaving only the loving flesh. Her nameless, blind body, without a thought, without a brain, met another anonymous body and joined it breathlessly" (67).

When Yankov realizes what he has done, he is at first ashamed, then accusatory, screaming that Anya has made him do it. Coolly, Anya agrees: "'Yes. I made you do it.' . . . She had meant him to take her; she had wanted to reduce her enemy to a ridiculous and abject squirming. She had forced him into the ridiculous antic of lust" (68). Yankov, the symbol of all the Jewish community's recriminations against Anya, is effectively manipulated by her seduction so that she comes out on top — in control, calm, and unencumbered. This becomes clear in her actions after he leaves. She takes off all her clothes, runs her hands all over her body, and affirms that nothing, really, has changed. She washes herself, particularly "the symbolic blood-stain, the token of her virginity" (69). In addition, although she has experienced a physical violation, her inner self has been untouched: "Her mind was as clear as snow, as clear glass. No heat would melt it away; no man had left his breath upon it. Nothing had happened to her, because her mind would not let it happen" (69). Anya affirms from this point on in the novel her complete independence from all others — whether it be the community or a particular man: "No man shall have power over me. . . . I shall not lie weeping for any man to comfort. . . . I need nothing" (72). Anya's affirmation here, however, is at best only partially fulfilled in the remainder of the novel; that is, while she avers that no man shall have power over her, ironically her life is defined in terms of her need for men.

Still, this sense of her inviolable self serves her well, since the Jewish community ostracizes her for her behavior with Vorontsov (they know nothing about her encounter with Yankov); yet she maintains her independence, taking control of her father's household after the death of her mother and even seducing Yankov a second time. In the days leading up to this second seduction it is clear that Anya, while insisting upon her independence, is at the same time a creature of intense sexual desire: "She had never been able to dismiss the thought of Yankov . . . for her arms and breasts and lips remembered contact with him . . . [and] she could not escape from wondering if they would be drawn together again to copulate in thick folds of cloth" (77). If sex is a weapon, then Anya intends it to be used doubly to her advantage: "Love is lust, and hatred is lust. Love wishes to enslave the body of the beloved, that he may lie beneath the feet; hate wishes to commit passionate outrage upon the hated body. Love aspires to lie as a slave beneath the onslaught of the lover, and hate makes one submit in ecstasy to any defilement. Her pleasure met her pain, and they clasped lovingly; they two were one" (77-78). Anya determines both to torture Yankov by seducing him and to luxuriate in the physical delight sexual consummation gives her.

These two leitmotifs — Anya's sexual appetite and her fierce independence — are played out repeatedly in the remaining seventeen chapters of the novel. However, unlike these early chapters in which on occasion Davidman gives us an inside view into the workings of Anya's mind, the remainder of the novel does not. Instead, we see Anya acting and responding to external stimuli and circumstances; while the early chapters prepare us in some ways for her coming sexual indiscretions and her willful, self-centered decisions, never again are we allowed inside the workings of her mind. What she does appears instinctive rather than reasoned, impulsive rather than thoughtful, and visceral rather than reflective. Furthermore, as the novel moves forward, her sexuality and strong sense of self are played out in terms of her relationship with four men: her unappealing husband, Cookeh; the young, virile Russian soldier, Colonel Miralov; the kindly but much older Yefim, a grain merchant in Odessa; and, late in the story, Shimka, her only true love.

Chapters seven through fourteen center on Anya's move from Shpikov to the town of Tulchin and her marriage to Cookeh, whose given name is Israel Spiegelglass.[18] His sudden introduction in chapter seven breaks the narrative flow of the novel, suggesting Davidman's clumsy attempt to shift the dramatic focus of the novel away from exploring the workings of Anya's mind toward her efforts to make peace with the Jewish community by doing what they expect: marry, have children, settle down, and become a good wife. Cookeh had been a weak, feeble-minded, and easily led child, always at the beck and call of his overly protective sister; once she saved him from being dragged away by a large sow who intended him to feed her litter of piglets. When he was fourteen he was apprenticed to Chaia Dinerstehn, a grocer who slowly groomed him into an effective salesmen; she taught him how to use his physical unattractiveness as a way to make customers feel sorry for him and thus buy even more than they may have intended. Because he eventually does become a good salesman — and thus a financial catch — the Jewish matrons begin scheming to secure him for their marriageable daughters.

After the death of Chaia's husband and Cookeh's sister, Chaia makes it clear that she is willing to marry Cookeh; however, he decides he only wants to marry a virgin. He consults a marriage broker who eventually arranges for him to marry the twenty-one-year-old Anya; throughout the marriage negotiations, Anya is very much involved, believing she can control and dominate him after they are married: "He is narrow and breakable — I could shatter him in my two hands into brittle splinters like cracked chicken bones." At the same time she feels almost mother-like toward Cookeh: "Here a swift lust to protect him, an aggressive and pathetic sort of love, came over her; to lie

---

18. As readers will recognize from Chapter 1, above, Tulchin is also the setting of her 1934 story "Apostate." Toward the end of the novel Davidman also reintroduces characters from this early story into the narrative and action of *Anya* (see below).

curled around him through the perilous night, while he, with his slack joints and hanging mouth folded like the bud of a flower, would be closed, weary and safe, in the circle of her body" (109-10). Nothing earlier in the novel has prepared us for this response, and, increasingly, Anya reacts instinctively rather than thoughtfully to the circumstances of her life. This is further illustrated in her actions that suggest she is getting married in order to fulfill the expectations of the Jewish community of Tulchin: "In this season the girl felt herself blessed among women. . . . It was not that the Jews came eagerly to talk to her; but at least they did not shun her, they did not look sidewise, they did not spit knowingly in the dust. Anya's hard weariness relaxed, and she thought her people were beautiful" (116).

Yet such moments are fleeting, and she always holds within a fierce independence. Emblematic is her decision to flout custom and refuse to cut her hair before her marriage; when the other women appeal to Cookeh to control his future wife, he says: " 'The child! . . . Is there not time enough to become a woman later? I do not wish' — his voice grew masterful — 'that she should cut her hair' " (120). When on their wedding night they consummate marriage, it is also clear that Anya is in control. Although she came to bed somewhat listlessly, feeling "only a kind of cold eagerness to have the troublesome beginning of her married life over," her feelings suddenly change once Cookeh enters the room: "Anya slipped softly downward in the bed without breathing, her body in that instant grown all one flame" (128). And when Cookeh slides into bed next to her, it is she who ravishes him and not vice versa: "He touched fingertips, he touched knees, he felt arms go about his shoulders, and something soft and living came out of the darkness to meet him, and all his confusions vanished in a warm delirium" (129). Soon found to be pregnant, Anya enjoys the acceptance of the Jewish community and on the surface appears happy and content; Cookeh is tender towards her, and she is satisfied with her life.

However, her willfulness soon leads to conflict as the other matrons come to resent both her physical beauty and her self-pity over how sick pregnancy makes her: "The matrons were faintly and doubtfully beginning to consider Cookeh's wife a queer one, with a good heart, doubtless, but wasteful, silly, given to vanities and trivialities" (147). Moreover, her heightened food cravings cause her to desire a lobster, a creature deemed unclean by Jewish custom. After Cookeh refuses to buy her a lobster, even consulting the local rabbi for counsel, Anya sets her will against him and wears him down so that eventually he gives in and purchases the creature for her. However, once she actually sees the lobster, Anya screams with fright and begs for it to be taken away, temporarily winning the confidence again of the Jewish matrons: "Anya's victory over temptation pleased them better than if she had never been tempted; for it provided excitement. They were grateful to her for another item on the ancient list of aberrations of pregnant women" (154). While the tone of this episode is satirical, the next stage in the relationship between Anya and Cookeh is darker and has repercussions throughout the remainder of the novel. When their son is born, Cookeh unknowingly creates a permanent wedge between himself and his wife by naming the child Yankov after his own father; in this act he sets Anya's heart against both him and "the child whom she could never touch without a faint, an inexplicable feeling of distaste" (160).

As their married life proceeds, outwardly Anya is timid and meek toward Cookeh, but inwardly she struggles with unhappiness: "It was not easy for her to realize that she was not satisfied, that she would never be satisfied, and that she did not particularly want satisfaction" (160). Cookeh assumes he has mastered Anya, but unwittingly every action he takes infuriates her. Furthermore, Anya breaks with the Jewish matrons when she is publicly criticized for showing too much affection for her child — although ironically she does so only to impress the women. She flies into a rage: " 'Not one kopeck do I care for what the women say of me!' . . . Why, said Anya [to herself], the Jews are enemies. I had forgotten. . . . What I make, they destroy . . . they are hatred. Always when I love a thing, their sneering faces and their eyes like hard brown nuts are there to frighten me. . . . I turn here and there looking for kindness, and I am met by hard stones, and I am bruised" (163).[19] Now despising Cookeh, she devises a way to break him: sitting together in their garden one evening, she demands that he kiss her for all to see. He refuses, so she says she will not enter the house until he does; although four times he implores her to come into the house, she waits him out, only entering the house at three in the morning.

Her willfulness grows stronger over the next three years as she gives birth to a sickly daughter whom she cannot love. Also, Yankov shows up unexpectedly one day and asks Anya if his sister-in-law, Shifra, whom he has impregnated, can stay with Anya until a month after the child is delivered. He offers her fifty rubles, and she agrees, all the while keeping the truth of

19. In one of the few instances of authorial intrusion, Davidman comments on Anya's blindness: "[Anya failed] to consider that it was perhaps she who would not let the Jews alone — her harsh colors, her bright passions, her demands being flung at the Jews like a knife, the tumult of her nature shaking the quiet, the obscure and fearful life of the Jews. To be noticeable had always meant, for them, to die" (164).

the situation from Cookeh. Anya falls out with Shifra when she discovers the girl pays regular visits to the Russian soldiers garrisoned nearby. Ironically, the Jewish matrons of Tulchin, not knowing the truth about Shifra, feel sorry for her, take her into their confidence, and pet her. Six weeks after Shifra's son is born, she is still living with Anya; although in some ways this disgusts Anya, in other ways it gives her delight because she feels superior to Shifra, particularly after she plans to reveal Shifra's sexual promiscuity to the Jewish matrons. However, before she can do this, Shifra is found beaten and raped by two Russian soldiers (she had made the mistake of arranging to meet both of them at the same time). Anya nurses her to health and is overjoyed when Yankov finally appears and takes Shifra back home. Throughout these chapters Anya's inner life is never explored; while we see that she is unhappy and miserable, Davidman never lets us really understand why. Instead, we only see Anya from the outside as she responds to the various incidents that make up these chapters.

Chapters fifteen through seventeen focus on the second man to hold Anya's attention, Colonel André Kyrillovitch Muralov. Sensual and passionate on the one hand yet tormented and fearful on the other, "he was nobody's idea of a soldier" (197). He had been posted to Tulchin in order to get him away from the War Department and from scheming women intent on trapping him into marriage. He was known as an aggressive lover, at times even sadistic, but this only attracted women to him even more. Bored and at the end of one of his affairs, he petitions for and is granted leave for a month, all the while hoping he can entice Anya, whom he has only seen once walking through the streets of Tulchin, to run away with him: "What he would give now . . . for something that could bleed in his hands; dark fire; an animal like himself; something he could take double handfuls of and dig his nails into, and beat, and cry on the breast of, and that would love him! The Jewess with yellow eyes he had seen walking in the street" (198). In the meantime, Anya, who longs to be free from her duties as wife and mother, is ready to bolt although she is not consciously considering such an act. When Muralov finds her alone in the street one afternoon, he manages to communicate to her that he is going to Odessa for a month (they do not speak the same language), that he wants her to come with him, and that she can meet him on the road at a cherry tree on the day he is leaving. Initially, she tries to put his invitation out of her mind, but she only succeeds in briefly fantasizing about this chance to escape from all that she loathes. On the appointed day, Anya is waiting for Muralov under the cherry tree and they ride off to Odessa. Throughout the pages leading up to this decisive action, Davidman does not give us an inside view of what Anya is thinking, nor does she offer a psychological exploration of Anya's inner life. While we know she is unhappy, her running away with Muralov seems arbitrary, spontaneous, and capricious, reinforcing our view that she is willful, sensual, and impulsive. Accordingly, we do not see her developing as a character; instead, we see her reacting as a character.

The month in Odessa is a sensual riot. Muralov showers Anya with lavish gifts, including expensive clothing, exotic food, and fine jewelry, delighted with his "amorous barbarian of a woman." Indeed, most of their time is spent in bed: "Blind, lost, childish with a passion that could not be bothered to count tomorrows, the prince and the woman clung to each other through night and day" (205). When his hands touch her, they "burned her like a fire" (206). Perhaps for the first time in her life, Anya gives no rein to her passion: "She would scrub herself with sweet-smelling soap all over and come bare into the room where André spread his arms wide, and they would roll on the bed, biting each other sometimes, rolling over and over and sometimes falling together on the floor. Or lying side by side for long hours they would touch each other lightly, and each touch was as sure and magical as an angel's wing. They did not speak much [since they do not speak the same language], but their bodies loved each other" (206-7). Anya even enjoys Muralov's rough sex:

> Snatching up his riding whip from a corner, the man flicked her with it, driving her about the room until she screamed just a little — for she knew he was not angry — and flung herself upon the bed. Then Muralov, with his face made at once coarse and fine by passion, set the fleshy heel of his hand upon her mouth and really beat her across the belly and thighs. But some obscure compunction in him kept him from hurting her very much, and the marks were gone in four days, so that at the time she liked it more than she suffered. She loved the look of his mouth, which he had forgotten to control. It was a good night for them. Besides, Anya remembered how Shifra had been beaten by two soldiers, and she said to herself, "It is good that he loves me." (210)

Like two animals, Muralov and Anya live entirely for the moment, seeking pleasure in ever more dangerous and sensually thrilling ways.

Throughout this wild month of love making, Anya never once thinks about Cookeh and her children; somehow she places them in a compartment outside her conscious mind, so intent is she on enjoying every moment of her thirty-day escape. Similarly, Muralov never once tries to find out anything about her life in Tulchin: "He did not know anything about her, if she had children and a house, if she had a husband" (211). Two sensualists — self-willed, self-centered, and self-pleasing — Muralov and Anya are completely taken up with their month of pleasure and care for nothing else. When the end of the month comes, Muralov makes a pathetic effort to tell Anya of his despair of life: "For two hours . . . Muralov spoke to her urgently and pleadingly in French. He knew she could not understand. Thank God that she could not understand. He spread his whole life out for her to look at; he gave her his unhappiness, and his lonely heart, and his violence and his unhappiness." Anya, not understanding a word, "sat unmoving, with a little smile like a doll" (212). Muralov's outburst is a sentimental, self-absorbed moment of self-pity. That he has no real interest in Anya beyond their month in Odessa is made clear after he drops her off on the outskirts of Tulchin: "He thought how well he loved her, and how little it mattered to him whether or not he ever saw her again" (214).

Lest we feel sorry for Anya, Davidman makes it clear that Anya has no illusions about some kind of future with Muralov. In addition, Anya does not come slinking back into Tulchin. Instead, she deliberately calls attention to herself by putting on one of her fancy, elaborate hats that Muralov had bought her and walks down the main street: "It came about that the Jews' eyes were struck by the hat before their minds were struck by Anya; it was one thing that the wanton should creep back to her home, but it was another and much greater thing that in doing so she should wear a hat upon her head" (215-16). Ever willful, Anya uses her hat as her way of rubbing the Jewish community's face in her rejection of their judgment and condemnation. Fiercely independent, Anya will not bow before societal pressure, nor show any remorse upon her return to Cookeh, in spite of the fact that he blames her desertion on the death of their infant daughter: "Anya went on with her work, setting water to boil in the samovar. If I keep silent, she thought, his talking will be over, and when he is finished it will be the same between us as before" (217). In fact, she never answers his questions about her running off with Muralov to Odessa, and he only ineffectually beats her when he discovers the bruises on her body left by Muralov's sadistic love blows. For some weeks she even continues to visit Muralov in his barracks, all the while thumbing her nose at the clicking tongues and wagging beards of the Jewish community: "Nor did Anya care anything at all for what the women said, nor for their spitting in the street, nor the silence of those who would not talk to her. She felt light and free. If they did not talk to her, good! Then she owed them nothing and could be free of their life" (221). The affair with Muralov ends when Anya gives birth to his stillborn daughter, and he becomes engaged to a young Polish girl. Throughout Anya's tryst with Muralov, we never see what is going on inside her mind; instead, we see her responding to external events and stimuli, always conscious of societal expectations, but never giving in to what others expect her to do.

Chapters eighteen and nineteen move the narrative ahead four years and we learn — through the gossips at Tulchin — that Anya has taken up with Yefim, a fifty-four-year-old widowed grain merchant. Almost running her over in his carriage one day, he instantly falls in love with her. He whisks her away to Kiev and — much in the fashion of Muralov — lavishes gifts upon her. For her part, Anya, bored and tired again with life in Tulchin, looks to Yefim not for love — "indeed [she] rather despised his gentleness" — but as another outlet for her willfulness: "Anya found it exhilarating to be so much the ruler of a man that everything done to her was as she wanted it done: she could make him perform any act or offer her any attention. Growing drunk with her power over him, she became intolerably capricious, which he loved" (232). In other words, for the first time in her life she controls a man, in stark contrast to her previous relationships with Shimka, Yankov, Cookeh, and Muralov. Like Chaucer's Wife of Bath, Anya now enjoys mastery in a relationship with a man. Although Yefim will not give in to her longing to be taken to Constantinople — he fears the Turks — he mollifies her by taking her to Odessa where she meets his two sons, Matvey and Kostya, students who are involved in revolutionary activities against the Russian government.

In many ways we might call these chapters "the education of Anya" as her involvement with the students broadens her mind and offers her glimpses of the larger world. She certainly is happy on several levels. First, "she liked being surrounded by young men." Second, she is free from the judgment of the Jewish matrons back in Tulchin. Third, though she struggles to understand the particular political motives urging on the young men, she identifies with them since "they were like her. They were rebelling" (238). When Matvey, the elder brother, begins to agitate for their group to engage in a spectacular and violent action as a protest against the government, Anya misses his point, caught up instead in trying to understand a much simpler concept: "What is this with a proletariat?" (241). Although it takes some time for her to comprehend their political rhetoric, eventually she acquires a basic understanding of the group's principles: "It was not right a man should bleed and die as a soldier for the comfort of Polish noblewomen. It was not right that some should have butter and roast meat while certain others had bread smeared with chicken grease. And where was the rightness in bowing down to the destroyer of Jews, Fonya the Tsar?" (244). After the group fails in an assassination attempt against the governor of Odessa, Yefim, his sons, and the other conspirators are arrested. Anya takes this all in stride, gathers up her most valuable clothes, pockets as much cash and silver as she can, and heads back to Tulchin, none the worse for wear and unaffected by what has happened to Yefim and the others. Once again we see only her instinctive and intuitive responses to an event that could have been the source of great internal rumination and personal reflection leading to a new understanding of herself, her environment, and her place in the world. Instead, we are given no insight into her psyche. Accordingly, this portion of the novel is the most episodic and least successful; if it was Davidman's intention to bring into her novel an effective portrait of nineteenth-century Russian revolutionaries in the tradition of Joseph Conrad's *The Secret Agent* (1907) and *Under Western Eyes* (1911), hers is a tepid effort.

Chapters twenty through twenty-three open with Anya back in Tulchin, once again living with the ever-patient, if hapless, Cookeh. Now in her mid-thirties, Anya is nonetheless still beautiful, perhaps explaining why Cookeh is so willing to let her return without recriminations. They live together quietly and peacefully. Two years later she gives birth to another stillborn daughter, and the Jewish community both feels sorry for her and assumes it is God's judgment on her scandalous behavior. Her only living child, sixteen-year-old Yankov, silently despises her, in part because he has become a zealous, devout Jew "possessed by the splendor and glory of Israel" (258). However, one day, after she tells him it is time they find him a wife, he says: "From what I have seen there is little honor in a wife. . . . A wife . . . can be the plaything of a colonel. Of grain merchants" (261). She flies into a rage, and Yankov unwittingly reawakens Anya's willfulness: "It was . . . unwise of the boy Yankov to reveal himself to his mother. For one thing, it called her back to life; again there was enmity, there was a contest, and she must put forth her strength. This was better than contending with Shifra, for Yankov was a man. Lying restless at night for the first time in years, his mother thought of ways to plague him" (262). Aware of Yankov's growing interest in young women, she hits on the perfect way to torture him: she invites many of them into her home. In addition, she teases him incessantly, one day causing him to smash a jewelry box that had been a gift from Muralov.

The strife between them is interrupted when, on her thirty-eighth birthday, Shimka, the only man she truly loved, appears back in town, two decades after having won Anya's heart. Predictably, and with no care for the consequences, she links arms with Shimka and openly walks through the streets of Tulchin to his squalid hut and "gave her body to Shimka, whom she loved, whom she had loved when they were both young and desperate, and who had never had her, twenty-two years before" (267). They leave Tulchin, live as gypsies, and for a time join a traveling band. Anya is reborn: "Her body had always been strong, but now for the first time she discovered the joy of using it. There is no joy in sleeking the clay floor, however much it demands of a woman's muscles; but to stride, endlessly, on and on into the blue singing distance: ah, that is good!" (269). After several months they fall in with a band of three thieves, and at this point Davidman introduces characters that first appeared in her 1934 short story, "Apostate," since the thieves are the sons of Nachman Goldschmidt. Also coming into the narrative is Chinya, the central character of "Apostate." It is some years since we last saw Chinya — who almost certainly served as the prototype for Anya — and she is now a "lion-hearted wanton" (273). Her three brothers want Shimka to join them; because he is unknown in the area and appears to be decent looking, they want to use him in order to gain the confidence of their prospective targets. Although Shimka is initially wary, eventually he accepts their offer to join them.

Ever the sensualist, Anya pays little attention to what Shimka has gotten himself into, entirely focused instead upon her pleasant life:

> This ease of every day, so comfortable in its passing that one cannot feel how it goes; food, sun, stove and tea, food and bed again, that is the stuff of my life. Man is my lover. He will come to me when he is tired, and I shall soothe his aching head by pressing it softly between my breasts. . . . Man is my lover and my son; I shall give him milk. . . . This is my happiness . . . not to know how the minutes pass; to do nothing in my days and yet be nourished by them; to be neither young nor old, but everlastingly alive in the arms of Shimka. The moment is now; the moment is forever. I have been with Shimka all my life. (276)

Anya is also delighted to find in Chinya the sister, friend, and confidante she had never had before. The two women are kindred spirits, cut from the same cloth: "[Chinya] was a strapping, tawny creature, who led with luxurious contentment the unquestioning life of an animal." Reference is made to the episode earlier in her life, when "in a hot moment of desire, she had tried to become a Christian in order to marry a certain moujik" (277), and how her three brothers had prevented the marriage, appearing at the last moment, disrupting the wedding, and beating her all the way home. However, we learn a new detail not found in "Apostate": "Chinya did not hold the episode against her brothers, for she had had her moujik after all, and it was easier to get rid of a man when you were not married to him" (277-78). Chinya is indeed a fit companion for Anya.

Anya's bliss, augmented by discovering she is pregnant by Shimka, is short-lived since the brothers, abetted by Shimka, torture and murder a reclusive miser. During the attack on the miser, Shimka receives what appears to be a harmless blow to the head. But after he returns to Anya that night, he dies, perhaps as a result of a blood clot in the brain. Devastated but undaunted, Anya returns to Cookeh and says, " 'I shall never go away again' " (287). Cookeh, who is patient and forgiving beyond measure, readily accepts her back; indeed, he had always believed "Anya would come back. A new and peaceful life would begin for them; their peace would be everlasting" (288). Anya's only challenge after her return is her son Yankov, who openly derides her for being pregnant with Shimka's child. Cookeh drives Yankov from their home and sets about getting him married off. Cookeh also works to rehabilitate Anya's reputation in the Jewish community, using a novel strategy — he affirms that she is mentally ill, and it works: "For a long time the Jews had been wondering whether [Anya] was a mere wanton or rather one afflicted by the Lord. The latter interpretation of her conduct was more credible to Israel; Jews went crazy with reasonable frequency" (291). David- man's satire here becomes more apparent as we observe Anya play along, even at one point offering a public confession for her past sins, especially for her seven months' desertion with Shimka, and pleading for the Jews to pray for her. Yet, it is all a sham, since she thinks to herself: " 'But, for all that, it was a good seven months.' And the smile curving the mouth of [Anya] was not precisely either humble or bewildered" (292).

The novel ends with Anya and Cookeh reconciled and seemingly happy. He accepts without resentment Shimka's son borne by Anya, as well as her decision that the three of them will emigrate to America where she believes her son will have an opportunity to enjoy a life filled with "milk and honey." During the final scene in which she names her son, Anya assumes a guise of self-righteous piety, announcing: " 'Hear Jews! . . . Four children have I lost in infancy. This son' — her voice lifted — 'this son I shall not lose. That it may bring him long life, I name my son Avrom, after our father Abraham. And he shall be like Abraham among our people!' " Outwardly placing her faith in the Jewish community and the Torah, Anya's last line in the novel ironically undercuts her religious cant: "But, for all that, it had been a good seven months" (296). While there is conflict, suffering, sorrow, and death in the story of Anya's life, she always rises above her potentially tragic circumstances, thus illustrating and affirming that she is a survivor. In every crisis she faces, she gets her way. And, as the ending of the novel reveals, she also gets the last laugh.

Anya is a modest achievement, particularly if seen in its proper light as a comic novel. There are many passages of effective description, and the dialogue is realistic and appropriate. Throughout the novel we see illustrated Anya's efforts to rise above the external circumstances thwarting her every desire. Accordingly, satire rather than irony is its controlling tone. No better example of this is that despite Anya's early claim that she will not be dominated by a man, the novel demonstrates just the opposite; in fact, in many ways her life is defined by her relationships with men. In addition, there are only two other significant women in the novel — Shifra whom Anya despises and Chinya whom she loves — but neither plays a major role in the novel; neither appears for more than ten pages or so and we never really learn much about their interior lives. It should also be noted that *Anya* is not concerned with matters related to morality. While it might not be fair to claim that Anya has no conscience, she certainly appears to be little bothered by her moral and ethical failures; she simply does not think about the impact of her sexual infidelities nor her parental irresponsibility. Characters in comic novels rarely worry very much how their actions may affect others because they are too busy finding their way in the world they inhabit — and usually it is a world that opposes them at every turn. This is not to say Anya should receive a free pass for her moral and ethical lapses. For instance, while we cannot hold her responsible for her stillborn children — although the Jewish community on more than one occasion does, seeing them as a sign of God's judgment — we can fault her for the neglect of her infant daughter who dies while she is away with Muralov. In addition, we can register genuine discomfort in her rejection of her infant son Yankov, especially since this rejection serves as the source of his later hatred for his mother. Yet in the end Anya is a survivor, not a heroine; she is a conniver, not a saint; she is a manipulator, not a pawn. Moreover, Davidman never suggests that she is offering Anya as an admirable character. The best way to think of Davidman's portrayal of Anya is through the lens of satire; she is not a character worth our pity, nor one we should emulate. However, neither should we despise her; she is a creature shaped, molded, and formed by the society she so vigorously attempts to escape.

Published only two years after *Letter to a Comrade*, *Anya* was an apprentice novel — after all, Davidman was only twenty-five when the novel appeared. While she had behind her an award-winning volume of poetry, a stint writing screen plays in Hollywood, a growing body of essays and re- views appearing in *NM,* and a handful of short stories, sustained narrative fiction was relatively new to her. And when we consider that it would be ten years before she published another novel — *Weeping Bay* in 1950 — we may safely conclude that writing fiction was not a priority for her during most of the 1940s. Moreover, as the next chapter will illustrate, several other matters conspired against her, contributing to her deferral of the writing of a second novel for almost a decade.

CHAPTER 7

Disillusionment to Faith: *Weeping Bay* (1950) and *Smoke on the Mountain* (1955)

By the mid-1940s Davidman's once zealous support of the CPUSA was waning. On the one hand, family interests began to consume her. On August 2, 1942, Davidman married William Lindsay Gresham. The birth of her two sons followed: David Lindsay Gresham was born on March 27, 1944, and Douglas Howard Gresham was born on November 10, 1945. The demands of being a wife and mother slowly superseded her former devotion to Communism. On the other hand, she began to read and study the basic principles of Communism — something she had neglected to do in her rush to join the CPUSA in order to right the wrongs of the world. Once she actually read the works of Marx and particularly Lenin, she lost faith in Communism, at least in its American expression. This gradual erosion of faith in a political system set the stage for her eventual movement to religious faith; however, rather than returning to her Jewish roots, Davidman became an "apostate," embracing instead Protestant Christianity. Throughout the months leading to her conversion she found herself increasingly under the influence of books by C. S. Lewis. While she continued to write (but not publish) poetry, her energies from 1945 to 1955 were given over primarily to letters and autobiography, the novel *Weeping Bay* (1950), and her nonfiction reflections on the Ten Commandments, *Smoke on the Mountain* (1955).

In "The Longest Way Round," Davidman recounts her reasons for her initial move toward Communism:

> My motives were a mixed lot. Youthful rebelliousness, youthful vanity, youthful contempt of the "stupid people" who seemed to be running society, all these played a part. . . .

I am not trying to excuse myself. I did something quite inexcusable; I entered the Party in a burst of emotion, without making the slightest effort to study Marxist theory. All I knew was that capitalism wasn't working very well, war was imminent — and socialism promised to change all that. (*Bone,* 90)

Yet, after her initial burst of enthusiasm for Communism, she says the "dry rot" began: "Like the fabulous snake that swallowed its own tail and vanished, the corrupt philosophy of Marxism devoured the very motives that made Marxists of us. Self-interest is the law, I was taught; the ultimate victory of the Party was my victory. . . . I was working for heaven on earth, in short, and that end justified all means. And so the means I used began to corrupt me" (*Bone,* 91). At the time this was happening, however, Davidman lacked a cognizant understanding of the political system she was so fervently embracing:

I had no idea what was happening to me, of course. Most American Communists are anything but scholars; as their leaders ruefully admit, they are unwilling to master Marxist theory, though it is true that the Party makes every effort to teach them. In consequence, Communist philosophy works on them by stealth. They do not see the deadly change from losing *self* in *class* to losing *class* in *self;* they never guess that they will end by justifying as "the future good of the working class" every imaginable indulgence of their own pride. (*Bone,* 91)

Although lacking an adequate philosophical basis for supporting Communism, Davidman pressed forward in her support of its policies, vaguely aware of an internal sense that what she was doing was based more on youthful passion than on reasoned reflection. Despite this internal inconsistency, she willingly sold her personal and literary integrity to Communism through her work for *NM.*

She traces the steps leading to her disaffection with Communism as twofold. First, she fell in love and married: "Presently I married a veteran of the Spanish [Civil] War — the writer William Lindsay Gresham. Together we made a startling discovery: marriage had ended, overnight, all our lingering interest in going to Party social gatherings! I realized then a hitherto unsuspected attraction for the young which the Communist Party shares with the church social — it is a great matchmaker" (*Bone,* 92). Now bored with Party meetings, her marriage and the subsequent birth of her son, David, dampened further her interest in Communism: "My little son was a real thing and so was my obligation to him; by comparison, my duty to that imaginary entity the working class seemed the most doubtful of abstractions. I began to notice what neglected, neurotic waifs the children of so many Communists were, and to question the genuineness of a love of mankind that didn't begin at home." And then after the birth of her second son, Douglas, she adds: "By 1946 I had two babies; I had no time for Party activity, and was glad of it; I hardly mentioned the Party except with impatience" (*Bone*, 92).

The second step in her movement away from Communism came as she finally began a proper study of Communism. "And so I did, at long last, what I should have done in the first place: I studied Marxist theory. It was a difficult and painful study. Inch by inch I retreated from my revolutionary position; fallacy after fallacy, contradiction upon contradiction, absurdity upon absurdity turned up in Lenin's *Materialism and Empirio-Criticism,* one of the basic textbooks of Marxist philosophers" (*Bone*, 95). She expressed her dismay in several letters. She wrote V. J. Jerome on January 21, 1948:

> By the way, I got an awful shock when I read [Lenin's] *Materialism and Empirio-Criticism.* What possesses us to offer *this* as a statement of our philosophy? No wonder we can never get anywhere with educated bourgeois thinkers! The book is pathetic; merely from the standpoint of construction it is rambling, repetitious to idiocy, irrelevant; its language, probably further corrupted by the translator, is of an almost hysterical violence and bad manners. Even the jokes ain't funny, they're just insults. As for its logic, it is unbelievable; the premises are wrong, the conclusions are wrong, and they're all non sequiturs anyway. He does not seem even to have understood the point under discussion, the question of whether sensory reality can be taken as the only or the whole reality; for his whole argument *depends* on the assumption of the absoluteness of sensory reality, and that is just the thing he is supposed to prove. . . .
>
> And what is still less defensible, by God, is the mediaevalism of our present approach; the endless reprinting, with superstitious reverence, of books like Lenin's *Materialism,* without the slightest attempt to develop Marxism, to use it as a science instead of a revelation from Heaven! (*Bone*, 52-53, 54)[1]

---

1. Later in this letter Davidman favorably contrasts C. S. Lewis with Lenin, noting in particular strengths she has found in *That Hideous Strength* (1945).

She further explained her disillusionment with Communism in an October 31, 1948, letter to William Rose Benét, thanking him for a recent poem, "To a Communist," which he had published in the *Saturday Review of Literature.* In the poem Benét had offered an even-handed evaluation of the failures of Communism while avoiding personal attacks:[2]

> It's quite true, I'm afraid, that Marxism is just another of man's hopeless attempts to foresee and control the future, and a crystal ball would have done nearly as well. . . .
>
> As for me, I had to have a direct and shattering experience of God, and then to plow my way through Lenin's *Materialism,* surely the world's most unreadable book . . . in order to find out that Marxism was philosophically nonsensical, logically unsound, historically arbitrary, and scientifically half false from the start and the other half overthrown by Einstein's first work. . . .
>
> [T]hank you . . . for giving us credit for our good intentions, no matter what road they paved. For almost all of us had them. I've met a few definitely paranoid communists, and a few embittered failures, but Lord knows the majority of us were just well-meaning half-educated schlemiels, and none a bigger schlemiel than I. We knew something was wrong with the world, and knew so little else that we were ready to fall for any glib way of putting it right. Some of us had to take the Sacred Writings of Marx and Engels on superstitious trust because we couldn't understand a word of them. Others, like me, were simply too lazy to read them — until we began to wonder if they really proved the case. (*Bone,* 79-80)[3]

2. "To a Communist," *Saturday Review of Literature,* October 23, 1948, p. 39.

3. In a letter to Aaron Kramer of January 26, 1948, Davidman writes of her work in *NM:* "We have, by our dishonest criticism, and I use the word advisedly, led a whole generation of young left-wingers to believe that technique does not matter, characterization and psychology and the sense of beauty and even the ability to write good clear English do not matter; as long as [one's] book is politically sound it's a book. We have destroyed not only Marxist criticism but Marxist creative writing for the time being. What has happened to the upsurge of the early thirties? Many competent writers have been forcibly driven away by the insistence of dishonest and half-literate critics on censoring their work" (*Bone,* 56-57). Also, in a later letter to Benét, Davidman gave her opinion as to the demise of *NM:* "What killed [*NM*] was simply the entire incompetence of its editors; they didn't know there was such a thing as a technique of editing, and refused to consider the possibility of learning it. They didn't know anything about their readers and did nothing to find out; their position was that reading *New Masses* was a moral duty, so it didn't have to be interesting" (February 1, 1949; *Bone,* 99-100).

Although a study of her letters written between 1945 and 1949 shows that she did not suddenly drop all Communist ways of thinking, it is clear she was moving away from it as an organizing framework for approaching life, thus linking her with many other lapsed American Communists of the time.[4]

Corresponding to her disaffection with Communism was her gradual movement toward Christianity. In "The Longest Way Round" she notes that very early in her life she was "haunted" by Christ (*Bone,* 84). And even when she claimed to be living as an atheist, she could not get away from him:

> This inner personality was deeply interested in Christ, and didn't know it. As a Jew, I had been led to feel cold chills at the mention of his name. . . . Nevertheless I had read the Bible (for its literary beauty, of course!) and I quoted Jesus unconsciously in everything I did, from writing verse to fighting my parents. My first published poem *was* called "Resurrection"[5] — a sort of private argument with Jesus, attempting to convince him (and myself) that he had never risen. I wrote it at Easter, of all possible seasons, and never guessed why. The cross[6] recurs through most of my early poems, and I seem to remember explaining that Jesus was "a valuable literary convention." (*Bone,* 86)

As she reflected back on her joining the CPUSA, she linked it to the faith she was being drawn to: "I think I was moved [toward Communism] by the same unseen power that had directed my reading and my dreaming — I became a Communist because, later on, I was going to become a Christian" (*Bone,* 90).

After she saw the holes in Communism, what stimulated her toward Christian faith were literary sources, particularly Lewis's *The Pilgrim's Regress, The Screwtape Letters,* and *The Great Divorce:*

4. For more on this, see Daniel Aaron, *Writers on the Left* (New York: Harcourt, 1961); Granville Hicks, *Granville Hicks in the* New Masses (Port Washington, NY: Kennikat Press, 1974); Irving Howe and Lewis Coser, *The American Communist Party: A Critical History* (New York: Praeger, 1957); David Madden, ed., *Proletarian Writers of the Thirties* (Carbondale, IL: Southern Illinois University Press, 1968); James E. Murphy, *The Proletarian Moment: The Controversy over Leftism in Literature* (Chicago: University of Illinois Press, 1991); Walter Rideout, *The Radical Novel in the United States, 1900-1954* (Cambridge: Harvard University Press, 1956); and Alan M. Wald, *Exiles from a Future Time: The Forging of the Mid-Twentieth-Century Literary Left* (Chapel Hill: University of North Carolina Press, 2002).

5. Joy Davidman, "Resurrection," *Poetry* 47 (January 1936): 193-94; *Naked Tree,* 15-16. See my earlier discussion of this poem in Chapter 1.

6. Another poem in which Davidman focuses upon the cross is "Againrising" from *Letter to a Comrade,* 81-82; *Naked Tree,* 148-49. See my discussion of this poem in Chapter 2.

These books stirred an unused part of my brain to momentary sluggish life. Of course, I thought, atheism was *true;* but I hadn't given quite enough attention to developing the proof of it. Someday, when the children were older, I'd work it out. Then I forgot the whole matter. That was all, on the surface. And yet, that was a beginning. Francis Thompson symbolized God as the "Hound of Heaven," pursuing on relentless feet.[7] With me, God was more like a cat. He had been stalking me for a very long time, waiting for his moment; he crept nearer so silently that I never knew he was there. Then, all at once, he sprang. (*Bone,* 93)

Her description of her conversion follows; her husband had called, saying that he was having a nervous breakdown, and she was full of fear for his safety:

For the first time in my life I felt helpless; for the first time my pride was forced to admit that I was not, after all, "the master of my fate" and "the captain of my soul."[8] All my defenses — the walls of arrogance and cock-sureness and self-love behind which I had hid from God — went down momentarily. And God came in.

How can one describe the direct perception of God? It is infinite, unique; there are no words, there are no comparisons. Can one scoop up the sea in a teacup? Those who have known God will understand me; the others, I find, can neither listen nor understand. There was a Person with me in the room, directly present to my consciousness — a Person so real that all my previous life was by comparison mere shadow play. And I myself was more alive than I had ever been; it was like waking from sleep. So intense a life cannot be endured for long by flesh and blood; we must ordinarily take our life watered down, diluted as it were, by time and space and matter. My perception of God lasted perhaps half a minute. . . .

When it was over I found myself on my knees, praying. I think I must have been the world's most astonished atheist. (*Bone,* 94)[9]

7. I discuss Davidman and Thompson's *The Hound of Heaven* (1893) in more detail in Chapter 9.

8. These phrases refer to the concluding lines of William E. Henley's "Invictus" (1888): "I am the master of my fate; / I am the captain of my soul." I discuss Davidman's use of these lines from "Invictus" in more detail in Chapter 9.

9. Perceptive readers will note how Davidman's characterization of herself as "the world's most astonished atheist" anticipates the way Lewis describes his own experience of conversion in *Surprised by Joy.* I discuss this and other instances of Davidman's literary influences upon Lewis in Chapter 9.

She goes on to say that, after this experience, "I snatched at books I had despised before; reread *The Hound of Heaven,* which I had ridiculed as a piece of phony rhetoric — and, understanding it suddenly, burst into tears. (Also a new thing; I had seldom previously cried except with rage.) I went back to C. S. Lewis and learned from him, slowly, how I had gone wrong. Without his works, I wonder if I and many others might not still be infants 'crying in the night' " (*Bone,* 95).

Her conversion took her back to the figure of Christ that had always "haunted" her:

> I had the usual delusion that "all religions mean the same thing." Fortunately I had learned my lesson, and this time I looked before I leaped; I *studied* religions, and found them anything but the same thing. Some of them had wisdom up to a point, some of them had good ethical intentions, some of them had flashes of spiritual insight; but only one of them had complete understanding of the grace and repentance and charity that had come to me from God. And the Redeemer who had made himself known, whose personality I would have recognized among ten thousand — well, when I read the New Testament, I recognized him. He was Jesus. (*Bone,* 96)

Because she believed in the divinity of Christ, she says it was only reasonable that she would accept orthodox Christian theology: "So what I was, it appeared, was a Protestant Christian, of the orthodox Trinitarian kind" (*Bone,* 96). Davidman's movement from disillusionment with Communism to Christian faith led her to conclude her autobiographical essay with a powerful affirmation: "I want to go deeper into the mystical knowledge of God, and I want that knowledge to govern my daily life. I had a good deal of pride and anger to overcome, and at times my progress is heartbreakingly slow — yet I think that I am going somewhere, by God's grace, according to plan. My present tasks are to look after my children and my husband and my garden and my house — and, perhaps, to serve God in books and letters as best I can. And my reward is a happiness such as I never dreamed possible. 'In His will is our peace' " (*Bone,* 97).[10]

---

10. The allusion is to Dante: "For in His will is our peace. It is the sea / To which all things existing flow, both those / His will creates and those that nature makes" (*Paradiso,* Canto III, 85-87).

Weeping Bay

Written in 1948, "The Longest Way Round" suggests that Davidman's newly realized Christian faith impacted the writing of her second novel, *Weeping Bay* (1950); at the same time, the novel reveals that she had not completely abandoned Communist ideals, although now they were expressed in less strident terms.[11] Indeed, both Christianity and socialism — especially the need for unionism — emerge as underlying influences throughout *Weeping Bay*. Several letters written during this time show how earnestly she was working on the novel. On February 7, 1948, she wrote Aaron Kramer: "My own work is progressing like mad; I'm working on the Canadian novel, for which I have a tentative contract, and doing occasional short stories; also laying the groundwork for a study of Marxist philosophy" (*Bone,* 73).[12] On January 4, 1949, she explained to William Rose Benét: "I'm all but finished with a novel for Macmillan (which I started eight years ago, B.C. — Before Children — at the [MacDowell] Colony)."[13] Six months later, on June 21,

---

11. In a letter of August 16, 1951, she writes:

Pretty hard for me to define exactly *what* I am, as you can see; I don't fall into any of the current categories. Politically, I have come to suspect that forms and organizations of government and class don't really matter a damn, that they are not causes but products, that any society will create them out of its own traditions and needs as a tree grows leaves, and that therefore any attempt to invent and impose a new system is as pathetically futile as the attempts to impose new languages like Esperanto. As a believer in original sin, though, I could hardly find anarchism either possible or desirable.

Am I radical or conservative? I think of all the squabbles about reorganizing the economic system as mere superficial tinkering; as far as I can see, there is no possible way of making an overpopulated industrial system work *at all.* "Too many people, not enough land!" to quote my own book. (*Bone,* 121)

The reference to her own book is drawn from the final chapter of *Weeping Bay* (New York: Macmillan, 1950). In answer to the question of why there is such hunger in Gaspé, the fisherman Hervé Kirouac says: "Too many people. Not enough land" (254).

12. Although she never published her study of Marxist philosophy, many of her letters from this time period reflect the essence of her thoughts; see *Bone,* 72-82 and 99-128. Regarding how her new faith was influencing her, she told William Rose Benét on February 1, 1949: "Since my conversion — I am now, believe it or not, a deaconess of the Presbyterian Church, and it feels odd to say the least. Oy! — since becoming a Christian, I am reveling in my new-found ability to admit my ignorance. In my old world, you just *had* to have an opinion on every conceivable subject that came up; an open mind was a moral offense. You can't imagine what a luxury it is to have no opinions where I have no evidence!" (*Bone,* 100).

13. Unpublished letter, DP Box 1, Series 1, Folder 2.

1949, she tells Chad Walsh:[14] "Macmillan has a novel of mine *Weeping Bay* — it's about the Gaspé peninsula — scheduled [for publication] for next spring" (*Bone*, 105).[15]

In brief, *Weeping Bay* tells the story of the hard lives of its townspeople. For most it is a life of unrelenting anguish, misery, poverty, and exploitation — the title of the novel serving as a not-so-subtle gloss on the ethos of the place. Caught between the forces of the Catholic Church and capitalism, characters are portrayed as grist for the mill; one after another finds himself or herself being beaten down, manipulated, or humiliated. Although it would be going too far to call the novel an example of proletarian literature, it surely marks its author as sharing to some degree the sensibility of those "who have clearly indicated their sympathy to the revolutionary cause."[16] Yet, Davidman prefaces the novel with an epigraph from John 21:17: "He saith unto him the third time, Simon, son of Jonas, lovest thou me? Peter was grieved because he said unto him the third time, Lovest thou me? And he said unto him, Lord, thou knowest all things; thou knowest that I love thee. Jesus saith unto him, Feed my sheep." Playing off Jesus' command to Peter to feed his sheep throughout *Weeping Bay*, Davidman waits until the final chapter to drive home her pointed rhetoric.

Among the large cast of characters (in an oddity for a novel, at the beginning Davidman lists the "persons of the book," much in the manner of a playwright), no one could be construed as the central voice of the novel; indeed,

14. Chad Walsh (1914-1991) was a longtime professor of English at Beloit College.

15. For contemporary reviews of *Weeping Bay*, see R. P. Breaden, Review of Joy Davidman's *Weeping Bay*, *Library Journal* 75 (February 1, 1950): 171; August Derleth, Review of Joy Davidman's *Weeping Bay*, *Sunday Chicago Tribune*, March 12, 1950, p. 4; Granville Hicks, Review of Joy Davidman's *Weeping Bay*, *New York Times*, March 5, 1950, p. 30; James Hilton, Review of Joy Davidman's *Weeping Bay*, *New York Herald Tribune Book Review*, March 12, 1950, p. 6; J. H. Jackson, Review of Joy Davidman's *Weeping Bay*, *San Francisco Chronicle*, March 7, 1950, p. 18; Review of Joy Davidman's *Weeping Bay*, *Kirkus* 18 (January 1, 1950): 8; Review of Joy Davidman's *Weeping Bay*, *New Yorker* 26 (March 11, 1950): 103; Review of Joy Davidman's *Weeping Bay*, *United States Quarterly Booklist* 6 (June 1950): 156; Mary Sandrock, Review of Joy Davidman's *Weeping Bay*, *Catholic World* 171 (June 1950): 171; Chad Walsh, "First Things First: How Does One Come to Know God?" *Presbyterian Life* 3 (May 27, 1950): 36-38; A. F. Wolfe, Review of Joy Davidman's *Weeping Bay*, *Saturday Review of Literature* 33 (March 18, 1950): 16.

16. Aaron, *Writers on the Left*, 283. In addition, because Davidman is attacking both Catholicism and capitalism, she is close to other "proletarian writers . . . [who] are under a solemn obligation to fight tooth and nail against philistinism in all its nauseating forms . . . [and] to rise above parochialism both of time and place" (Arvin Newton, "A Letter on Proletarian Literature," *Partisan Review*, February 1936, p. 14).

the lack of a main character seriously undercuts the potential power of the story. Often we are given short vignettes in a rapid fire of characters; while this technique provides a broad overview of the townspeople, we never have a fully developed, psychologically nuanced, and experientially convincing point of view. This means the novel lacks a unifying device, undercutting what might have become a compelling story of human misery and social disharmony. Without a central character, it is difficult to empathize with the plight of the townspeople, despite their lives of quiet despair.

Two characters might have served as the central voice of the novel. The first, M. l'Abbe François-Xavier Desrosiers, has just returned to the home of his youth in order to organize a Catholic trade union in the local iron factory. As a young priest, Desrosiers is keen to improve the working and living conditions of the factory workers, especially as he remembers how hard it was growing up in Weeping Bay. However, he has an inflated sense of his own abilities and only a superficial understanding of human nature. For instance, his first act is to set up his office in a room in the town's main hotel: "He nailed his sign in place with short, careful taps. In a small way, he was now a symbol of what he stood for, the Carpenter who worked with His hands. What was more, by this physical act did he not establish an obvious brotherhood between himself and the workers of Weeping Bay?"[17] Although he is aware of how he is prone to romanticize himself, this does not stop him from succumbing to heroic dreams. After he has an initial meeting with the factory owner, M. Evangéliste Boisvert — who not surprisingly sees the priest as a threat — Desrosiers "began to make plans. What a different town Weeping Bay would be when he got through with it! At the back of his mind there had always lurked the vision of a town . . . [with] white streets, clean sunshine, and singing people. A dim procession of singing people, flower-garlanded, forever made its way to some place of worship" (26).

However, the young priest fails to see that by setting up his office in the hotel, he has cut himself off from the very workers he means to help. He naively believes that because he nails a sign to a door signifying a union office, the workers will flock to him. In fact, no one comes to see him. He tries going to the factory entrance and handing out leaflets, but the only worker who takes a leaflet cannot read. After several weeks of this, he is nearing despair when he is finally approached by Hervé Kirouac, the one factory worker brave enough to talk about organizing a union. Kirouac tells Desrosiers he has helped organize unions in the past; his brash confidence,

---

17. *Weeping Bay,* 22; subsequent references in the text.

his disdain for the local authorities (including both the church and the local police force), and his penchant for cursing offend the priest: "But this is not a gang of water-front radicals — this is the Catholic Syndicate. Heavens, man, we have the blessing of the Pope!" (40). Still, Kirouac makes Desrosiers see that by having his office in the hotel he has cut himself off from the men he wants to help. Eventually, the priest goes to live in the home of the poorest family in the town, the Carons.

While living with the eight members of the family in their two-room house, Desrosiers receives an education about the human condition not available to him back in the hotel. He learns that abortions — over which he is morally outraged and spiritually shocked — are the common resort of townswomen since as Catholics they are denied access to contraceptives. He learns that the local parish priest, M. le Curé Philémon Chouinard, is the best businessman Weeping Bay has ever had for a priest — his main preoccupation is overseeing a weekly Grand Bingo event sponsored by the church — and he implicitly conspires with Boisvert against Desrosiers' efforts to organize the union. He learns that the local police chief, M. Clodomir Chouinard, brother of the parish priest, is a cruel womanizer who relentlessly pursues young women, in some cases raping and beating them, all the while hiding behind his position and wielding his power ruthlessly. He witnesses the anguish and crushing poverty of Amable and Elaine Caron, the former crippled by a factory accident and now unable to work and the latter caught up in having child after child, including three who are deaf and dumb. And at the end of the novel he learns that his romantic dreams about the difference he would make in Weeping Bay were just that — dreams, and empty ones at that. Yet readers never identify with Desrosiers, and while we are interested in the things he learns, Davidman rarely gives an inside view of his character. Like the other characters in the novel, the young priest is a pawn she moves about the board — useful in achieving her various polemic purposes, but not one we identify with or care about.

The second character who might have served as the controlling voice of *Weeping Bay* is Hervé Kirouac, the hardened former fisherman who now works as a die-stamper in the factory. In addition to his disdain for clerical and civil authorities, Kirouac is sexually frustrated by his wife's refusal to use contraceptives. His wife, Marie, initially holds dogmatically to the Catholic Church's position against the use of contraceptives; she views sex primarily as a means of producing more children. Her faith is unassailable: "She was so sure of herself inside, so sure of herself and of the Church, that no argument could really capture her attention. You could not raise even enough doubt in her mind to make her stop sewing" (17). Kirouac, on the other hand, who is a good father to his five children, despairs at having more. They have fierce arguments — at one point he says to her, "Your priest with the pretty voice . . . you love him better than me" (17) — over the use of contraceptives, with Marie believing their use involves mortal sin leading to damnation and with Hervé believing more children would damn their lives with more debt and financial ruin. They reach an impasse: Marie is eager to have sex with Hervé, but he will not for fear of another child: "So it is this . . . I won't sleep with you without the rubber, and you won't sleep with me with" (18). Tensions escalate between them; they are so estranged that later Kirouac visits a carnival prostitute.

Frustrated sexually, Kirouac channels his energies into helping Desrosiers organize the union. Because he is trusted by the other factory workers, Kirouac convinces many to attend meetings about setting up a union. After several meetings, more than a dozen men, including Kirouac, form a union. But just as they plan to confront Boisvert, he calls them together and summarily fires them, all under the watchful and protective eye of the police chief, Chouinard. Instinctively, Kirouac knows they have been betrayed. When he tracks down the "rat," Odilon Ouellet, Kirouac attacks him on the factory floor, and both are severely injured when they roll into a die-stamping machine: Odilon's face is almost crushed and Kirouac loses two fingers. Kirouac is arrested while Odilon — who is shunned by family and friends — commits suicide a few days later. Hervé Kirouac's arrest becomes the catalyst for mending his marriage. When Marie hears what has happened, she rushes to the jail and asks Desrosiers to help her get her husband freed. When he hesitates, she says: " 'Priests . . . you're all in it together.' The words were quiet; the tone was the worst blow Desrosiers had ever had. He stared for a moment at the decent, shabby, faded woman who had so stricken him . . . 'You are all liars together' " (216). Eventually Hervé and Marie are permitted to see each other; as they reconcile and love flows between them, it is clear there will be no further arguments about contraceptives. Marie has lost respect for the rigid rules of the Church; her disillusionment with its priests and their lack of compassion for the people they are supposed to minister to leads her to place her love for her husband above the strictures of the priests. While Hervé's character is the strongest in the novel, he is rarely on stage. He plays an important role in Desrosiers' effort to set up a union and his relationship with Marie is compelling, but his is not the central or unifying voice throughout the novel.

Before offering an overall assessment of *Weeping Bay,* I return to the

John 21:17 epigraph. Christ's injunction to Peter, "feed my sheep," is an ironic echo throughout the novel since Davidman portrays the Catholic clergy at best as misguided, such as we see in Desrosiers, or at worst as perfidious, such as we see in M. le Curé Philémon Chouinard. The Church, Davidman would have us believe, is hardly interested in feeding its sheep; instead, it is primarily interested in feeding itself. Even Desrosiers, who comes to Weeping Bay intent on organizing a union in order to help the workers get better wages, better working conditions, and a better life, ends up selling out — although to be fair he leaves the town after negotiating Kirouac's release from prison on the curé's condition that he stop trying to organize the union. In the tense scene where the deal is cut, Desrosiers ironically says to Chouinard: "All the same . . . the sheep should be fed" (238). Desrosiers' words fall on deaf ears as the Church's intransigence, duplicity, and indifference trump the love Christ would have it demonstrate.

The source of Davidman's antipathy for Catholicism is hard to trace, although she may have shared with other Jews the belief that the Catholic Church was at least partially complicit in the persecution of the Jews before and during World War II.[18] Other hints of her misgivings about Catholicism can be found in "The Longest Way Round" and in several of her letters. At the end of "The Longest Way Round," while explaining why she joined the local Presbyterian church, she says: "My beliefs took shape; I accepted the sacraments as meaningful but not magical; I recognized the duty of going to church, while I rejected the claim of any church to infallibility and an absolute monopoly on divine authority" (*Bone*, 96). Later experiences with the publication of *Weeping Bay* also affected her. In her May 29, 1951, letter to Kenneth Porter she wrote: "I hope you like *Weeping Bay* — if you can find a copy. The book was quietly suppressed at Macmillan's home office by an ardently Catholic sales manager, for reasons you'll understand when you

18. For more on this, see Doris L. Bergen, "Catholics, Protestants, and Christian Anti-semitism in Nazi Germany," *Central European History* 27, no. 3 (1994): 329-48; David Black-bourn, "Roman Catholics, the Centre Party and Anti-Semitism in Imperial Germany," in *Nationalist and Racialist Movements in Britain and Germany before 1914*, ed. Paul Kennedy and Anthony Nicholls (London: Palgrave Macmillan, 1981); Donald J. Dietrich, *Catholic Citizens in the Third Reich: Psycho-Social Principles and Moral Reasoning* (New Brunswick, NJ: Transaction Publishers, 1988); Ernst Christian Helmreich, *The German Churches under Hitler: Background, Struggle, and Epilogue* (Detroit: Wayne State University Press, 1979); Franklin H. Littell, "Christian Anti-Semitism and the Holocaust," in *Perspectives on the Holocaust*, ed. Randolph L. Braham (Boston: Kluwer-Nijhoff, 1983); and Franklin H. Littell, *The Crucifixion of the Jews: The Failure of Christians to Understand the Jewish Experience* (New York: Harper & Row, 1975).

read it. They've since fired the guy and sent me an implied apology, but too late to do me any good. Oh, well, here's a chance for me to practice Christian forgiveness, if I can stop gnashing my teeth long enough" (*Bone,* 119). On August 16, 1951, she told Porter: "Since you've read *Weeping Bay,* you are not likely to think me pro-catholic; but I fear Catholics are quite right in pointing out that Calvin was the ancestor of capital!" (*Bone,* 121).

The irony of the Catholic Church's indifference to the plight of the poor is completed in the final chapter when Kirouac, now working as a fisherman, encounters the whiskey-drinking Protestant lay preacher[19] whom he first met at the carnival and who had at that time quietly slipped into his pocket "L'Evangile de St. Mathieu." Kirouac, thoroughly jaundiced by his encounters with the Catholic Church, finds hope in the words of the lay preacher, particularly in the words he shares from the old hymn "Good Shepherd, Feed My Sheep":

If you want . . . to go to Heaven,
Over on the yonder shore,
Keep out the way of the bloodstained banners,
Oh, good shepherd, feed my sheep.

One for Paul and one for Silas,
One for to make my heart rejoice.
Cain't you hear them lambs a-crying?
Oh, good shepherd, feed my sheep. (250)[20]

---

19. Davidman's use of the carnival is directly related to the influence of her husband, Bill Gresham, who had grown up around carnivals; moreover, his novel *Nightmare Alley* (New York: Rinehart, 1946) is set in a carnival, and he later published the nonfiction book *Monster Midway: An Uninhibited Look at the Glittering World of the Carny* (New York: Rinehart, 1953). About the lay preacher, she wrote Porter on August 16, 1951: "The whiskey-drinking preacher of *Weeping Bay* is my Southern husband's contribution — he's known plenty of them" (*Bone,* 123).

20. Here is the text of the hymn:

If you want to get to heaven,
Over on the yonder shore,
Keep out of the way of the blood-stained bandits [or banners],
Oh, good shepherd,
Feed my sheep.
One for Paul and one for Silas,
One for to make my heart rejoice,
Can't you hear my lambs a-crying?
Oh good shepherd, feed my sheep.

Using the hymn as a bridge, the preacher gently begins to invite Kirouac to take into his heart and mind the gospel message, suggesting that direct interaction with the Bible — without benefit of a priest's interpretations — is the best way to encounter God: "Maybe Jesus don't need no priest for His telephone wire. Maybe the blessed Carpenter has got Him a way of boring a hole right straight into a man's heart" (250). Kirouac then thinks out loud: "You mean it is not all a lie, invented to feed them on roast chicken? You mean that this thing was true once? That there was once a man who was poor and knew the children of the poor? That it was true He came from God to the poor?" (251). The preacher then urges Kirouac to read chapters five through seven from the Gospel of Matthew — Jesus' Sermon on the Mount: "Go on, read it. I tell you, brother, we're put into this world for some purpose, ain't up to us to try and figure it out. Leave that to God. But having kids hungry ain't in it. That ain't any of it" (251). Then he alludes to 1 Corinthians 13:13: "There's three things above all else a man's got to have: faith, hope, and love. And the greatest of these is love" (252).

The preacher, after pledging to help Kirouac start organizing a new union, ends his sermonette by singing from the hymn one more time:

> Stay out the way of the gunshot devils,
> Oh, good shepherd, feed my sheep.

If you want to get to heaven,
Over on the yonder shore,
Keep out of the way of the long-tongued liar,
Oh good shepherd,
Feed my sheep.
One for Paul and one for Silas,
One for to make my heart rejoice,
Can't you hear my lambs a-crying?
Oh good shepherd, feed my sheep.

If you want to get to heaven,
Over on the yonder shore,
Keep out of the way of the gun shot devils,
Oh good shepherd,
Feed my sheep.
One for Paul and one for Silas,
One for to make my heart rejoice,
Can't you hear my lambs a-crying?
Oh good shepherd, feed my sheep.

One for Paul and one for Silas,
One for to make my heart rejoice,
Cain't you hear them lambs a-crying?
Oh, good shepherd, feed my sheep. (256)

The effect on Kirouac is electric: " 'So that — *it was for that they nailed Him to the cross!'* He turned and shouted in a great voice, 'Séverin, Séverin! Open up a bottle for me and my friend. I celebrate a Mass right here. No priest! I drink it myself, by God, by God in Heaven!' " (256). The preacher, now a fisherman like Kirouac and the others, is more a fisher of men than all the combined members of the Catholic clergy in Weeping Bay. Unlike the abbé and curé — whose religion has an outward, external, material focus that lacks genuine spiritual depth and human compassion — the whiskey-drinking preacher best feeds the sheep.[21]

Weeping Bay is not as effective a novel as is *Anya*. While it is technically well-written — including crisp, tight prose, lively pacing of the narrative and plot, and finely crafted sentences — it fails to draw readers into the plight of the people of Weeping Bay. As we witness character after character encounter brutal and unforgiving realities, our inability to empathize with them leaves us curiously untouched. Deaths by horse cart accident, self-induced abortion, and drowning ought to pull us closer to the characters; instead, we remain emotionally unconnected. Perhaps this is because we sense the polemic behind the story — as Davidman would have it, the Catholic Church is a rigid theocracy, a self-interested oligarchy, and a materialistic monolith.[22] As she had done earlier in her political poems in support of the CPUSA, here in *Weeping Bay* she sacrifices art for propaganda. While she does show, especially in some very effective descriptions of the Gaspé landscape, more often than not we feel she is trying to tell. In doing so, Davidman undercuts the verisimilitude she means to

21. Another biblical passage that Davidman echoes throughout the last chapter of the novel is John 10, particularly verses 11-15: "I am the good shepherd: the good shepherd lays down his life for the sheep. The hired hand, who is not the shepherd and does not own the sheep, sees the wolf coming and leaves the sheep and runs away — and the wolf snatches them and scatters them. The hired hand runs away because the hired hand does not care for the sheep. I am the good shepherd. I know my own and my own know me, just as the Father knows me and I know the Father. And I lay down my life for the sheep."

22. It would disingenuous and unfair to argue that her hatred for Fascism during her CPUSA days was replaced by similar feelings toward the Catholic Church after her conversion; at the same time, it is important to observe at least her pointed indignation toward a church that she believed shackled rather than liberated its adherents.

create in the narrative and leaves readers unmoved. Perhaps, too, we sense she is more driven to write into the novel aspects of her newly realized Christian faith than she is guided by the artistic principles of a novelist.

At about the time *Weeping Bay* was published, Davidman began writing C. S. Lewis. Davidman's entrée to Lewis was through the American literary critic Chad Walsh, who had published the first critical study of Lewis in 1949, *C. S. Lewis: Apostle to the Skeptics.*[23] Davidman sought out Walsh, and a friendship resulted. In one of her first letters to Walsh, on June 21, 1949, she indicates their mutual affinity for Lewis:

> We more than share your feeling for [C. S.] Lewis; with us it was not the last step but the first that came from reading his books, for we were raised atheists and took the truth of atheism for granted, and like most Marxists were so busy acting that we never stopped to think. If I hadn't picked up *The Great Divorce* one day — brr, I suppose I'd still be running madly around with leaflets, showing as much intelligent purpose as a headless chicken. But I wouldn't have picked up *The Great Divorce* if I hadn't loved fantasy, and I wouldn't have loved fantasy if I hadn't, as a twelve-year-old moping in the school library, found *Phantastes.*[24] It had exactly the effect on me that Lewis describes only more blurred around the edges and with less positive consequence. . . . My taste for fantasy was something I was once ashamed of; got rebuked sternly by Marxist authorities for bringing "Astounding Stories" into the *New Masses* office. . . .
>
> What I am working round to is, yes we would dearly love to talk about Lewis' work, particularly (of course) about what it is doing to our *own* novels. (*Bone*, 104-5)

With Walsh's encouragement, she eventually writes Lewis and captures his attention. Warren Lewis indicates this in his diary, *Brothers and Friends:* "Until 10th January 1950 neither of us had ever heard of her; then she appeared in the mail as just another American fan, Mrs. W. L. Gresham from the neighbourhood of New York. With however the difference that she stood out from the ruck by her amusing and well-written letters, and soon J and she had become 'pen-friends.'"[25]

23. Walsh, *C. S. Lewis: Apostle to the Skeptics* (New York: Macmillan, 1949).

24. George MacDonald, *Phantastes: A Faerie Romance for Men and Women* (London: Arthur C. Fifield, 1905).

25. *Brothers and Friends: The Diaries of Major Warren Hamilton Lewis,* ed. Clyde S. Kilby and Marjorie Lamp Mead (San Francisco: Harper & Row, 1982), 244. Davidman's first

On January 27, 1950, she writes to Walsh and intimates something of what she had written to Lewis on January 10 as well as Lewis's response; at least part of their discussions had concerned the "believability" of Gospel stories related to Jesus:

It's partly one's knowledge of psychology — for instance, if the Apostles had been romancing they would never have told so many stories which made them look silly. Nor would their immediate followers. They would have said, "*We* knew Him when, *we* were the extra-special faithful who understood Him perfectly, *we* were the ones appointed to govern the rest of you!" If they had lied, they would have been lying for their own advantage, surely? Instead of which — continual rebukes, and "He that would be first among you, let him be last!"

And, similarly — and in addition to Lewis' reasoning on this point — anyone who thinks Jesus could have been a paranoid with delusions of grandeur has only to read up on *real* paranoids, in the asylum and out, and see what they sound like.[26] History is full of self-appointed Messiahs, and they all sound the same, mad with pride. The humor and commonsense of Jesus never came from a disturbed mind.

But mostly, I think, what convinced us was our sense of the difference between fiction and life. Fiction is always congruous, life usually incongruous. In fiction there is a unity of effect, of style; the people all say exactly what they should say to be in character and in the mood. And all the effects are heightened, arranged. If there *is* an incongruous reaction, that too is obviously arranged — either for humor or for some plot reason; and it looks as blatant as a movie double-take. . . .

Well, the Gospels are full of these little incongruities — like the cut-

---

letter to Lewis has not survived. However, her letter to Walsh soon after suggests something of the content of her letter to Lewis. For more, see below.

26. Lewis had given a series of radio broadcasts for the BBC during World War II that were later published in America as *The Case for Christianity* (New York: Macmillan, 1943). The passage Davidman has in mind here is the following:

I'm trying here to prevent anyone saying the really silly thing that people often say about Him [Christ]: "I'm ready to accept Jesus as a great moral teacher, but I don't accept His claim to be God." That's the one thing we mustn't say. A man who was merely man and said the sort of things Jesus said wouldn't be a great moral teacher. He'd either be a lunatic — on a level with the man who says he's a poached egg — or else he'd be the Devil of Hell. You must make your choice. Either this man was, and is, the Son of God: or else a madman or something worse. (45)

off ear of the high priest's servant.[27] That's a thing that happened; no one could have invented it. . . .

But mostly it's just that I know the sort of thing that people make up, and this ain't it. I suppose that's what Lewis feels too, when he says we couldn't have invented it, and also what Tertullian meant when he said *Credo quia impossibile.* (*Bone,* 111-14)[28]

A lively correspondence developed between Davidman and Lewis, one enjoyed as much by Warren Lewis as by his brother.[29]

In the summer of 1952 Davidman sailed to England and invited Lewis to lunch with her in Oxford.[30] In fact, Lewis and George Sayer met Davidman and her friend Phyllis Haring for lunch at the Eastgate Hotel on September 24, 1952.[31] According to Sayer, Lewis "was delighted by her bluntness and her anti-American views."[32] Lewis, who obviously enjoyed being with Joy, reciprocated and invited her to luncheon at his rooms in Magdalen College, and then followed this up with the very unusual invitation that she spend Christmas at his home, the Kilns. On December 9, 1952, Lewis told his friend Belle Allen: "We have just had a 'pen friend' of long standing, from New York . . . stopping with us; she . . . is delightful — a rolling stone, authoress, journalist, housewife and mother, and has been 'doing' England. . . . She comes back next week before sailing for America, and we look forward to hearing

---

27. John 18:10.

28. Tertullian's statement is Latin for "I believe it because it is impossible."

29. In *Brothers and Friends* Warren wrote:

In the winter of 1952 she visited Oxford. I was some little time in making up my mind about her; she proved to be a Jewess, or rather a Christian convert of Jewish race, medium height, good figure, horn rimmed specs., quite extraordinarily uninhibited. Our first meeting was at a lunch in Magdalen [College], where she turned to me in the presence of three or four men, and asked in the most natural tone in the world, 'Is there anywhere in this monastic establishment where a lady can relieve herself?' But her visit was a great success and a rapid friendship developed; she liked walking, and she liked beer, and we had many merry days together; and when she left for home in January 1953, it was with common regrets, and a sincere hope that we would meet again. (244-45)

30. In the next chapter, using Davidman's August to December 1952 unpublished letters, I explore in more detail her time in England and her meetings with Lewis.

31. Phyllis Haring was a writer who lived in London; Davidman had first met her through correspondence. She is referred to as Phyllis Williams by George Sayer and Lyle Dorsett, but Douglas Gresham recalls her name as Haring.

32. See George Sayer, *Jack: C. S. Lewis and His Times* (San Francisco: Harper & Row, 1988), 214-15.

her experiences."[33] Lewis was both delighted over and overwhelmed by Joy's Christmas visit. On December 19, 1952, he wrote his godson, Laurence Harwood: "I am completely 'circumvented' by a guest, asked for one week but staying for three, who talks from morning till night. I hope you'll all have a nicer Christmas than I. I can't write (write? I can hardly think or breathe. I can't believe it's all real)."[34] Lyle Dorsett observes that "it is likely that Joy was already falling in love with C. S. Lewis [even before her meeting him. Her cousin, Renée] believed that [Joy] had fallen in love with Lewis's mind during their extended period of correspondence, and since Joy's marriage was a shambles, it does not require an overly active imagination to believe this. Lewis perhaps was growing infatuated with Joy; at least he delighted in her company, or he never would have continued the round of luncheons."[35]

Smoke on the Mountain

In the next chapter I will explore in greater detail the literary evidence we have for how Davidman's romantic feelings for Lewis may have developed during this time. I have included here the information about how Davidman and Lewis began their relationship as a lead-in to a discussion of her last published book, *Smoke on the Mountain*, particularly since Lewis eventually wrote the foreword for the English edition of the book.[36] Davidman's letters do not reveal the impetus for her decision to write on the Decalogue. Nor can we say with certainty when she first began work on *Smoke*, although she had completed a draft of it by late 1952; in her January 25, 1953, letter to Walsh she writes about her stay at the Kilns during December 1952: "[Jack had] time to go over my own Decalogue book with me (about 50,000 words of it) and tell me how to fix it; he liked it quite well, thank heaven" (*Bone,* 138).

Lewis's suggestions may have been incorporated when two of the chap-

---

33. C. S. Lewis, *Collected Letters* (hereafter *CL*), vol. 3: *Narnia, Cambridge, and Joy, 1950-1963*, ed. Walter Hooper (London: HarperCollins, 2006), 260.

34. *CL*, 3, p. 268. In the next chapter, see my excerpts from her December 19, 1952, unpublished letter to her husband Bill about this visit.

35. Dorsett, *And God Came In: The Extraordinary Story of Joy Davidman* (New York: Macmillan, 1983), 86. For more on this, see Abigail Santamaria, *Joy: Poet, Seeker, and the Woman Who Captivated C. S. Lewis* (New York: Houghton Mifflin Harcourt, 2015), chs. 9 and 10.

36. *Smoke on the Mountain: An Interpretation of the Ten Commandments* (Philadelphia: Westminster, 1953; London: Hodder & Stoughton, 1955); hereafter *Smoke*.

ters first appeared in the journal *Presbyterian Life:* "Into the Full Light" appeared on April 4, 1953, and "God Comes First" appeared on May 2, 1953.[37] Walsh was intrigued by the idea of turning these two chapters into part of what became *Smoke,* writing to Davidman on March 6, 1953: "Are you planning to publish the Decalogue in book form? I imagine Macmillan would snap it up for publication after it appears in *Presbyterian Life*" (*Bone,* 143). Lewis's advice and Walsh's encouragement about her plans for a book on the Ten Commandments, as well as her growing frustration with her husband Bill, are suggested in her March 10, 1953, letter to her cousin Renée: "And the more I see of [Bill] the more impatient I become to get away; so I'll do something as soon as this book [*Smoke on the Mountain*] is out of the way. . . . I've got my last two revisions off to *Presbyterian Life,* thank God. But *now* I'm getting the whole book in shape for Bernice,[38] and I find I've got to rewrite the first article!" (*Bone,* 145).[39] She also tells Renée on April 16, 1953: "My first article came out in *Pres. Life* at last! Actually they used the last one first; it looked pretty good and I've had a bit of fan mail" (*Bone,* 146).

Smoke is a book of several strengths.[40] For example, Davidman uses her own extensive learning to great advantage. Although she does not wear her learning on her sleeve, she is quick to cite Egyptian, Babylonian, Syrian, Persian, Greek, Roman, and Jewish patterns of thought as well as principles from Buddhism, Hinduism, and Islam. Not surprisingly, she interacts with and draws conclusions from her engagement with both the Old and New Testament — the Decalogue and the Gospels in particular. Her facile grasp of Scripture and her Jewish ethnicity inform much of what she says. Moreover, she is cognizant of Protestant and Catholic thought and remains balanced

37. "Into the Full Light," *Presbyterian Life* 6 (April 4, 1953): 12-13, 26-29; it is chapter 11, "Light of Light," the last chapter in *Smoke.* The second essay, "God Comes First," appeared in *Presbyterian Life* 6 (May 2, 1953): 12-14; it is the first chapter of *Smoke.*

38. Bernice Baumgarten was Davidman's literary agent and on the staff of the literary agency Brandt & Brandt.

39. In the same letter she suggests that her husband, Bill, had a hand in shaping the original article, "Into the Full Light": "Bill did it, or most of it, in his best rhetorical style — and I think it stinks" (*Bone,* 145).

40. For contemporary reviews of *Smoke on the Mountain,* see L. R. Miller, Review of *Smoke on the Mountain, Library Journal* 79 (September 1, 1954): 1496; Review of *Smoke on the Mountain, Kirkus* 22 (September 15, 1954): 661; Review of *Smoke on the Mountain, Christian Century* 72 (February 16, 1955): 72; Review of *Smoke on the Mountain, Saturday Review of Literature* 38 (March 5, 1955): 31; Review of *Smoke on the Mountain, Journal of Bible and Religion* 23 (April 1955): 157; Review of *Smoke on the Mountain, Times Literary Supplement,* May 6, 1955, p. iii.

in her comments upon both. Occasionally she alludes to Fascism and Communism, but she never gets side-tracked from her discussion of the Ten Commandments. From her close studies of English literature related to her master's course work and thesis, she brings in material from Anglo-Saxon writings, Shakespeare's *King Lear,* Dr. Samuel Johnson, William Blake, and Charles Dickens, along with writings by G. K. Chesterton, Charles Williams, and Lewis.[41] Nor does she neglect other expressions of art, at one point using Charlie Chaplin's film *Monsieur Verdoux* (1947) to drive home a point.

A second strength is that Davidman, as in her earlier movie and book reviews, is a bold and direct prose stylist. For instance, her descriptions of God are memorable. Early on she says, "we are in danger of forgetting that God is not only a comfort but a joy. He is the source of all pleasures; he is fun and light and laughter, and we are meant to enjoy him."[42] Humanity, she claims, is "God-haunted" (21), and our latching onto idols reveals our effort to have a god we can control (33). About Christ, she writes:

> For many contemporaries God has dwindled into a noble abstraction, a tendency of history, a goal of evolution; has thinned out into a concept useful for organizing world peace — a good thing as an idea. But not the Word made flesh, who died for us and rose again from the dead. Not a Personality that a man can feel any love for. And not, certainly, the eternal Lover who took the initiative and fell in love with *us.* (132)

Although she writes less frequently about the Holy Spirit, her few remarks are memorable: "If we are to be saved, it must be by the one power that is built into a man at his beginning and that he does not have to make with his hands — the power of the Holy Spirit, which is God" (39).

The third strength is that she follows a similar rhetorical strategy in each chapter. Her chapter titles are interpretative. About not stealing, her title is "You Can't Cheat an Honest Man," and about not coveting her title is "The Moth and the Rust," an allusion to part of Jesus' Sermon on the Mount.[43] Immediately following the chapter title is the relevant biblical passage from the Ten Commandments. Then, when she begins the chapter, she starts with

41. She cites or refers to Lewis's books almost a dozen times.

42. *Smoke,* 14-15; subsequent references in the text.

43. Matthew 6:19-21: "Do not store up for yourselves treasures on earth, where moth and rust consume and where thieves break in and steal; but store up for yourselves treasures in heaven, where neither moth nor rust consumes and where thieves do not break in and steal. For where your treasure is, there your heart will be also."

a modern fable or anecdote. In her chapter on keeping God's name holy, she imagines rites at a Black Sabbath, including a human sacrifice made "holy" by chanting magical god names; the chapter about keeping the Sabbath holy is prefaced by an imaginary Martian student visiting Earth who, while writing his thesis, notes that on Sundays most humans may be found sunning themselves on a beach rather than attending a house of worship; and the chapter about not bearing false witness employs the story of Titus Oates, the seventeenth-century English perjurer who invented the Popish Plot — the supposed Catholic conspiracy to murder Charles II — a particularly wicked lie that led to the execution of over a dozen people and a long-lasting legacy of suspicion and distrust toward Catholics in England. After these modern fables or anecdotes, she systematically works through how the biblical commandment — especially its disregard — is in evidence in mid-twentieth-century American society.

Fourth, her ability to "translate" the important biblical principle expressed by each commandment into the modern vernacular is very effective. This is particularly evident in Chapter 9, "Jesting Pilate." In her discussion of the prohibition against bearing false witness, she expands it to show how this sin involves itself in others: "The false witness, the wicked heart, the lying tongue, and the troublemaker were early recognized as aspects of the same man and the same sin" (107). Moreover, she suggests that "when Christ came, his fiercest wrath was for the hypocrite, the living lie whose every action is a false witness to his own virtue" (108). She relates Pilate's question to Christ, "What is truth?," to the "lie of the skeptic bound hand and foot in despair, who rather than face his own sins will even doubt his own reality; the question that hints that there is no such thing as truth" (108). Deftly she observes how Pilate's jest is still with us, "for he may have represented the very modern view that truth is after all a relative and subjective affair, an agreed-upon convention, a matter of expediency — and that therefore we are justified in doing anything that seems expedient, even as Pilate" (108). Davidman then considers the lies of the gossip, advertiser, journalist, and politician, and notes the most fundamental of lies: "We lie to ourselves about ourselves. Not for profit or power; but for pride" (112). Yet, and this is true of each chapter, Davidman closes the chapter on the upbeat, pointing out that "the way to freedom . . . was shown us long ago; it consists in the honest confession and repentance that alone can open our hearts to the Comforter" (114). Throughout the chapter her ideas are clear and easy to grasp, and her language is straightforward, crisp, and precise.

Other examples of her ability to translate significant biblical ideas into

the modern vernacular appear in each chapter. About the first command-
ment, she writes: "Whatever we desire, whatever we love, whatever we find
worth suffering for, will be Dead Sea fruit in our mouths unless we remem-
ber that God comes first" (29). The essence of idolatry, she claims, "is the
attempt to control and enslave the deity" (33). Regarding the third com-
mandment, she argues that "profanity does not insult God — a man cannot
insult God. But it does cripple man" (44). The key to keeping the Sabbath
is "looking beyond the world to the Love that sustains it" (58). Honoring
parents is important "lest your children dishonor you. Or, in other words, a
society that destroys the family destroys itself" (61). Christ, she affirms, laid
upon his followers the need to protect the weak, "and it is obviously impos-
sible to do that without sometimes having to fight the strong. . . . It follows
that killing a man is not the worst thing you can do to him" (77). Davidman's
chapter on adultery — no doubt informed by her husband's multiple infidel-
ities — broadens to reflect her appreciation for the heart of Christ's words
regarding sexuality: "Every statement our Lord made about sexuality works
to protect women and to awaken men to their own responsibilities" (89).
Similarly, she casts a wide net concerning theft: "The thief is not only he who
steals my purse, but also he who steals my trade; and he who underpays me,
and he who overcharges me; and he who taxes me for his own advantage
instead of mine; and he who sells me trash instead of honest goods" (100).
The way to avoid envying what others have is "to want God so much that we
can't be bothered with inordinate wants for anything else" (127). Christ's two
commands in the New Testament challenge us to "have enough belief in the
love of God to trust it to run our lives" (130) and to be willing to "lose many
worldly advantages if we love our neighbors as ourselves; we may even lose
our lives. But then, that is what we were told to do" (138).

At the same time, there are weaknesses in *Smoke*. For instance, often in
her zeal to convince, she makes brash claims that are unsupported. She also
has a tendency to make her battering-ram arguments in sequences of topic
sentences, each begging more nuanced development. And in some places
she verges on launching into a jeremiad, reminiscent of her days writing for
NM and the CPUSA. But perhaps the book's greatest weakness is our feel-
ing that *Smoke* — for all its good sense, striking directness, vivid language,
and biblical insights — was written more because of Davidman's need to
make money than because of deep spiritual convictions. Of course, there is
no dishonor in writing to earn a living; nor am I suggesting she sold out in
the sense of compromising her literary and spiritual integrity when writing
Smoke. At the same time, there is the lingering feel throughout the book

that Davidman rushed to get the chapters written in order to bring in some badly needed cash.

There is plenty of evidence in her letters of this. She tells Bill Gresham on March 16, 1954, that the English rights to publishing *Smoke* "won't pay much; I'm lucky if I clear £50 on it for an advance, but considering everything I haven't done badly on a book that has yet to see print. And the bit of money will at least buy me a few nylons" (*Bone*, 184). In her May 10, 1954, letter to him she says that Lewis "has done a perfectly lovely preface for the English edition of *Smoke on the Mountain,* but I'm afraid it's just too late for the American edition. If only the blasted book sells!" (*Bone*, 192).[44] On November 4, 1954, she writes Bill: "I'm getting my teeth into *Queen Cinderella* — provisional title for my biography of Mme. de Maintenon. . . . There's miles of reading to do, but I think I ought to be able to sell it on an outline and a few specimen chapters; the story's sure-fire. I don't hope much for *Smoke on the Mountain,* which is just out in the States . . . but the biography smells to me like a money-maker if I can get it done" (*Bone,* 224-25). On April 29, 1955, she tells Bill: "[*Smoke* is] doing fairly well here — has sold 3000 already, mostly on the basis of Jack's preface and some extraordinarily good reviews in church publications. There ought to be a little money in it eventually, though since most of the sales are paperbacks it won't be much" (*Bone,* 246). Another way to put this is that we can make a good guess regarding when and how she started working on *Smoke,* and that her motives for writing *Smoke* combined both the biblical and the commercial.

Weeping Bay and *Smoke* were Davidman's last published books.[45] While

---

44. Lewis begins his foreword by briefly reviewing Davidman's success with *Letter to a Comrade,* even citing from several of the poems. Then he shows that he has carefully read her "The Longest Way Round" before pronouncing that "in a sense the converted Jew is the only normal human being in the world" (7). He goes on to commend her style, her knowledge of the Law, and her reticence to pontificate: "The author is not a quack with a nostrum. She can only point, as in her concluding chapter she does point, to the true Cure; a Person, not a set of instructions" (9). His only critique is that Davidman quotes from him when he believes she needs "no pen save her own to express [her ideas]. But every old tutor (and I was not even that to Miss Davidman) knows that those pupils who needed our assistance least are generally also those who acknowledge it most largely" (11). Lewis also shares with others his praise of the book. On April 6, 1955, he writes Dorothy L. Sayers about the book: "I hope you've read Joy Davidman's *Smoke on the Mountain,* an ex-Communist, Jewess-by-race, convertite, on the X Commandments and, I think, really good" (*CL,* 3, p. 596).

45. It is worth mentioning here that she published three short pieces at about this time: "Theater Party," *Bluebook* 88 (February 1949): 16-17; "A Little Bird Told Her," *McCall's,*

the former lacks the energy and passion of *Anya*, it merits our attention as evidence of her determined efforts at fiction. The latter recalls the fervor of Davidman's Communist nonfiction book and movie reviews that appeared in *NM*. Neither, however, is the final word on her literary ability. For that we need to turn to the next chapter and the astonishing sequence of love sonnets she wrote to Lewis.

February 1951, pp. 44, 112, 115-17; and "It's Right to Marry Young," *Redbook*, November 1952, pp. 40-41, 72-73 (with her husband, Bill).

CHAPTER 8

A Naked Tree: Joy Davidman's
Love Sonnets to C. S. Lewis (1952-1956)

One important biographical gap in the story of C. S. Lewis and Joy David-
man concerns the nature of their relationship between 1950 (when they first
began corresponding) and 1956 (when their civil marriage occurred). As I
suggested in the last chapter, by the time Davidman came to England in the
summer of 1952 she was probably already in love with Lewis. Until recently
we knew of only a few letters that survived from this period, so biographers
were left to speculate about the details of how their relationship blossomed
from *agape* into *philia* and thence to *eros*.[1] However, because of the newly
discovered letters and poems in DP, part of this gap may now be bridged. In
particular, there is an astonishingly beautiful sequence of forty-five love son-
nets that Davidman wrote to Lewis.[2] While "breathtaking" is an often over-

---

1. In his letter to Dom Bede Griffiths of September 24, 1957, Lewis notes this progres-
sion: "It is nice to have arrived at all this by something which began in Agape, proceeded
to Philia, then became Pity, and only after that, Eros. As if the highest of these, Agape,
had successfully undergone the sweet humiliation of an incarnation." C. S. Lewis, *Collected
Letters* (hereafter *CL*), vol. 3: *Narnia, Cambridge, and Joy, 1950-1963*, ed. Walter Hooper
(London: HarperCollins, 2006), 884.

2. Moreover, there are many other previously unknown poems concerning Lewis; I
note five here as indicative. "Bread-and-Butter" sestina (*Naked Tree*, 268-69) appears in Joy's
unpublished letter of October 15, 1952, to Bill Gresham. She says the poem, which recounts
details of her visits to Oxford, impressed Lewis. "Ballade of Blistered Feet" (*Naked Tree*,
267-68) is a comic recounting of a drenching walk that she, Lewis, and Warren took some-
time during another of her visits to Lewis. The sonnet "Threat" (*Naked Tree*, 271), which
she dates as February 10, 1953, is a poem anticipating what will happen when she returns
to Headington; it shares no similarities with Sonnet IX in the forty-five sonnet sequence I
discuss in this chapter. "Valentine" (*Naked Tree*, 272) is a sonnet; she dates it February 14,

used term, it aptly expresses the nature of these sonnets; they offer stunning evidence of Davidman's spiritual struggles with regard to her feelings for Lewis, her sense of God's working on her selfish, demanding, love-starved, and lonely life, and her increasingly mounting frustrations with Lewis for keeping her at arm's length emotionally and physically. In another regard, the sonnets are brilliant evidence of Davidman's skill as an artist. She proves to have a facile hand at the sonnet form, and the "conversational" nature of the sonnets is reminiscent of the poetry of John Donne, particularly his "Holy Sonnets."[3] In this chapter I review the important details about Lewis and Davidman's relationship as revealed in her unpublished letters between August and December 1952, introduce and discuss the love sonnets, and offer a brief discussion of their artistic merits and biographical implications.

Many of Davidman's unpublished letters between August and December 1952 report on her activities, the places she has visited, and her delight (for the most part) in all things English. For instance, she writes Renée on August 16, 1952: "We went to Trafalgar Square and Piccadilly and the [Westminster] Abbey and the Thames — walked our legs off and enjoyed every bit of it. It's no use describing the Abbey, one must see it — an enormous stone jewel. Same for many other buildings. . . . It would take a lifetime to *know* London, but I've done a lot in three days!"[4] In addition to London sightseeing, she reports on meeting Mrs. Charles Williams and on day trips to Canterbury and Dover, and on September 14 she tells Bill that she will be off to Oxford the next day. It was during that visit that she met Lewis for lunch at the East-gate Hotel on September 24.[5] The next letter we have is to Bill on September 30; here she relates details of her trip north to Scotland, including visits to Edinburgh, Aberdeen, Carlisle, and Dumfries.

By October 4 she has returned to London, and her letters from this point forward contain numerous references to her meetings and conversations with Lewis. She tells Bill that "Jack introduced me to pork-pies washed down with cider one day at the famous Bird and Baby [the Eagle and Child] pub; very good" and "I'm trying to write Jack a bread-and-butter letter in the form

---

1953. It shares similarities in tone with many of the sonnets in the sequence, but it (or variations of it) does not appear in the sequence. Another poem is "A Sword Named Joy" (*Naked Tree*, 273), which she dates February 23, 1953; see the text of this poem in note 84 below.

3. The sonnets as a narrative sequence are also reminiscent of William Shakespeare's sonnets 126-54 and many of the lyrics of Alfred Tennyson's *In Memoriam*.

4. DP, Box 1, Series 1, Folder 6; all the subsequent unpublished letters cited are from this folder.

5. For more on this, see Chapter 7, note 29.

of a sestina" (October 4); "Jack was very pleased with the sestina, which turned out really good"; she alludes to publishing either an interview with or article about Lewis (October 13); "I'll enclose my sestina, which seems to have knocked Jack for a loop — he being one of the few people who can tell how hard that sort of thing is" and "Damn it, Jack's not lecturing this term after all, so I don't get to hear him. But I'm gonna show him my poetry and see what he thinks" (October 15); "On November 10th, [Doug Gresham's] birthday, Jack is talking to a group of children in London and I shall be there; wish the boys could be, too" (October 29); "As for That Man [Lewis], he is certainly fond of me and rather attracted by me, but not enough to disturb his peace of mind (thank goodness); and if it were ten times as strong a feeling, his belief would still be stronger. Funny; I've never before been with a man who looked at me and talked to me like that and then did not make a pass — and, do you know, I half like it! I'll be a Christian yet" (November 3); "Am going to Oxford on the 17th to hear [Jack] lecture on Hooker" (November 8); "When Jack came [in the room to lecture on Hooker] he at once began to look around anxiously, nodded abstractly to one or two people he knew, and went on looking. I didn't realize he was looking for me until he saw me, gave me a delightful sunburst of a smile, and sat down content"; and "By the way, Jack really is the cleverest and most effective lecturer I've ever heard. Hooker's Laws of Ecclesiastical Polity, and the rising Calvinism of Elizabethan times, are hardly subjects made to order for keeping an audience roaring with laughter; but he did it" (November 23).

The last letter Davidman writes Bill from England at this time is during her Christmas stay at Lewis's home, the Kilns. It is notable especially for the insights it provides about both his and her writings:

I'm having a most wonderful time. Jack is relaxing on vacation — which means he is only editing his book on [Edmund] Spenser,[6] writing his book on prayers,[7] answering nine hundred letters a morning (most of them fantastic), interviewing the assortment of creatures who depend on him for guidance, beginning work on the O-hell[8] proofs (which I've been

---

6. This may refer to draft versions of what eventually became either *Studies in Medieval and Renaissance Literature,* collected by Walter Hooper (Cambridge: Cambridge University Press, 1966) or *Spenser's Images of Life,* ed. Alastair Fowler (Cambridge: Cambridge University Press, 1967).

7. This may refer to a draft version of what eventually became *Letters to Malcolm: Chiefly on Prayer* (London: Geoffrey Bles, 1964).

8. This refers to Lewis's *English Literature in the Sixteenth Century Excluding Drama,*

privileged to read before *any* other human, unless you count typesetters and such) and incidentally going over my article and being an enormous help.[9] It's such a joy to have a reader who really *understands* what I'm talking about! By the way, he liked best a great deal that *Presbyterian Life didn't* like; such things as the Martian introduction to the Sabbath piece, which he roared over, and said should be used separately if they wouldn't have it, the idea could be used for a book. (December 19, 1952)[10]

Davidman's letters from August to December 1952 do not suggest that she and Lewis were yet being drawn together romantically; however, they do reveal the importance of writing for both of them, the frequency with which they met, and the friendly nature of their relationship.

Yet a certain kind of intimacy had developed between them since she talked to Lewis about her unhappy marriage. On February 27, 1953, she writes Walsh:

> I never felt I could talk to anybody about my married life, in the past. But when this new situation developed [Bill and Renée had begun a sexual relationship while Joy was in England] I asked Lewis for advice and told him a good deal of the story — an expurgated version, at that. Some of it I simply can't put into words. Anyhow Lewis strongly advised me to divorce Bill; and has repeated it even more strongly since I've been home — Bill greeted me by knocking me about a bit, and I wrote Lewis about that.[11] So now I'm rid of the feeling that it's my duty to go on! (*Bone*, 140-41).

In this same letter she confides to Walsh that she was planning to return to England with her two boys: "I hope to take the children to England and bring them up there — not so much because I'm completely in love with

---

vol. 3 of the Oxford History of English Literature series (Oxford: Clarendon Press, 1954). Lewis spent roughly ten years researching and writing the book, and it became so burdensome that he joked to friends about his OHEL (O Hell) book: O[xford] H[istory] E[nglish] L[iterature] book. In the preface to the book, Lewis thanks a number of people, including "Miss Joy Davidman for help with the proofs" (vi).

9. This appears to refer to what became chapter 4, "Day of Rejoicing," of *Smoke on the Mountain*.

10. In her January 25, 1953, letter to Walsh she offered more details about the visit; see *Bone*, 138-39.

11. Lewis's letters to Davidman advising her to divorce Gresham have not survived. On occasion he wrote correspondents about divorce; see his letter of March 2, 1955, *CL*, 3, p. 575.

England, though that's part of it, as because living is so much cheaper there and I'll be able to live decently on what Bill can pay" (*Bone,* 141). From this time forward Joy and Bill lived together infrequently and were planning to divorce.[12] In early November 1953, Davidman and her two boys sailed for England.

Once Davidman returned to England we might have expected to find a number of letters between her and Lewis; however, apparently none of these letters has survived.[13] Her surviving letters to others from the end of 1953 until the civil marriage between Davidman and Lewis reveal many visits and frequent time spent together, but nothing about a growing romantic relationship. It is to the sequence of forty-five love sonnets Davidman wrote to Lewis that we must turn to explore this fascinating development.

There are a number of important general observations to make about the sonnet sequence to Lewis. First, as I discussed above, three other love sonnet sequences appear in her earlier unpublished poetry.[14] These earlier sonnet sequences recount the painful internal recriminations a female lover makes against herself as she suffers the anguish of unrequited love, and they illustrate Davidman's penchant both for the sonnet form and for using poetry as a rhetorical tool; that is, these sequences are "arguments" with herself, her desired lover, and/or her actual lover. Each sequence demonstrates a woman who has experienced romantic love as all-consuming and reveals a mind given to obsessive, compulsive, and possessive thoughts regarding sexual love.[15]

The second important general observation concerns matters related to the composition of the sonnets. Most of the love sonnets to Lewis exist in multiple drafts in the DP, although the differing versions show little revision — often a word or punctuation mark is the only variance.[16] The varying

12. For more on this, see *Bone,* 142-59.

13. And perhaps there were not many anyway; with Joy living in London, their personal visits to each other (as well as an occasional phone call) may have replaced the need for many letters.

14. I discuss these earlier love sonnet sequences in Chapter 1.

15. The sheer number of her love sonnets — including the sequence to Lewis, she wrote over sixty — is striking because it contrasts dramatically with the paucity of sonnets in her published work. There are only four sonnets among the more than seventy poems she published during her lifetime. Perhaps Davidman's unpublished sonnets were both poems and a journal; that is, because she could write sonnets so effortlessly, they may have served as the primary literary venue for her most private, intimate, and self-revealing thoughts.

16. Also of note is that the sonnets give the impression, especially the early ones in the sequence, of being easily composed — casual readers may think Davidman was able to dash

drafts often carry titles, and a number are dated.[17] Most were written between 1949 and 1954, revealing that some were written well before Lewis and Davidman met. These matters of composition point out, I believe, that the sonnets were initially conceived of as separate poems. It was only at some point later — perhaps when Davidman was especially frustrated by Lewis holding her at arm's length emotionally and physically — that, recalling her three earlier love sonnet sequences, she decided to put the poems together in the sequence as we now have it.[18] One instance arguing for a later pulling together of the separate sonnets into a sequence is most revealing; the last love sonnet in the sequence, XLIV, is dated by Davidman as having been written in November 1939, more than a decade before she wrote her first letter to Lewis.[19] One conclusion we can draw from this is that the sonnet sequence to Lewis was a deliberate, conscious decision by a gifted artist who wanted the poems to accomplish two things: to indicate boldly her passion for Lewis, and to serve as a piece of sharp rhetoric intent on persuading him to return her affections. Moreover, as an experienced poet, Davidman knew her individual sonnets could be woven together into a sequence that might accelerate the kind of relationship she wanted to have with Lewis. If this is the case, the sequence gives evidence of Davidman as both advocate and artist.

The third general observation concerns the relationship between the individual sonnets and the sequence as a whole. Although each sonnet is complete in itself — telling, if you will, its own little story — it is easy to discern a larger story or narrative as we read through the sequence. Accordingly, within the sequence many of the sonnets are "conversational"; that is, sometimes Davidman is speaking to herself, sometimes to Lewis directly or indirectly, sometimes to God, sometimes to former lovers, sometimes to no one in particular, and sometimes to several of these at the same time. Throughout the sequence Joy's narrative tone or mood vacillates between despair and hope, anger and resignation, desire and shame, longing and self-

---

them off in a moment or two. This view of the sonnets as "artless" is deceptive; Davidman was a conscious craftswoman, and she used all her skills as a poet in this extraordinary display of her creative talent.

17. In my discussion below I will indicate by title if other drafts of the sonnets are found in DP.

18. The entire sequence, a prefatory sonnet followed by forty-four more titled with Roman numerals, appears in DP, Box 1, Series 4, Folder 24; the sequence is now published in *Naked Tree*, 282-307.

19. See in her index in DP, Box 1, Series 4, Folder 27.

denial, scheming and confessing, plotting and humiliation, *eros* and *agape,* passion and reason, the flesh and the spirit, a fierce desire to possess and a frustrated acquiescence to give up, and desperation and resolution.

Before we look more closely at the sonnets, we see that Davidman provides the following chronological structure for the sequence:

A prefatory sonnet
Sonnets I-IV grouped under the subtitle "America, 1951"
Sonnets V-VIII grouped under the subtitle "England, 1952"
Sonnets IX-XVI grouped under the subtitle "America, 1953"
Sonnets XVII-XLIV grouped under the subtitle "England, 1954."

This suggests we are to read the first four sonnets as if they concern Davidman's life and search for love before her first visit to Lewis. Sonnets V through VIII highlight events and emotions related to her first trip to England and her initial meeting with Lewis in the fall of 1952. While we might think IX through XVI will focus upon her return to America in 1953 and the eventual break-up of her marriage to Bill Gresham, actually they center on her hopes and dreams of returning to England and forging a closer relationship with Lewis. By far the largest group, Sonnets XVII through XLIV, explores in great detail the nature of Davidman's efforts to forge that relationship. In the discussion that follows I have attempted to communicate above all else Davidman's arresting, provocative, and sharply penetrating voice, intent on saying what she feels and getting what she wants. Although I provide some informational footnotes in my discussion of the sonnets, I refrain from editorializing on the content of the sonnets until the end of the chapter.

The Love Sonnet Sequence

Prefatory Sonnet

In the prefatory sonnet, whimsically entitled "Dear Jack," Davidman self-effacingly suggests she is sending him the sonnets, even though they are flawed: "The trouble with them, as I think you'll see, / Is that I do the trick too easily, / In fifteen seconds from desire to deed."[20] She says that in the

---

20. About the allure of writing sonnets, Davidman wrote Aaron Kramer on September 9, 1946: "The sonnet is always a temptation to a good technician to be too clever" (*Bone,* 47).

past she often dashed off sonnets like this, causing her words to rush beyond her art. Still, "I have made such and such / Rhymes in your honour, sir, and here's the lot." She confesses that after Lewis reads them he may not think them very good; her poems may fail, but he should not miss her intention in sending him the sonnets: "And if you think the sum of it not much, / Remember it's the only gift I've got; / As our slang has it, funny as a crutch — / The verse may be a joke; the love is not."[21]

Sonnets I-IV

Sonnets I-IV, although set by Davidman as "America, 1951," and thus well before her actual meeting with Lewis, nonetheless concern her romantic longings for him. Sonnet I introduces one of several different tones Davidman expresses in the sequence — here one of desperation at having fallen in love another time: "Begin again, must I begin again / Who have begun so many loves in fire / And ended them in dirty ash?" She tells herself that she should stop her passion at this very moment, saving both herself and Lewis from the agonies of love. Yet that resolution is quickly dismissed; since she cannot stop her feelings, she will measure them out a teaspoon at a time: "I'll measure my affection by the drachm."[22] At the end of the poem she settles on being Lewis's friend and follower, rich in affection but loath to ask for more than that: "Honoured sir, I am / Somewhat your friend; as far as courtesy / Requires, your servant; not at all your slave. / I love you far too well to give you love."[23]

In Sonnet II Davidman admits to a shocking truth: "Having loved my love tonight with you between, / My lord, I pray you of your courtesy / That I may give as much as he gives me; / Lie mouth to mouth, skin upon naked skin, / Joy upon joy." That is, she confesses that as she made love that night with one man, her husband, Bill, all the time she was presumably thinking of Lewis. Her lips, breasts, all her flesh pressed against Bill, and she did try, she really did try, to give him her heart and soul as well, but she could not. Therefore, "because you have my heart, he has my bed," and she claims she gave him her body freely, willingly. The one thing she does not want Bill to

---

21. Although Davidman does not date this poem, I suggest it was written after the entire sequence was completed, perhaps sometime in 1954 or 1955.

22. A very small quantity.

23. This sonnet is dated April 8, 1951. Another draft of this sonnet is titled "When It Was Already Too Late."

know is this: "Nor ever let him guess / How I, staring above his quiet head, / Knew, in the lonely midnight afterward, / The terrible third between us like a sword."[24] In short, she prays Bill will never know that while she lay with him, her eyes were searching the darkness for Lewis, aware at every moment that he lay between them like a sword.[25]

The lighter tone of Sonnet III contrasts with that of the two previous sonnets, in part because its focus is not upon Lewis but instead upon the nature of romantic love. Rather than reflecting desperation or deception, Sonnet III muses that love is all-consuming and fickle. She says love is a constant nag, eating away at one's heart and mind. It kills and quickens; it is fleeting and eternal; it refreshes and empties; it is sustaining and insatiable. It drains your soul while at the same time over-filling your heart's blood. It leaves you wide-eyed and jittery: "Love will empty you and love will fill you / With the fluids that keep your heart pumping / And your eyes alive and your nerves jumping." In addition, love leads to madness: "Love will go crazy if the moon is bright. / You can be very sure it will not kill you, / But neither will it let you sleep at night." In short, the sonnet claims that while love certainly will not kill, do not expect it to give peace, rest, or satisfaction.[26]

Sonnet IV continues the theme of love's all-consuming nature, although with a darker undertone and a return to her feelings for Lewis: "Let me not lie about it; there are worse pains. / There is seeing your children shot before your face. / There is being buried alive in the shallow graves / Where afterward the torn sods heaved in vain." Still, she argues, losing one's lover is indeed painful: "There are many deaths and several sorts of life / That are much worse than what I feel for you; / And yet this loss is loss, this love hurts too." So, she wonders, is her loss of Lewis no more than a pinprick, a splinter in the finger, or a tick bite? If that is the case, she at first affirms that she can take it, but then quickly changes her mind: "I would not do you the wrong of / Pretending that I sicken and must die. / Believe me, I am sound — Why, no; I lie."[27] She asserts it is false bravado to assert that she can live without Lewis.

---

24. The poem is dated by Davidman as 1948 or 1949. Another draft of this sonnet is titled "Premonition" and a third draft includes at the end in Davidman's hand this note: "In a moment of insight, for CSL."

25. Perceptive readers may recognize in her use of the sword metaphor one Lewis uses later in *A Grief Observed* to describe Davidman. More on this below.

26. Another version of this sonnet is "Definitions" in folder 21; she dates it as March 1940 in her poetry index in folder 27.

27. I date this poem as September 1938. The first nine lines of this sonnet appear as stanza II in the poem "Notes on an Obsession"; *Naked Tree*, 79.

Sonnets V-VIII

Sonnet V is a transitional one, moving from the first four sonnets set in America, 1951, to the next four set in England, 1952. In the sonnet Davidman congratulates herself for how often in the past she has been patient and gentle with the pathetic men who loved her. When they wept on her shoulder, blubbering their love, she fought her impulse to backhand them: "I have not slapped them on the crying lips / When they came to me and bleated love / And weakness, and despair; I have been kind." She played nice, becoming their refuge and harbor. Yet sooner or later everyone is supposed to get in the queue where love is dished out, bit by bit. She ends the poem hoping and praying it is her turn: "Here I am, and what have I deserved? / Here I hunger, waiting; I am cold."[28]

Sonnets VI-VIII are the first ones directly addressing Davidman's initial meetings with Lewis. Sonnet VI alludes to her first meeting with Lewis. She recalls vividly that day in September: "My lord and love, the yellow leaves were sailing / Confusing sorrowful air and earth together / Between two rivers, in the wistful weather, / Sky changing, tree undressing, summer failing; / September."[29] The autumn leaves, gold and red, rushed by them in the blustery breeze as they walked between the Isis and the Cherwell Rivers. Yet she also calls to mind how the nearby bells from Magdalen College tolled ominously, banging out unfriendly portents about their love: "Even the bells in Magdalen tower[30] were ringing / Death to the drooping afternoon, and never / A merry note to comfort him, for neither / Angels nor larks had any heart for singing." Still, when she remembers that day it is with aching delight: "That was no golden season for lover and lover / But for dying light and bright things falling. / And yet, not too forlorn a memory: / Oxford, autumn leaves, and you, and me."[31]

She continues her reverie about this initial meeting in Sonnet VII. As they walked between the two rivers, the rain fell furiously and lashed against them so violently they could barely hear one another. The force of the lashing rain made her melancholy and caused her to think about how time might kill all her hopes of love with Lewis: "I have forgot / Innumerable joys,

28. I date this poem as sometime in 1940.
29. See above about her meeting Lewis for the first time on September 24, 1952, in the Eastgate Hotel in Oxford.
30. This refers to the famous tower at Magdalen College, Oxford, where Lewis was a don from 1925 to 1954.
31. This sonnet is dated December 10, 1952. Another draft is titled "First Meeting."

that dreaming of / Might have made night less dreadful all the years / I am to bear without you." Now she believes all her hopes for love with Lewis are ludicrous. It is impossible that he will ever love her, leading her to the tender final lines: "Even tears / Fade and leave blank eyelids; only not, / O love, this bitter endless pain, my love."[32] Sonnet VIII extends this poignancy as she claims she has obeyed Lewis, perhaps alluding to his check — either covertly or overtly — on her romantic feelings for him: "I brought my love obedience; cupped my hand / And held submission to his thirsty mouth, / A cooling water in a burning land." She suggests that first he was delighted with her attentions, but soon "he led me to an open door / And sent me and my empty soul away / Saying I must not love him any more." It is as if Lewis had told her to leave, please, with both her heart and soul, and forget about him. When she heard that, however, she decided she would obey him no more: "But now at last I learn to disobey."[33]

Sonnets IX-XVI: America, 1953

Sonnets IX-XVI are set in America during 1953. This was a painful year for Davidman as her marriage to Bill failed, in no small part because he had begun an affair with Joy's cousin, Renée Rodriguez Pierce, while Davidman was in England.[34] Perhaps reacting against her anguish, Sonnet IX imagines the day when she will return to Headington, the village outside Oxford where Lewis's home, the Kilns, is located: "If ever I go back to Headington / I'll go on foot, some breezy day in spring, / With new leaves winking at the yellow sun / And subtle sounds of water murmuring / A silver word." In this pleasant reverie she imagines floating on the wind: "I shall come lightly as a flower or leaf / Dancing on April wind — and bring you, Jack, / Something a little sweeter than my grief."[35] She promises that during this visit she will not dump her pain on him; instead, she will be smarter, happier, and wiser,

---

32. This sonnet is dated Christmas 1952. Another draft is titled "Sonnet of Memories."

33. This sonnet is dated "S. S. Franconia, January 1953." After her first visit to Lewis in the fall of 1952, the *S. S. Franconia* was the vessel Davidman sailed on when she returned to New York, suggesting that she wrote the poem during her voyage home. Another draft of this sonnet is titled "Sonnet of Misunderstandings."

34. For more on this, see *Bone,* 131-37; Dorsett, *And God Came In,* 89-102; and Santamaria, *Joy,* chs. 11 and 12.

35. This probably refers to Davidman having shared with Lewis the deteriorating state of her marriage to Bill Gresham during her 1952 trip to England.

leading her to one of her most upbeat endings: "O may the rooks caw to the rising sun / For joy, when I come back to Headington."[36]

Yet Sonnet X returns to the desperation of earlier sonnets. She baldly confesses that she has made Lewis into an idol: "Why, you may call the thing idolatry / And tell no lie; for I have seen you shine / Brighter than any son of man should be; / And trembled, and half-dreamed you were divine, / And knelt in adoration." She admits that she is giving him the devotion that belongs only to God: "You are not God, and neither are you mine." Her desperation threatens to lead to self-mutilation with an Old Testament precedent: "The pagan priesthood, honouring their Baal, / Slashed themselves till they bled, and so have I, / Yet neither they nor I to much avail; / The fire was out, and vacant was the sky."[37] She claims that just as the pagan priests cut themselves, bleeding out the "proof" of their faith, so she has done the same regarding her passion for Lewis with no more success than the Baal worshipers. And, yes, she knows she has been wrong to do this. Still, she is helpless to resist her idolatry: "Sir, you may correct me with your rod. / I have loved you better than I loved my God."[38]

Rhetoric, not desperation, characterizes Sonnet XI. She readily agrees with the arguments Lewis has apparently listed as to why he cannot love her; she even admits his reasons are persuasive and potent. They could darken the sun, stop the tides, reverse the rain, cause flowers to smother bees, and stifle the wind. Even more, his arguments could make heaven out of hell, hell out of heaven. But she says two can play that game:

> The argument that keeps the sun in power
> Over his children, makes the firefly glow,
> Adorns the summer with her proper flower
> And decorates the winter with his snow,
> Makes dead men rise and promises come true —
> Such reasons do I have for loving you.

She attempts to turn the tables on Lewis, affirming that the same force — the force that keeps the sun shining, that pushes the flowers out of the earth,

---

36. This sonnet is dated February 11, 1953. Another draft is titled "Hopeful Sonnet."

37. Here Davidman alludes to the confrontation between Elijah and the prophets of Baal recorded in 1 Kings 18. See especially 1 Kings 18:25-29.

38. This sonnet is dated February 14, 1953, interestingly enough, Valentine's Day. Another draft is titled "On Her Love Saying That She Loved Him Too Well."

that blankets winter with snow, that raises the dead, that promises truth — compels her to love him.[39]

In Sonnet XII Davidman introduces an idea that readers will not find stated anywhere in Lewis's writings: that he had a penchant for blondes.[40] This put Davidman at a distinct disadvantage since she was a brunette, and in her mind an aging one: "I am not Queen Helen,[41] sir; I have no gold / Framing the perfect sorrow of my face; / The best of me is merely commonplace, / And I am tired, and I am growing old, / My mirror says." She laments the way she has seen her beauty erode away — skin that once glowed fresh and alluring, now sags. Frankly, she knows how little she has to attract him:

> What I am saying is that I have nothing
> To give you that you possibly could want;
> A double handful of the barren earth
> Is all I am, a skull touched up with paint,
> A thing to move your laughter or your loathing;
> Still, you may have my love for what it's worth.[42]

Here her desperation comes close to self-pity, yet even so she cannot stop loving Lewis.

Self-pity continues in Sonnet XIII and is augmented with bitterness: "I said it did not hurt. My lord, I lied; / Painted my mouth into a smiling shape / Before the mirror, taught my heart to ape / Happiness; wore the dagger in my side / As if it were a jewel." When Lewis rebuffed her feelings for him, she fooled him into believing it did not bother her even though it hurt, and

---

39. This sonnet is also dated February 14, 1953, making it another Valentine's Day sonnet. Another draft is titled "Of the Laws of Nature."

40. See also Sonnets XX, XXII, and XXXI. It is worth noting that medieval and Renaissance love literature elevates women with the fairest skin and golden hair, ideas of which Lewis was very cognizant. In her reference to Helen of Troy Davidman may also have been having something of a private joke with Lewis since her first name was Helen.

41. In Greek mythology Helen of Sparta — better known as Helen of Troy — was hailed as the most beautiful woman in the world. As a representation of ideal female beauty, Helen became the object of many lovers. She eventually married Menelaus, king of Laconia, a Greek province. Entranced by her beauty, the Trojan prince, Paris, kidnapped Helen and took her to Troy. Her legendary beauty, "the face that launched a thousand ships," resulted in the Trojan War in which Menelaus led Greek warriors against Paris and his allies.

42. This sonnet is dated August 1, 1953. Another draft is titled "The Inveterate Present-Giver."

continues to hurt like hell: "Now I roll in hell / My wheel of agony, and burning stones / Eat their slow acid way into my bones / Etching the secret that I would not tell." The simple truth is that she cannot stop loving him. Perhaps when she dies she will stop cursing God for this agony: "Eternity may teach my idiot brain / Not to blaspheme against God's gift of pain."[43]

Her desperation intensifies in Sonnet XIV. She wonders what she will do when words no longer help her cope with the pain of unrequited love. What will she do when she runs out of poems to write about her feelings? What will she do when her tortured sonnets, conceived at midnight and birthed at sunrise, no longer suffice? What will she do when she has gone to God in prayer to no avail?

> Always, after the praying and the poor gabble
> Of sobs, and the twisting in the lonely bed,
> And the clever spiderwebs I weave in my head
> To catch you with, I sit down at my table
> And stare at nothing, neither God nor you;
> Sir, at the end of words, what shall I do?[44]

After she has wrung her hands to redness, after sleepless nights scheming about how to catch Lewis in her web as a spider catches a fly, after she reaches the end of despair, what in God's name will she do?

In Sonnet XV desperation and bitterness give way to self-loathing and self-recrimination. Addressing her own "insatiate" heart, Davidman accuses it of despising an *agape* or unselfish love for Lewis, intent instead on *eros:* "Must holiness be hunted like a beast, / Tricked like a man, entangled in a snare / Woven of such poor stuff as womanhair?" Heart, she says — you that are never satisfied — cannot you be happy that you found meaning, purpose, and hope when you were filled with pure, simple, and honest *agape*? Do you, oh heart, have to debase even this kind of love? "Must you try to trap him in your bed, / A fire and valour to appease the lust / Of your cold empty arms? and yet you must."[45] In effect, she asks her heart: Do you have to be Venus's slave? Are you that desperate for sex? And her heart's reply is simply: Yes. She is helpless in the throes of her passion for Lewis.

43. This sonnet is dated March 20, 1953. Another draft is titled "Non Dolet" (Latin for "it does not hurt" or "no regrets").

44. Another version of this sonnet is titled "To My Love Who Told Me to Write Verses" and dated February 22, 1953.

45. This sonnet is dated January 8, 1953. Another draft is titled "Apropos of the Unicorn."

Davidman concludes this section of the sonnets set in America, 1953, with Sonnet XVI, one that adopts the distant, objective tone of a woman reflecting on the final stages of a love affair: "At the last hour the few important things / She kept firm hold of, had not much to do / With what she said and suffered, what he knew / Or thought about it all; or even love."[46] Just before the affair ended, the woman grasped at straws, blindly grabbing for anything that might sustain her. She had given up the pain of trying to figure him out and ceased from remembering her many nights of tortured tossing and turning in bed — wishing beyond hope that he would be there: "She had outlived the agony of wonder / What he was really like inside his head, / Forgotten the harsh nights and lonely bed." But there was one thing she simply could not get out of her mind: "One thing remains, / One arrow still may burn, while flesh is flesh; / The accidental beauty of his face."[47] At this point in her life, for Davidman that face was Lewis's.

Sonnets XVII-XLIV: England, 1954

The final group of sonnets builds to an emotional climax after which Davidman tries to come to grips with the possibility that Lewis may never accept her as a lover. Sonnet XVII, like XVI, is distant and objective. The woman seems reconciled to the end of the matter: it is over, darkness covers all, and in a starless and moonless night sky she feels a deathly cold breeze: "Cold, cold the funeral wind. And of our bones / What shall be made but rubbish? Never rain / Whimpers to this trash in undertones / Of resurrection; spring comes not again." The world will burn, the ocean retract in frost. Yet, if possible, she is willing to face all this — and even worse — with her lover: shoulder to shoulder, arm to arm, hand to hand: "Yet one eternal moment let us stand / Against the encroaching dark. Give me your hand."[48]

---

46. Sonnet XVI is a slight variation on the sonnet form since it contains fifteen lines rather than the normal fourteen lines. This poem also appears as stanza III in the poem "Notes on an Obsession," a poem that I date as September 1938; if my dating is correct, this may explain the distant, objective tone of this sonnet as it was originally addressed not to Lewis but to one of her earlier lovers.

47. I date this sonnet as September 1938.

48. I date this sonnet as sometime in 1938. Another draft is titled "Fimbulwinter." In Norse mythology Fimbulwinter was a three-year winter (with no intervening summers) ushering in Ragnorak, the final battle that would end the world. I think Davidman uses

Sonnet XVIII returns to addressing Lewis directly. Davidman dismisses Lewis's offers of *agape:* "I think, my lad, you learn your charity / By rote and not by heart. 'Tis very well / For flights of angels, as I hear you tell, / To shower love on all men equally." It is as if she says to him that it is all well and good for him to say "God loves you." That's not the point. She does not want that kind of love: "But you and I were made for other ends, / And you are something short of angel yet; / And if you smile upon the thing you hate, / 'Tis kinder to your enemies than friends." She accuses him of running from passionate love, and what he calls love — Platonic love, affection, friendship — does nothing to whet the flesh. She does not want his kindness or pity: "Less charity, my angel, might be more."[49] Davidman wants not Lewis's charity or pity; she wants the warmth and intimacy of his body.

Davidman introduces in Sonnet XIX the notion of a trinity — herself, Lewis, and Christ. However, the sonnet is not a spiritual acquiescence; that is, she does not just "leave it in God's hands." She admits she is in an odd mess: "Here are three pair of wings caught in one net; / Three sets of silken feathers, as the bird / Stoops to the fowler's lure, and most ill met; / My love and I, with Christ to make the third." Was there ever an odder trinity? "And one of us has mud-bedabbled wings, / And one of us has wings washed clean as sun; / And one of us planned this and other things / Before the howling planets were begun." What a threesome! "Here are three unlikely birds indeed! / A jackdaw[50] in a peacock company / I strut, until they peck me and I bleed, / Since I am black and they are bright to see." It is as if she is a rook caught between an eagle and a phoenix. Still, even though she is the "odd man out," her heart burns brightly with love, for both Lewis and Christ: "Yet I've a fire at heart shall make me shine / Fit for my human love — or my divine."[51]

Despite the somewhat upbeat ending of Sonnet XIX, in Sonnet XX Davidman revisits desperation and bitterness, and recalls Lewis's penchant for blondes first mentioned in Sonnet XII. It appears she has confronted Lewis about her need for more than *agape* or affection:

---

the term metaphorically, suggesting that her romantic relationship has gone through the equivalent of a killing winter.

49. This sonnet is dated February 23, 1954.

50. The common name of the daw, a small crow that frequents old buildings and church towers; it is easily tamed and taught to imitate the sound of words.

51. I date this sonnet as sometime in 1954 or 1955.

My love, who does not love me but is kind,
Lately apologized for lack of love,
Praising the fire and glitter of my mind,
The valour of my heart, and speaking of
Affection, admiration, bitter scraps
Men fling the begging woman at the door.

She goes on to suggest that Lewis says he cannot love her the way she wants, that he even thinks it is a compliment when "he said that I had beauty of a sort / Might do for other men, but not for him." But what really cuts her heart is when she realizes that he rejects her "not for love of God, but love of blondes!"[52]

Her frustrations with Lewis's lack of response to her physical desires becomes increasingly intense in Sonnet XXI. Her rhetoric heightens so that she claims she used to be a woman until his rejection gutted her. She compares Lewis to a butcher who hangs a lamb's carcass in the shop window, cutting off a piece at a time for any passerby. She asserts he has done the same thing to her; she is a dead carcass feasted on by a fire bird, fit for neither offal pile nor graveyard. While she should hate him, she does not; she remains a helpless woman in love: "And yet the horror is a woman still; / It grieves because it cannot stroke your hair." Her anger, frustration, and bitterness easily give way to her powerful feelings for Lewis.[53] However, her anger with Lewis is ameliorated in Sonnet XXII: "It is not his fault he does not love me; / It is not his fault he does not know / Any anesthetic word to give me / When the devil makes him tell me so." But neither can she help loving him. If only "I had / Brighter-coloured eyes and paler hair, / I might, it seems, be turned to gold and glad / By the same luck that leads me to despair." Who should she blame then? If it is God Lewis wants, so be it. She, on the other hand, stands stricken, numb, and mute. And for that she "shall not pardon God."[54]

God also becomes the focus of Sonnet XXIII as Davidman complains to him about her state: "Lord, when you laid your treasure on my back / To carry for myself, you did not say / What pricks and thorns set thick along the way / Would scratch the heart out of me." She also blames God for not telling her that winning Lewis's love would involve suffering, that it would be an uphill

---

52. This sonnet is dated January 22, 1954. Another draft is titled "Gentlemen Prefer . . ."

53. I date this sonnet as sometime in 1938.

54. I date this sonnet as sometime in 1954 or 1955. Another draft is titled "The Problem of Pain."

climb, that the stars would look on coldly and dispassionately, that the daylight would sear her eyes, and that everyone watching would blink her into invisibility. What God calls a treasure — suffering — she calls a burden, and it is one she cannot bear: "Lord, you must take your treasure back again; / A precious gift, and I shall mourn its loss; / But only You have strength to bear the Cross."[55]

The pains of unrequited love give way at the beginning of Sonnet XXIV to the joy of her memories of first loving Lewis: "When I first loved you, daylight sang and blazed / With angels; the incarnate miracle / Rang in my heart like ocean in a shell, / The sky was loud with God." Stunned by such delight, she felt compelled to write poems about it, giving expression to the only real talent she has. So she wrote sonnet after sonnet, believing she was pleasing both God and Lewis. Her sonnets, she admits, were weak, shrill, pathetic whimperings. But when Lewis found out about them, he was appalled and ordered her to stop: "You heard, and trod / That crying down, and taught me to forsake Him. / Love, you have sent me back to my own place, / A silence where there is not even God." In effect, if she cannot write her sonnets, she is bereft of both God and Lewis. She is left alone in the hollow, silent cell of her soul.[56]

Sonnet XXV revisits the self-loathing and self-recrimination of Sonnet XV. She resolves that because Lewis will never love her, she should stop her pathetic complaining: "He is gone; / You will not have him back for all your weeping. / The man is not for you." He was never meant for her, and it does not matter if she lies awake all night in silent agony or whether she cries her eyes out. In fact, when she weeps, Lewis just prays harder for her. It would not matter if she could break the bars of hell and ascend the walls of heaven, because "you should not have him." He doesn't want her: "He is God's lover not yours, and he is fled / Beyond the ultimate stars." She imagines Lewis with God, probably praying for her in his prayer closet. For a moment she resolves to leave him alone: "In God's name, leave him / To Christ, to angels, to the risen dead." But this is just a brief instance of clear-eyed sanity: "No, follow. Some day he may need to use / The tatters of your soul to wipe his shoes."[57]

---

55. This sonnet is dated January 22, 1954. Another draft is titled "Backslider."

56. This sonnet is dated February 16, 1954. Another draft is titled "The Sweet Cheat Gone."

57. This sonnet is dated February 2, 1954. Another draft is titled "Ich Grolle Nicht" (German for "I bear no grudge" or "I do not chide"). Drawn from the well-known sixteen-song cycle of Robert Schumann, *A Poet's Love* (1840), Davidman's title "Ich Grolle Nicht" is from the seventh song in the cycle; the texts for the sixteen-song cycle are from the *Lyrisches Intermezzo* (1822-23) of Heinrich Heine.

Davidman muses in Sonnet XXVI about how her poems may profit someone else in the future. In writing her sonnets she compares herself to a miner digging out precious ore. Miners, like her, have problems; they have smashed fingers and are waist deep in water that pushes the ore further and further away. As time ticks by, the miners slip toward death — the gold just barely out of reach. It is the same when she thinks about Lewis, her precious ore, and remembers their walks in the autumn gold: "So I / Store my memories of you. The gold, / The sweet, the dreadful; how I took your arm / And climbed a hill of bracken all aflame / With sunset lights." Accordingly, she hopes her sonnets might assist another woman in the future: "Some woman who is cold / In bed may use my words to keep her warm / Some future night, and recall my name."[58]

Frustration and bitterness appear again in Sonnet XXVII, recalling the angst of Sonnet XXI. Davidman posits that a torturer could hardly have been more cruel to her than Lewis; indeed, she says Lewis should have stripped her soul to pay off debts, have thrown her into a fire to keep him warm, have drunk her blood for wine, have eaten her flesh for food, or have shattered her fingers for pegs. Or he could have sired his children of lust on her. Instead, he kills her with kindness:

> Instead you put my hunger on a ration
> Of charitable words, and bade me live
> On air, and wear a mask of smiles to dress
> The bare indecency of desolation;
> You asked for nothing, you would only give.
> Dear cruelty, you should have wanted less.

The ending implies that although Lewis always says he wants nothing, that all he wants is to help her, by keeping her at arm's length he is most cruel and unfeeling.[59]

For the first time in the sequence, Sonnet XXVIII intimates that Davidman has awakened Lewis's feelings: "O I did wrong to wake you from that sleep / Whose splendour glimmered on your eyelids; wrong / To thrust between you and the airy shapes / That fill your dreams with rainbows." He

---

58. This sonnet is dated January 31, 1954. Another draft is titled "Powerful Rhyme," and the original title, "Aere Perennius" ("more lasting than bronze," which comes from the third book of Horace's *Odes*), has been struck through.

59. This sonnet is dated February 18, 1954.

has been living in realms untouched by passion, unlike her world that is "a tangled web of sins and groans." Yet she dreamed that while he was sleeping he "turned in sleep and cried my name / To be a playmate for you in a land / Too lovely and too lonely for most men." But then she cursed herself: "I woke you to my disillusion. Blame / The credulous heart that must misunderstand; / For I did wrong. Sleep, sleep, and dream again." She was wrong to awaken his feelings, so she tells him to close his eyes to passion and to dream of his passionless days of old.[60]

I judge Sonnet XXIX to be the most moving, tender, and poignant of the entire sequence. Rather than engaging in more rhetoric or further expressing her desperation and frustration with Lewis, Davidman develops a powerful conceit that gives voice to all her feelings:

> There was a man who found a naked tree
> Sleeping in winter woods, and brought her home,
> And tended her a month in charity
> Until she woke, and filled his quiet room
>
> With petals like a storm of silver light,
> Bursting, blazing, blended all of pearl
> And moonshine.

Imagining herself as the tree and Lewis as the gardener, Davidman suggests that in his attentions to her, Lewis caused her to blossom with love. Moreover, "he, in wonder and delight, / Patted her magic boughs and said: Good girl." Predictably, the tree, excited to have pleased the gardener, did more than just bloom:

> Thereafter, still obedient to the summer,
> The tree worked at her trade, until behold
> A summer miracle of red and gold,
> Apples of the Hesperides upon her,
> Sweeter than Eden and its vanished bowers . . .
> He said: No, no, I only wanted flowers.

In rejecting her love, Lewis is like a gardener who chastens a tree for producing fruit from its blossoms. Such chastening goes against the very reason the

---

60. This sonnet is dated February 18, 1954.

blossoms opened in the first place, and by implication Lewis is unfeeling in trying to suppress her love for him.[61]

Davidman again addresses God in Sonnet XXX, this time comparing herself to one of the thieves crucified next to Christ: "Talking to you as one crucified thief / To another; Lord, will you not tell me why / You have spread-eagled me on a black sky, / Nailed through my fingerbones with nails of grief / Forever?" She wonders "what are you buying with my pain?" Is some future good going to come out of her agony, are the nails through her hands going to purchase relief for someone else, or will some other poor soul be saved by her suffering? If that is the case, then all right; you are, after all, God: "You are welcome to all you rob me of; / You may filch the lot and be forgiven, / Blood and breath and laughter, tears and love." But she does make a simple request: "Only this one prayer; do not let me die / An idiot sacrifice, not knowing why!"[62]

Sonnet XXXI does not provide an answer to the conclusion of Sonnet XXX. Instead, Davidman shares a message she has heard from God: a warning against her physical pursuit of Lewis: "The God I worshipped said: Woman, no tricks. / Such magic as you have of lip and eye / And fingers straying on a sleeve, and sly / Caressing words, forbear. You must not vex / My prophet at his prayers." Denied the use of her smiles, fetching eyes, wandering fingers, or flirtatious words, she is cornered into replying: "I will try." On top of this pain and before she can catch her breath, she imagines Lewis "like a drunken sailor / Choosing in a brothel from a crowd / Of whores" saying: "What, little Brownie, there? Not half! / I'll have a blonde or nothing!" But even more pain follows as the final insult is her sense that even God is amused by her suffering: "And far away within an evil cloud / I heard the thing that I had worshipped laugh."[63]

In Sonnet XXXII Davidman returns to the subject of Sonnet XXVIII — that she has awakened Lewis's feelings for her. The opening lines allude mockingly to Matthew 4:18-20: "Has He made you a fisher of women, then? / Was it He who taught you how to bait / The hook you caught me through the heart with?" Unknowingly — at least at first, she implies — Lewis had hooked her, drawing her to him like a fish on a line. But of course she was a willing catch. Perhaps it was wrong, she suggests, for the two of them to angle for the other

---

61. I date this sonnet as sometime in 1954 or 1955.

62. This sonnet is dated March 1, 1954.

63. This sonnet is dated May 9, 1954; this is the latest date Davidman assigns to any of the sonnets.

in life's choppy seas: "My friend, if it was sin in you and me / That we went fishing for each other in / The troubled waters of life, let honesty / Compel ourselves to carry such a sin." Surprisingly, and against all that has compelled her up to this point in the sequence, Davidman suggests that they should check their growing feelings for each other; not to do so would compromise Lewis's role as a spiritual mentor to many and bring dishonor to God: "And let us not, with self-deceiving lies, / Kiss and betray Him to His enemies."[64]

Such caution is rejected in Sonnet XXXIII as Davidman returns to desperation and bitterness. This time lashing out at God, she addresses Lewis: "Forgive me that I turn my bitter tongue / Against you sometimes. None of them are true, / The harsh and jagged words. If there was wrong, / It was done by God and not by you." In a metaphor Lewis later adopted in *A Grief Observed*, she posits God as a vivisector: "He used you for His knife. Since I am dying / Of His long vivisection, need you wonder / If I cannot forbear a moment's crying / Against the steel that saws my throat asunder?" Lewis is only God's dagger, dissecting her like a rat in a laboratory. Lewis should not blame himself if she loves him to distraction; it is God's fault: "Blame Him who let [the world] be so badly made / That I, because I love you, must be hurled / To bloody ruin by your helping arm; / I know you never meant me any harm; / And yet, I know that I have been betrayed." God, not Lewis, has deceived and tricked her.[65]

But no, Davidman says in Sonnet XXXIV, neither God nor Lewis is to blame for her anguish. The blame falls fully on her: "No, it was neither you nor God, but I / Whose nature drove the dagger in my side / So deadly near my heart; if I should die / Of loving you, call it a suicide." Could she have acted differently? She is not sure, but she knows she would not have loved Lewis any differently than she has. Her rage is not against God or Lewis or even herself. And she resolves to go forward, introducing for the first time in the sequence the love and care she has for her two sons, David and Douglas: "Only, when I see my children sleeping, / I think I have a task to keep alive for; / But they and I must take our chance on God. / Let it be as He wills, and no more weeping."[66] Davidman's honest confession and open admission of her struggles with God, Lewis, and herself mark this as one of the most moving sonnets in the sequence.

Sonnet XXXV is another poem exploring Lewis's now awakened feelings

---

64. I date this sonnet as sometime in 1954 or 1955.
65. I date this sonnet as sometime in 1954 or 1955.
66. This sonnet is dated March 10, 1954.

for Davidman. She teases Lewis, mocking his thoughts that he could rely solely on the love of God, noting as well that he has failed to account for feelings and emotions, especially those in a woman like her. Even though he sees his mistake and tries to back off, it is not that easy: "No good to cross yourself, no help to run, / No use to mumble prayers beside your bed." Now he is "haunted by a woman-skeleton / With pits of grief for eyes, nodding its head / And clicking comments bitter as a bone." The final line is one of pity: "Child, it is dangerous to raise the dead." She chides Lewis's naiveté, and her introduction of Lewis's childlikeness forms a bridge to the next sonnet.[67]

Lewis's incredible innocence concerning the nature of romantic love is the focus of Sonnet XXXVI: "The monstrous glaciers of your innocence / Are more than I can climb; I might have braved / Platoons of dragons, or a fiery fence, / But walls of ice defeat me." Indeed, she says, it is his childlike innocence — not his sexual purity — that thwarts her: "Being saved / More by childishness than chastity." Surely, she reminds him, hell is thought by some to be a lake of ice. Then, in lines recalling John Donne's elegy "Going to Bed," she makes a sardonic inside joke:

> O my Antarctica, my new-found land
> Of woman-killing frost! but could I dare
> More than the least touch of a casual hand;
> Could I but come upon you in your bed
> And kiss you at my leisure — why, my lad,
> You might forget the colour of my hair.

Her reference to Lewis's "cold" responses to her desires for emotional and physical intimacy alludes to lines in Donne's elegy.[68] Jack, she says, you are my Antarctica, my Newfoundland, my continent of ice! If only I could come to you at night, slip into your bed, and press my lips to you! Then, I believe, you'd no longer care that I am a brunette.[69]

Davidman wishes she could reverse gender roles with Lewis in Sonnet XXXVII so that she might unthaw him: "I wish you were the woman, I the man; / I'd get you over your sweet shudderings / In two such heartbeats as the cuckoo sings / His grace-notes in!" However, since such a switch is not

---

67. This sonnet is dated May 9, 1954, the latest date Davidman assigns to any of the sonnets.

68. For more on this, see the discussion below.

69. This sonnet is dated May 9, 1954.

possible, "I play the games I can / With eye and smile." He thinks his scruples make him virtuous. Perhaps, she says:

> Call it your virtue if you like; but love
> Once consummated, we recover from;
> Not so, love starved forever. Thus you have,
> With this device of coldness, made me tame;
> Your whipped adoring bitch, your tethered slave
> Led on the twin leashes of desire and shame.[70]

Love, she argues, sustains, nourishes, and redeems. Thwarted love, on the other hand, damns — it festers, rots, and decays. Thus, Lewis's icy mountain freezes her out, leaving her a fawning dog, a pathetic bitch held in check by chains of passion and humiliation.

Building on the pathos of this sonnet, Sonnet XXXVIII takes the argument one step further. Invoking again the idea first explored in Sonnet X of Lewis being an idol, she acknowledges that heaven is embarrassed by her worship of him: "Yes, I know: the angels disapprove / The way I look at you. Creation weeps, / Observing how my naughty finger creeps / Along your sleeve." She admits that even Satan will not waste his time on her ill-fated desire for Lewis. Nonetheless, she says, a recent incident sustains her now:

> But one day, riding on the upper deck
> Of a large, red, respectable Oxford bus
> You in the seat in front, and I behind
> Coveting the back of your nice neck
> Where your hair curls — why, I might lean and kiss;
> Somehow I do not think that God would mind.[71]

Davidman simply cannot lessen her feelings for Lewis; it is not going too far to claim here that she is lusting after him, while trying to believe at the same time that God would not condemn her longings.

Lust gives way to a desire for physical intimacy in Sonnet XXXIX. Davidman makes an impassioned personal appeal to Lewis, stripping herself and opening herself to Lewis's pity: "Do not be angry that I am a woman / And so have lips that want your kiss, and breasts / That want your fingers

---

70. This sonnet is dated May 9, 1954.
71. I date this sonnet as sometime in 1954 or 1955.

on them; being human / I need a heart on which my heart can rest." Such desires, she argues, are only natural: "Do not be angry that I cry your name / At the harsh night, or wear the darkness through / With blind arms groping for you in a dream; / I was made flesh for this, and so were you." Blame God, not her, for her desires, since she has spent the last three years of her life bloodying her fists against the iron door of Lewis's resistance. Those same bruised and bleeding hands "could still caress / The naked body of love with ecstasy, / And might have ways to teach you tenderness / More than you have learned from all your prayers."[72]

Sonnets XXXIX and XL combine as the climactic poems of the sequence. Davidman adopts the metaphorical approach she first used in Sonnet XXIX, but here she is not a naked tree; instead, her sonnets are lilies beckoning Lewis to love her: "I brought lilies in my hands, tigerspotted, / Bloodthroated lilies, coloured with gold and death, / Stained with the opal world, veined and netted / With patterned pride. I waited, holding my breath." But Lewis "would not have them." Next she tries to sanctify the sonnets: "Then I dipped my lilies / In vats of purity, freezing them to crystal / Lightbearers, chalices of morning chill, / Mystery silver as dew on every petal." Still, Lewis "would not have them." Enraged, she tells herself bitterly:

> Down, you lilies, down,
> Let hellmouth eat your beauty. Woman, take
> Two nails instead and hammer for his sake
> The spikes where they should go, till there has grown
> Within each empty hand a brilliant rose
> Of sacrificial blood. He might have those.[73]

What more can she do to win Lewis's love? Lewis's rejection of her is a cruelty, and self-crucifixion is one possible response. This is the moment of highest tension in the sequence; she has finally spent herself and can no longer generate the energy necessary to try to win Lewis's heart.

Accordingly, Sonnet XLI is a quiet reflection in which Davidman essentially says: OK. It is over. I have done all I can to win his love, and I will find consolation in friendship: "Love me or love me not; nevertheless autumn / Scatters bright bonfires of leaves upon the ground, / Patterns with swirls of leaves the river water; / We shall find horse-chestnuts, bright and

---

72. I date this sonnet as sometime in 1954 or 1955.
73. This sonnet is dated March 30, 1954. Another draft is titled "Flower Piece."

brown, / The right shape for your fingers and mine." She is resolved to live on, drawing strength from long autumn walks by the Cherwell when the two of them will gather chestnuts together. She knows he cannot love her the way she wants: "You cannot / Love me at all, but there will be spring days / Striped with cloud and daffodil like banners; / We'll drink our beer among anemones / Another time, perhaps." She finds solace in the prospect of such a relationship:

> And I shall call
> The laughter that lies sleeping in your voice
> To wake, or finish poems when you begin them;
> The sterile years have starry moments in them.
> Love me or love me not, the leaves will fall,
> And we shall walk them down. I have my joys.

Mere friendship is not really what she wants, but it is something. One way or the other, time will press forward, and at least she will be by his side. Although she says friendship is its own kind of joy, her words are more a sigh than an affirmation.[74]

Sonnet XLII is another reflection, this time a tender one upon all that she finds precious in Lewis: "You are all the gold of all the rocks / Precious in my fingers; brighter things, / Lucid gold, netted in a brook, / Of the rising sun." Moreover, he is a songbird, a flame, a constellation, a sunrise, God's sweet laughter, and a summer's thunderstorm. Yet she knows she is punishing herself when she celebrates Lewis in these ways since she will never have him in the way for which her heart longs. Still, "now and then, / By God's grace, I am given a moment when / The shadow of pain is lifted from my eyes / And I rejoice to see how gold you are."[75] There are moments when God gives her great peace, lifts her suffering, and allows her to see how precious Lewis truly is, taking away her greedy, selfish, self-seeking heart.

The penultimate sonnet, XLIII, continues Davidman's reflections as she frankly admits she has been foolish in pursuing Lewis: "What a fool I was to play the mouse / And squeak for mercy! What had you to give / So small a creature when it wanted love?" Lewis, she muses, could never have given her what she needed. He is a lion to her mouse; nonetheless, he has drawn her to him. So she curses statues of kings, giving vent to her disappointment,

---

74. This sonnet is dated May 1954.
75. This sonnet is dated May 1954.

and wraps herself in courage: "Now I snarl at bearded kings / Upon Assyrian friezes, prop the doors / Of Agamemnon's town, provide a skin / That Hercules can wrap his valour in." So she claims the lioness in her roars to the lion in him: "Wake up and take the sun! His golden paws / Itch like mine to play with you. 'Ware claws!"[76]

In Sonnet XLIV Davidman concludes the sequence with quiet acquiescence:

> Now, having said the words that can be said,
> Having set down for any man to see
> My blood and body in plain poetry;
> Having displayed my sickness; brought to bed
>
> Publicly; what advantage shall I have
> To be thus naked to the questioner?
> How shall it serve, how shall it profit her
> Gaining the kingdom, locked outside your love?

Her sonnets are testimony to all she has had to say. She has opened her heart for all to see — particularly Lewis — yet what good has it done? She wonders if her sonnets have mattered at all to him. She does not care if she wins the world's acclaim if she does not win his heart. The final lines are an impassioned plea — not desperate or bitter, but wistful and winsome:

> Open your door, lest the belated heart
> Die in the bitter night; open your door,
> My lord. Admit the traveller to the fire.
> Here is the quiet light, the silent shore
> Beyond the foaming world; here is the chart
> Of the last journey, past the last desire.[77]

Analysis of the Sequence

The artistic merits of the sonnets are significant. Davidman displays an ease and facility with poetics, including the use of alliteration, anaphora, asso-

---

76. I date this sonnet as sometime in 1954 or 1955.

77. This sonnet is dated November 1939. Another draft is titled "Postscript."

nance, consonance, half-rhyme, caesura, and enjambment throughout the sequence. Many of the sonnets employ the standard rhyme scheme of the English sonnet — *ababcdcdefefgg* — but she also frequently varies the first eight lines as *abbacdde* and the last six lines as *efgefg, efeffe,* or *effegg.* On a few occasions she comes near to the rhyme scheme of the Italian sonnet — *abbaabbacdecde* — but her variations include, for example, *abbaabbacddcee, abbaaccadeffde,* and *abbacddceffeaa.* The sonnets also typically employ iambic pentameter or slight variations of that meter. Irony and self-deprecating wry humor are used to great effect. Structurally and rhetorically, the poems work on some occasions as three quatrains and a couplet, on other occasions as an octave and sestet, and not infrequently a combination of these as in two quatrains and a final sestet.

However, the chief artistic merit of the sonnets is the way Davidman weaves them together into a narrative, most often via the device of an imagined dramatic conversation. The influence of John Donne (1572-1631) at this point is apparent.[78] In his *Songs and Sonnets* (1635) he uses the dramatic persona to great effect, creating poems that verge on being dramatic monologues; moreover, often the focus of his poetry is sexual frustration, conquest, or intimacy. For instance, in "The Flea" Donne creates the oddest (and funniest) of conceits when his male persona tries to woo a woman into bed, suggesting that, since their two bloods are now mingling in the body of a flea that has bitten both, they are already "one" flesh: "This flea is you and I, and this / Our marriage bed and marriage temple is."[79] Although less subtle and more urgent than Donne in her wooing of Lewis, Davidman uses a similarly pleading tone in her Sonnet XXXIX:

Do not be angry that I am a woman
And so have lips that want your kiss, and breasts
That want your fingers on them; being human
I need a heart on which my heart can rest;

78. We should not be surprised to find Donne's influence on Davidman as she was deeply read in the poetry and prose of sixteenth- and seventeenth-century England. Her MA thesis at Columbia University gives evidence of this; "My Lord of Orrery" concerns the life and writings of the English Renaissance figure Roger Boyle, Lord Broghill, First Earl of Orrery (1621-1679). In addition, Davidman recommended to one correspondent that he read "as much as you can take" of Donne, listing him as one of the "indispensable" English poets (January 26, 1948; *Bone,* 68).

79. All quotations of Donne's poetry are taken from *The Complete Poetry of John Donne,* ed. John T. Shawcross (Garden City, NY: Anchor, 1967).

Do not be angry that I cry your name
At the harsh night, or wear the darkness through
With blind arms groping for you in a dream;
I was made flesh for this, and so were you. (*Naked Tree,* 304)

A more obvious example of Donne's influence occurs in Davidman's Sonnet XXXVI. There she complains that Lewis's sexual innocence (this is almost certainly hyperbole) is like a mountain of ice she cannot scale. This leads her to say:

O my Antarctica, my new-found land
Of woman-killing frost! but could I dare
More than the least touch of a casual hand;
Could I but come upon you in your bed
And kiss you at my leisure . . . (*Naked Tree,* 303)

In Donne's elegy "Going to Bed" a man urges his female companion to join him in bed as he delightedly watches her undress, at one point exclaiming: "License my roving hands, and let them go, / Behind, before, above, between, below. / O my America, my new-found-land, / My kingdome, safeliest when with one man man'd, / My Myne of precious stones." Assuming Lewis read Davidman's sonnet, I imagine he had an enormous laugh at this allusion.

Donne's greatest influence upon Davidman's sonnets, however, may be found in his own sonnet sequence, "Holy Sonnets."[80] Donne's persona is alternately angry, desperate, resolute, tentative, pleading, helpless, confident, fearful, complaining, burdened, and relieved — emotions displayed as well throughout Davidman's sequence. This is nowhere more evident than in the best-known of Donne's sonnets, "Batter My Heart," where the persona strips his soul bare before God. In the opening quatrain Donne's persona criticizes God for being too kindly, too gracious in dealing with his sin: "Batter my heart, three person'd God; for you / As yet but knocke, breathe, shine, and seeke to mend." Deeply cognizant of his sin, Donne's persona demands more of God: "That I may rise, and stand, o'erthrow mee, and bend / Your force, to breake, blowe, burn and make mee new." In the remainder of the poem he illustrates time and again how helpless he is in controlling the sin that binds

---

80. Donne wrote nineteen of these sonnets. While it is doubtful that he planned them consciously as a sequence, readers have long seen the many links and connections between them, especially the presence of a unifying dramatic persona.

him, thus ending with this hyperbole: "Take mee to you, imprison mee, for I / Except you enthrall mee, never shall be free, / Nor ever chast, except you ravish mee." The fact that Donne's persona demands that God spiritually rape him as the only means of overcoming his sin is offensive to some readers, but it captures masterfully the conflicting emotions within Donne's persona and underscores his own condition of near spiritual death.

Another example of Donne's intense introspection occurs in "I Am a Little World Made Cunningly." In this sonnet his persona muses on the mystery of the human condition, particularly our dual nature — part flesh and part spirit. Sin, however, triumphs over both parts and threatens damnation to the whole. He calls upon God to "power new seas in mine eyes, that so I might / Drowne my world with my weeping earnestly, / Or wash it if it must be drown'd no more." A similar desperation appears in "What If This Present Were the World's Last Night?" Here Donne's persona longs for his soul to "mark" his heart with the image of Christ crucified in the hope that this picture will bring him spiritual strength and solace. In almost every one of Donne's "Holy Sonnets" we find an intense personality focusing upon itself with deep and profound introspection; this is the picture of a soul on the edge of a precipice, teetering on the edge of emotional breakdown, sliding off a ledge into despair.

Even a cursory review of Davidman's sonnets to Lewis reveals a similarly self-absorbed persona. For instance, Sonnet II is a bald admission that while she was making love to one man, all the time she was thinking of another man:

> Having loved my love tonight with you between,
> My lord, I pray you of your courtesy
> That I may give as much as he gives me;
> Lie mouth to mouth, skin upon naked skin. (*Naked Tree*, 283)

In Sonnet XIII she focuses upon the pain of unrequited love:

> I said it did not hurt. My lord, I lied;
> Painted my mouth into a smiling shape
> Before the mirror, taught my heart to ape
> Happiness; wore the dagger in my side
> As if it were a jewel. (*Naked Tree*, 290)

In Sonnet XV her self-recriminations are poignant:

> Is it not enough, insatiate heart,
> That a most silver and miraculous horn
> Stabbed you once with splendor, struck apart
> Your ironbound defenses, and made glad
> The outward thrust and rush of your freed blood?
> . . . .
> Must you try to trap him in your bed,
> A fire and valour to appease the lust
> Of your cold empty arms? and yet you must. (*Naked Tree,* 291)

A final example comes from Sonnet XXVII:

> Dear cruelty, you should have wanted more;
> You should have cut me into scraps of gold
> To pay your taxes with, or burnt me for
> A bonfire to defend you from the cold;
> . . . .
> Instead you put my hunger on a ration
> Of charitable words, and bade me live
> On air, and wear a mask of smiles to dress
> The bare indecency of desolation;
> You asked for nothing, you would only give.
> Dear cruelty, you should have wanted less. (*Naked Tree,* 298)

As these few excerpts illustrate, the central, unifying device of Davidman's sonnet sequence to Lewis is its arresting, provocative, and sharply penetrating voice, and one reminiscent of Donne's.

There are multiple lines of biographical inquiry suggested by the sonnets — so many so that they are beyond the scope of this study. Accordingly, in what follows I offer exploratory, not exhaustive, comments.

Numerous questions are raised by the sonnets. The most fascinating ones concern whether or not Lewis ever read the sonnets. If so, when did he read them? That is, what evidence suggests that he did? I speculate that he probably did read the sonnets, perhaps sometime after May 9, 1954, since this is the latest date we have for the writing of any of the sonnets (XXXI and XXXV). The strongest internal evidence for his having read the sonnets (or at least some portion of them) comes in the prefatory sonnet ("Here are some sonnets you may care to read"; *Naked Tree,* 283) and in Sonnet XXIV (I "learned what I must do / With my one talent that had gone to waste, /

Unwanted gold. I spent my love at last, / Brought it to God in bringing it to you"; *Naked Tree,* 296). Other sonnets offer less compelling evidence, but are suggestive. For example, Sonnet XIV says:

When I have said all the words, what shall I do?
When all the rhymes are paired and I have sung
Whatever tunes are nested in my tongue,
And have made all the promises, false and true — ... (*Naked Tree,* 290)

In addition, if we read the "Apples of the Hesperides" produced by the naked tree in Sonnet XXIX as her sonnets, it makes the poem's ending — "He said: No, no, I only wanted flowers" (*Naked Tree,* 299) — consistent with Lewis's rejection of her sonnets noted in Sonnet XXIV.[81] We could apply a similar metaphorical reading to Sonnet XL:

I brought lilies in my hands, tigerspotted,
Bloodthroated lilies, colored with gold and death,
Stained with the opal world, veined and netted
With patterned pride. I waited, holding my breath.
He would not have them. (*Naked Tree,* 305)

That is, the lilies could be metaphors describing her sonnets.[82] A final piece of evidence occurs in the last sonnet in the sequence, XLIV:

Now, having said the words that can be said,
Having set down for any man to see
My blood and body in plain poetry;
Having displayed my sickness; brought to bed
Publicly; what advantage shall I have
To be thus naked to the questioner? (*Naked Tree,* 307)

This internal evidence, while not insignificant, must be viewed as limited and insular. So, is there any external evidence that Lewis read the sonnet sequence? His letters do not provide direct evidence, although scholars may want to reread them with an eye to possible allusions to Davidman's poetry. Here I

---

81. Of course the "Apples" here could refer to her passionate love for him as opposed to the "flowers" of her friendship love.
82. Or the lilies could refer to her passionate love.

advance three possible pieces of external evidence, all linked to Lewis's *A Grief Observed*. The first, and I offer this quite tentatively, occurs in Sonnet II, where Davidman writes about having sex with one man (almost certainly her husband, Bill Gresham) while thinking of another man (almost certainly Lewis):

> Because you have my heart, he has my bed,
> And let him have it then conditionless
> With all my heart; nor ever let him guess
> How I, staring above his quiet head,
>
> Knew, in the lonely midnight afterward,
> The terrible third between us like a sword. (*Naked Tree,* 283)

Her use of the word "sword" in the sonnet calls to mind what Lewis says about Davidman in *A Grief Observed:* "[She] was a splendid thing; a soul straight, bright, and tempered like a sword."[83] Later he adds: " 'She's in God's hand.' That gains a new energy when I think of her as a sword. Perhaps the earthly life I shared with her was only part of the tempering. Now perhaps He grasps the hilt; weighs the new weapon; makes lightnings with it in the air. 'A right Jerusalem blade' " (*Grief,* 50). That fact that Davidman and Lewis use the same metaphor — describing the other as a sword — may be coincidental. But perhaps not. Perhaps Lewis selected the metaphor because he recalled how Davidman had once applied it to him.[84]

---

83. *A Grief Observed* (London: Faber and Faber, 1961), 35; hereafter *Grief,* with subsequent references in the text.

84. Moreover, Lewis may at some point have read Davidman's "A Sword Named Joy" (*Naked Tree,* 273). Douglas Gresham writes of "a soapstone-handled Arabian dagger which Mother had bought for Jack as a present and Jack had passed on to me after Mother's death" (*Lenten Lands: My Childhood with Joy Davidman and C. S. Lewis* [New York: Macmillan, 1988], 212). Almost certainly this is the "sword" she refers to in her poem. Davidman dates the poem as February 23, 1953:

> If you love me as I love you,
> No knife can cut our love in two!
>
> On Christmas Day I gave my lord
> An old and wicked Persian sword
> To cut his finger on; and he
> Did cut it most obligingly,
> But would not let me kiss it well.
> On Christmas morning it befell,
> And all the bells of Oxford then

My second example is perhaps stronger. In Sonnet XXXIII Davidman refers to God as a vivisector:

> Forgive me that I turn my bitter tongue
> Against you sometimes. None of them are true,
> The harsh and jagged words. If there was wrong,
> It was done by God and not by you;
> He used you for His knife. Since I am dying
> Of His long vivisection, need you wonder
> If I cannot forbear a moment's crying
> Against the steel that saws my throat asunder? (*Naked Tree*, 301)

She suggests that she is dying because of God's long vivisection of her. Readers familiar with *A Grief Observed* will recall how many times Lewis uses exactly the same idea to describe his view of God as he struggles with his grief. For instance, he says: "I am more afraid that we are really rats in a trap. Or, worse still, rats in a laboratory. . . . Supposing the truth were 'God always vivisects'?" (26). In another place he thinks: "But the real question is whether [God] is a vet or a vivisector. . . . And I can believe He is a vet when I think of my own suffering. It is harder when I think of hers" (34). While not conclusive, the fact that both use the same notion that God is a vivisector may offer external evidence that Lewis read the sonnet sequence.

The third piece of evidence I draw from *A Grief Observed* to support the argument that Lewis read Davidman's sonnet sequence and may have been influenced by it is, I believe, the most compelling: both works are intensely subjective and introspective, and in the case of Lewis this intensity

---

Were crying goodwill unto men!
O it was very bad indeed
To bring a gift that made him bleed,
It was unchristian and inhuman;
But still, the creature's name is woman —
A knife is a true lover's gift,
Old poets say; and so with thrift
She saved her pennies, had no rest,
Till she had found of knives the best,
Curved as sweetly as her breast.
And he has hung it on his wall,
And yet, he loves her not at all.

If you loved me as I love you,
No sword could separate us two!

is not something we find in his other books. We could select almost any of Davidman's sonnets as example. One will suffice. In Sonnet XXX she writes:

> Talking to you as one crucified thief
> To another; Lord, will you not tell me why
> You have spread-eagled me on a black sky,
> Nailed through my fingerbones with nails of grief
> Forever? What are you buying with my pain?
> Is it worth jewels, can you ransom souls
> With this poor coin of wounds, these bleeding holes
> Knocked in a human heart? (*Naked Tree,* 299-300)

Examples of Lewis's raw emotion in *A Grief Observed* are ubiquitous. Early in part one he writes: "Not that I am (I think) in much danger of ceasing to believe in God. The real danger is of coming to believe such dreadful things about Him. The conclusion I dread is not 'So there's no God after all,' but 'So this is what God's really like. Deceive yourself no longer'" (9-10). Later in the same section he notes: "Cancer, and cancer, and cancer. My mother, my father, my wife. I wonder who is next in the queue" (14). In part two he says with some bitterness: "Oh God, God, why did you take such trouble to force this creature out of its shell if it is now doomed to crawl back — to be sucked back — into it?" (18). Still later in this section he says:

> "Because she is in God's hands." But if so, she was in God's hands all the time, and I have seen what they did to her here. Do they suddenly become gentler to us the moment we are out of the body? And if so, why? If God's goodness is inconsistent with hurting us, then either God is not good or there is no God: for in the only life we know He hurts us beyond our worst fears and beyond all we can imagine. If it is consistent with hurting us, then He may hurt us after death as unendurably as before it. (24-25)

I need not provide additional examples. My point is that Lewis may have been profoundly influenced to write so personally and introspectively as a result of reading Davidman's sonnet sequence.[85] After all, Joy, he says, was "my pupil and my teacher" (*Grief,* 39). That she may have "taught" him how

---

85. Of course, Lewis was an extremely gifted writer and may have adopted the personal, introspective tone of *A Grief Observed* without reading the sonnet sequence. Losing Davidman may have been more than enough to lead him to write the way he does in *A Grief Observed.*

to write so personally is drawn out further in his poem "All This Is Flashy Rhetoric about Loving You":

> Only that now you have taught me (but how late) my lack.
> I see the chasm. And everything you are was making
> My heart into a bridge by which I might get back
> From exile, and grow man. And now the bridge is breaking.
> For this I bless you as the ruin falls. The pains
> You give me are more precious than all other gain.[86]

The marked contrast between the tone of *A Grief Observed* and almost everything else Lewis wrote has proved problematic. Certainly some readers have been so taken aback by *A Grief Observed* — particularly its pathological exploration of suffering, anguish, and faith — that they have posited various theories about the work, including that it is not autobiography but instead fiction.[87] The truth, however, may be as simple as Lewis following the lead of Davidman's love sonnet sequence.

If Lewis did read the sonnets, when did he read them? My best guess is that Davidman gave them to Lewis sometime as early as just prior to their civil marriage on April 23, 1956, or as late as sometime shortly after October 18, 1956, immediately after she was diagnosed with bone cancer.[88] In either case, reading the sonnets may have so moved Lewis's heart (and what man would not be both stricken and flattered by receiving such a testimony of love?) that it served as the catalyst transforming his feeling for Davidman from *agape* to *philia* and thence to *eros*. Moreover, as I suggested at the beginning of this discussion, Davidman constructed the sequence at least in part rhetorically, intent on persuading Lewis to love her the way she desired to be loved. If so, and if successful, the sonnet sequence helps to explain why Lewis married Davidman . . . twice.

---

86. *The Collected Poems of C. S. Lewis: Critical Edition,* ed. Don W. King (Kent, OH: Kent State University Press, 2015), 396.

87. See Mary Borhek, "*A Grief Observed:* Fact or Fiction?" *Mythlore* 16 (Summer 1990): 4-9, 26; George Musacchio, "C. S. Lewis' *A Grief Observed* as Fiction," *Mythlore* 12 (Spring 1986): 24-27; and Noelene Kidd, "*A Grief Observed:* Art, Apology, or Autobiography?" *The Canadian C. S. Lewis Society* 97 (Spring 2000): 4.

88. Doug Gresham suggests that if Lewis read the sonnets "I bet it was not until after they were married. Knowing Jack as Mother did (and I also did), she would have known that had he received them earlier, he would have taken off for the dark side of the moon rather than get involved" (email to the author, April 24, 2015).

Other lines of inquiry regarding the sonnet sequence (among many) include addressing the following questions: How might this sequence have impacted Lewis's writing of *Till We Have Faces, The Four Loves, Letters to Malcolm: Chiefly on Prayer,* and other late works? What are Lewis biographers going to make of the sequence? What are those who revere Lewis going to make of the sequence? What are those who dislike Lewis going to make of the sequence? What are Davidman biographers going to make of the sequence?[89] What are those who dislike Davidman going to make of the sequence? Without doubt the sequence illustrates the extent of Davidman's feelings for Lewis and reminds readers of earlier published poems that focus upon romantic love, particularly those appearing in *Letter to a Comrade.* For instance, in "Sorceress Eclogue" she says: "I shall kiss you with your mouth sticky with honey / your eyelids stuck together with sleep; / the summer shall enclose us in the heavy heat . . . / I shall put my hands over your hands / and feel the blood beginning in your arm / and run my hands over the hair on your arm" (*Naked Tree,* 130-31). "Il Pleure dans Mon Coeur" is equally sensual: "Only turn your lips to my lips and let your hair / lie in my hand or tangle in my hand, / and fall asleep, and let your body stand / between my sorrow and the weeping air" (*Naked Tree,* 123). A final example comes from "Night-Piece": "Keep warm, / My lover. Lie down lover. If there is peace / Arrested in any memorable fragment of time / I have shut you in with it and drawn circle" (*Naked Tree,* 117). The emotional intensity of Davidman's earlier love poems appears in pronounced and extended fashion in her love sonnet sequence to Lewis.

Joy Davidman was passionately attracted to C. S. Lewis. Sonnet XXIX gives perhaps the best expression of this where she describes herself as a naked tree in the middle of a frozen wood that is nurtured to life by Lewis's friendly attentions, kindnesses, and compassion; but at the end of the poem he finds he has gotten more than he bargained for:

There was a man who found a naked tree
Sleeping in winter woods, and brought her home,
And tended her a month in charity
Until she woke, and filled his quiet room

With petals like a storm of silver light,
Bursting, blazing, blended all of pearl

---

89. In her biography of Joy, Abigail Santamaria calls the sonnets "private poems" that Davidman wrote to console herself. See *Joy,* chs. 9-13.

And moonshine; he, in wonder and delight,
Patted her magic boughs and said: Good girl.

Thereafter, still obedient to the summer,
The tree worked at her trade, until behold
A summer miracle of red and gold,
Apples of the Hesperides upon her,
Sweeter than Eden and its vanished bowers . . .
He said: No, no, I only wanted flowers. (*Naked Tree,* 299)

If she wanted more than friendship, we can hardly blame her. Warren Lewis certainly did not: "In the summer of 1955 [Davidman] hired a house in Headington . . . and she and J[ack] began to see each other every day. It was now obvious what was going to happen."[90] And then, after their civil marriage, Warren adds: "Joy, whose intentions were obvious from the outset, soon began to press for her rights, pointing out with perfect truth that her reputation was suffering from J[ack]'s being in her house every day, often stopping until eleven at night." That Lewis himself was blind to what was happening is very doubtful. He may have resisted at first his own feelings as well as Davidman's advances. However, eventually, he relented, finally accepting fruit from the naked tree, the very fruit he had helped to nourish. Davidman's sequence of forty-five sonnets is a stunning testimony to this as well as to a woman who was both a gifted poet and a determined lover.

That she and Lewis eventually enjoyed the kind of love she longed for is hinted at in several letters. On February 13, 1957, Davidman wrote Chad and Eva Walsh from her bed in the Wingfield Hospital, Headington, where she was being treated for bone cancer: "I was very merry last weekend and Jack and I had a gay time in my room with lots of sherry and kisses. *What* a pity I didn't catch that man younger" (*Bone,* 307). On February 28, 1957, she writes Bill Gresham: "[We've been] wrong about the Englishman's supposed coldness. The truth about these blokes is that they are like H-bombs; it takes something like an ordinary atom bomb to *start* them off, but when they're started — Whee! See the pretty fireworks! He is mucho hombre, my Jack!" (*Bone,* 309). The intimacy Joy hints at in these letters was not limited to their physical and emotional relationship; as we will see in the next chapter, Joy also had a profound effect on Lewis as writer.

90. *Brothers and Friends: The Diaries of Major Warren Hamilton Lewis,* ed. Clyde S. Kilby and Marjorie Lamp Mead (San Francisco: Harper & Row, 1982), 245.

CHAPTER 9

Last Things (1954-1960)

Smoke on the Mountain was Davidman's last published work, but it did not mark her last efforts at writing. Her letters show that she produced a 25,000-word novella, *Britannia over Brooklyn,* and began work on two nonfiction pieces: a biography of Mme. de Maintenon (1635-1719), given the working title *Queen Cinderella,* and a theological treatise, *The Seven Deadly Virtues.* In addition, she assisted Warren Lewis in his research into seventeenth-century French history; typed manuscripts for other writers, including the detective novelist Kay Farrer; and wrote a handful of short stories. Perhaps most importantly, she had collaborative roles in several of C. S. Lewis's books written in the mid to late 1950s. All of Davidman's writings of this period were born from her desperate need for money. Bill Gresham was consistently late and short with the funds his divorce obligated him to send her, so Davidman was forced to try to earn a living by writing since as an American citizen she was severely restricted by British law from holding down a regular job. In this chapter I explore Davidman's last literary activities and offer a final assessment of her as a writer.

It appears Davidman may have been working on *Britannia over Brook-lyn* even before her move to England in 1953. She writes Bill on January 24, 1954: "I'm getting back to the typewriter myself. On rereading my Britannia story, I realize that it's far too compressed, ought to be a novelette; so I'm reworking it as a three-part serial, fifteen to twenty thousand [words] or so" (*Bone,* 172). As had been the case on several earlier occasions during their marriage, Davidman notes how she is drawing on Bill's collaborative influence: "My Britannia story progresses as well as the cold will let it. I've done about four thousand words so far and am just reaching the point where the original story began; you're quite right about milking the scenes — I keep remembering what you taught me about that as I go, and boy am I squeezing both emotion and suspense out of it now" (February 4, 1954; *Bone,* 174).[1] However, she confesses that her progress is halting: "Britannia progresses pretty well, but it's a new length for me and a lot of trial and error involved. I think it'll come out somewhere about 20,000 [words], but I may want to expand still further" (February 8, 1954; *Bone,* 177). Several weeks later the writing was going much better: "My Britannia story has grown into a young novel; 18,000 words on paper already, and about 5,000 to go. Boy, I'm pulling out all the stops on this one. I've even got a group of American prisoners, penned in the local church and told ironically to sing hymns, defiantly breaking into Yankee Doodle! . . . Corn, but marketable corn, I hope" (February 26, 1954; *Bone,* 181). By the middle of March 1954 she had finished the novella at 25,000 words and sent it off to her agent. Davidman had great hopes of earning some much-needed cash, but the book was never picked up by a publisher; she records its death on June 26, 1954: "I've just had a regretful note from [my agent] that Collier's has no room for Britannia" (*Bone,* 205).

A close reading of *Britannia over Brooklyn* reveals why the book was never published, and Davidman herself instinctively knew the reason: it was, as she had written Bill, "corn" — a formula-driven story with wooden characters, a tired plot, and a predictable ending. The heroine of the story, Britannia van Ryden, is the wife of Colonel Jan van Ryden, an officer in the army of George Washington. Britannia, who had lived much of her life as a gypsy, is cut from the same cloth as Chinya from "Apostate" and Anya: strong-willed, clever, rebellious, resourceful, restless, not easily managed, and passionate. When, after a defeat by the British, her husband makes a brief stop at their home in Long Island in order to burn papers incriminating local men loyal to Washington, Britannia's only concern is keeping him home, safe from the war. When van Ryden insists he must leave to lead the defense of the fort on the heights of Brooklyn, she is furious: "He must go wild himself, set up liberty poles and cry huzzah for General Washington and off to battle along with hotheads from the Massachusetts and Virginia colonies. I had liberty enough, till I met him. What is Jan van Ryden to me? The sudden rage brought her up short, her hands clenched, shivering. She

---

1. In a later letter she noted how important collaboration had been for the two of them: "Incidentally, I imagine that some of the trouble you're having in writing is the same as mine: the difficulty of breaking up a team. We were a good team; we each had what the other lacked, and I hated to dissolve it. A pity that your ego made you resent the collaboration so much" (June 26, 1954; *Bone,* 205).

growled once in her throat almost like a wild animal."[2] Still, her passionate
love for him tempers her anger: "For a moment they stood staring at each
other, their eyes full of the hunger and anger of love. A gray, aching light, the
dreary forerunner of dawn, had begun to filter through the curtains and add
a bleakness to the pale guttering candles. In a moment, Britannia thought,
he will have his arms around me, and then I shall be helpless as I always am,
I must let him do as he likes then."

After van Ryden leaves, the story moves quickly and predictably. A Brit-
ish officer arrives and is billeted in Britannia's home; during the evening she
flirts with him, gets him drunk, and elicits critical military intelligence from
him. Despite van Ryden's strict command that Britannia stay at home and
not get involved in the rebellion, the next morning she slips out of the house
and begins a quest to find him. Assuming a disguise from her gypsy past,
she hopes to move unnoticed but encounters a British patrol; many of the
men want to arrest her, but a kindly sergeant lets her go. Her next adventure
involves running into a gypsy clan; one of the young gypsy men falls in love
with her and threatens to carry her away until his mother prevents him.
After this she is arrested by a different British patrol and taken to the officer
in command — of course, it is the same officer that she had earlier billeted in
her home. He does not recognize her as Britannia, so he tries to seduce her;
using her wits, she plays along, but drugs the wine they are sharing and so
is able to make her escape. After several other scrapes — including injuring
her ankle — and helped by the young gypsy man, she finally hobbles her
way to van Ryden.

However, when she tries to tell him the military information she has
obtained, instead of being pleased to see her he is angry: "I mind you told
me my fortune, three years since, when the devil prompted me to come
back and steal you from your caravan to make you part of it. 'Twas a lying
fortune you told, Britannia my wife. Well, you have found the roads you
wanted, and a companion for them. Get out, in God's name! . . . Go off with
your naked gypsy, if he'll have you, and let me be!" Eventually van Ryden
learns the truth of his wife's heroic efforts to save him and his men, and all
is made well between them:

> They had only a moment or two for explanations and kisses then, for Jan
> had much to do. Stammered apologies from the man; forgiveness from

2. Two manuscripts of the novella are available in DP, Box 1, Series 5, Folders 45 and
46; all quotes from the novella are from Folder 45.

Britannia, who could understand far better than he knew what tricks fatigue and nerve-strain may play with one's fidelity; stammered gratitude, between quick keen questions. There were officers to hear Britannia's story, and rush off to wake up still senior officers; there was a camp to rouse, a regiment of Marblehead fishermen who must be set to row with muffled oars and get the little army across to New York before dawn.

The final lines of the story underscore its patent ending: "She was asleep; the man wrapped his coat about her. The moon had come into its own now; under that cool whiteness the boat drove westward, toward the dim New York shore and beyond it the unimaginable continent and the untraveled hills." Britannia, in the end, is a tame Chinya, a domesticated Anya, a marketable heroine; unfortunately for Davidman, she did not deliver a marketable book.

Concurrent with *Britannia over Brooklyn,* Davidman was working on *Queen Cinderella.* On February 19, 1954, she tells Bill: "As soon as I get Britannia off my neck (it's growing longer and longer, drat it) . . . Warnie [Warren Lewis] keeps suggesting that I collaborate with him on a life of Mm. de Maintenon, Louis XIV's morganatic wife" (*Bone,* 179).[3] On May 19, 1954, she adds:

> If I could get one good sale I'd tackle the biography of Mme. De Maintenon; Warnie's sent me a full outline of the lady's life complete with book and page references all the way, and *what* a life; born in the workhouse, mysterious childhood visit to America, married as a girl to brilliant paralyzed poet, widowed, gets to be governess to the king's bastards and next thing you know she's reformed the king and married him! Her hobby was a girl's school she founded and she used to pop out of the royal bed at dawn, tear off to the school, help get the children up and teach a few classes herself. Do I hear a movie sale? (*Bone,* 197)

Six months later Davidman was still doing research for the book, but apparently had not begun writing the manuscript: "I'm getting my teeth into *Queen Cinderella* — provisional title for my biography of Mme. de Maintenon; what do you think of it? Warnie's lent me some of his treasured books. There's miles of reading to do, but I think I ought to be able to sell it on an

---

3. Françoise d'Aubigné, Marquise de Maintenon, was the second wife and untitled queen of King Louis XIV of France. By all accounts she encouraged an atmosphere of dignity and piety at court, founding in 1686 an educational institution for poor girls at Saint-Cyr.

outline and a few specimen chapters; the story's sure-fire . . . [and] smells to me like a money-maker if I can get it done" (November 4, 1954; *Bone,* 224-25). For the next seven months Davidman worked on researching the book. She writes Bill on January 24, 1955, that she is "trying to work as fast as possible myself; my book looks like being a humdinger, and if I grind out a few chapters and an outline I ought to be able to sell it. But the research takes forever" (*Bone,* 236). Indeed, in many ways she was thwarted by the research the book required, complaining about it in many of her letters. Throughout the spring she continued to work steadily on the book, sending out a 5,000-word outline to several publishers. However, on July 11, 1955, she writes Bill with the bad news: "Macmillan, drat them, has turned down the synopsis of my *Queen Cinderella,* and so has H[odder] and S[toughton]. Looks as if I'll have to write it first" (*Bone,* 253).[4] Her last reference to the book is August 26, 1955 (*Bone,* 258), after which she effectively abandoned it.

About the time she gave up on it, she schemed up a more promising book, *The Seven Deadly Virtues.* The first mention of this book occurs in her letter to Bill of May 23, 1955: "Fortunately my publishers here are eager for my two new books (I dreamed up another religious one called *The Seven Deadly Virtues* half an hour before I had to talk to the publisher) and are talking about giving me a contract and advances on just outlines. I've got *SDV* outlined already, and am working on [*Queen Cinderella*]" (*Bone,* 248).[5] While her initial planning for the book was slapdash, she managed to get an advance for it, telling Bill on June 2, 1955: "Hodder and Stoughton here are going to take my *Seven Deadly Virtues* book and I'll get 100 pounds advance. Even minus agent's fees it'll be a big help — that is, if I can get the tax people to let me keep it!" (*Bone,* 251).[6] In her notes for *The Seven Deadly Virtues* (perhaps the very prospectus first given to her publisher), Davidman leaves a record of how the book might have developed:

> *The Seven Deadly Virtues* is planned as an attempt to rehabilitate virtue in the popular vocabulary; that is, to free the concept and the very word itself from the associations of drabness, dullness, triteness, harshness and above all sham which they have acquired. This can best be done, I think, by distinguishing between the real virtues, which lead to humility, happi-

4. Her outline of *Queen Cinderella* has not survived.

5. Davidman's notes for *The Seven Deadly Virtues* appear in DP, Box 1, Series 2, Folder 13. A draft of the prologue for this book appears in DP, Box 1, Series 5, Folder 67.

6. For a copy of her contract with Hodder and Stoughton, see DP Box 1, Series 3, Folder 17; for the royalty agreement, see DP Box 1, Series 3, Folder 19.

ness in love, from their Pharisaical or worldly counterfeits, which can only lead to pride, misery, and hate. My intention is to do this not by praising true virtue, which has become a dull and trite exercise, but by satirizing the false ones in such a way that the true will appear through contrast. Thus I intend to begin with an introductory fable describing a modern prig and Pharisee who dies and presents himself confidently at the door of Heaven. He lists all the ways in which he is "not as other men." . . . The seven following chapters begin with, as illustrations, instances of Mr. Pharisee's attempts to practice each virtue — very disastrous and self-righteous attempts. There follows an examination of all the various misinterpretations we usually make, turning justice into inflexibility, fortitude into insensibility, and so on. . . . Each chapter will end with a definition, through instances and analysis, of what *real* temperance, or *real* hope are like, and with some practical guides to learning them. The book concludes with a return to our Pharisee at the gates of Heaven, and a description of the judgment he receives and of the manner in which he takes it. His fate is not explicitly stated as a final damnation; it is suggested that he will repent in time.[7]

In many ways Davidman was planning to organize *The Seven Deadly Virtues* as she had done *Smoke on the Mountain,* especially by using an anecdote or fable to begin each chapter.

By July 1955, she had received a contract on the book from Hodder and Stoughton (*Bone,* 254).[8] However, work on the book did not go well. On October 10, 1955, she tells Bill: "I hate writing on theological subjects but it seems to be going all right, and Jack is being very helpful with it" (*Bone,* 262). Four months later she is even more distressed about her progress, confessing to Bill: "I'm having a hard time myself trying to write my *Seven Deadly Virtues* book, which I don't in the least feel like doing — how did I get into this theology racket anyway? The trouble is that while I like Christianity well enough, I hate Churchianity; as far as I can see, every organized church in the world ends either by missing the point and tangling itself in trivialities, or by contradicting the point altogether" (February 14, 1956; *Bone,* 278). On April 13, 1956, she intimates to Bill that Hodder and Stoughton were getting impatient with her lack of progress, especially since they had given her sev-

---

7. These notes are available in DP, Box 1, Series 2, Folder 13. In addition, see Box 1, Series 5, Folder 67 for a partial draft manuscript.

8. A copy of this contract dated July 18, 1955, is available in DP Box 1, Series 3, Folder 17.

eral advances: "None of Bernice's [her American agent's] frantic letters and cables ever reached me; God knows where they were sent. I know I gave Brandt this address a long while ago! My London agent finally told me she was trying to get me and I wrote to her. It's all about the *Deadlies,* which aren't finished yet on account of various troubles" (*Bone,* 285). Despite Lewis's help on the book, a signed contract, and several advances, by the end of summer 1956 Davidman essentially stopped work on the book.[9]

In addition to these three unrealized books, Davidman did smaller writing and editing jobs as a way to make ends meet. For example, in the case of Warren Lewis, she played a significant role helping him to edit and correct three of his books. On July 30, 1954, she tells Bill: "Incidentally, I've been reading copy on Warnie's new book for him (mostly for spelling — the Lewises have a family failing of being unable to remember when and where *i* comes before *e* or the reverse)" (*Bone,* 210-11). Regarding her help on this book, *The Sunset of the Splendid Century* (1955), in the foreword Warren Lewis thanks "my friend Joy Davidman for her great kindness in correcting the proofs."[10] He also credits her in the foreword to his *Assault on Olympus* (1958): "[Thanks] to Joy Davidman for her patient kindness in pruning the first draft and recommending certain excisions."[11] Davidman did even more on this book, writing Bill on March 16, 1955: "I finished the index of Warnie's new book for him — he's in a nursing home with fibrositis and flu — and his publisher was so pleased with the job I did on it that she asked if I would do indexes professionally and said she'd send me some now and then. They pay from 15 to 25 pounds apiece for them, and I can do one in a week or little

---

9. Notes for what appear to be two other books Davidman was thinking about at around this time have survived. *Bright Reason Will Mock Thee* (the title is drawn from Shelley's poem, "When the Lamp Is Shattered") would have explored the idea that "not by reason were we first persuaded, but by revelation . . . Revelation: the unanswerable Fact, the presence of God. Once experienced, how could it be questioned? Not that day, or that year. Revelation became the point of departure from which Reason must begin to work" (DP Box 1, Series 2, Folder 13). The other book, *Chosen for What? The Problem of the Christian Jew,* would have been a historical review of the "problems" facing the Jew converted to Christianity and then the posing of a possible "solution": "Reeducation of the Jew; recognition of the problem by the Gentile, and assistance, without *either* blind hostility or excessive encouragement. The Jew will only be free of his curse when he can recognize himself to be a miserable sinner like everyone else; instead of something special!" (DP Box 1, Series 5, Folder 49).

10. *The Sunset of the Splendid Century: The Life and Times of Louis Auguste de Bourbon Duc du Maine 1670-1736* (London: Eyre & Spottiswoode, 1955), 10.

11. *Assault on Olympus: The Rise of the House of Gramont between 1604 and 1678* (London: Andre Deutsch Ltd, 1958), 8.

more if I try; so it will be very worth while, if anything comes of it" (*Bone,* 241). Perhaps most poignantly, Warren Lewis dedicates his *The Scandalous Regent* (1961) to "My Sister-in-Law, Joy Davidman," and then adds in the foreword: "I have to acknowledge gratefully my indebtedness to my sister-in-law Joy Davidman for her kindness in reading my manuscript and for making many valuable suggestions."[12]

Davidman also did some typing for Kay Farrer (1911-1972), whose detective, Richard Ringwood, appears in her three novels, *The Missing Link* (1952), *The Cretan Counterfeit* (1954), and *Gownsman's Gallows* (1957). Farrer, one of only a few of Lewis's friends who had befriended Davidman, employed her to provide a complete typescript of *Gownsman's Gallows*. While thankful for the chance to earn some money, Davidman had a low opinion of the novel, writing Bill on May 2, 1956: "I'm nearly finished typing Kay Farrer's new detective story for a little extra money; painful job — she writes like an angel but plots like — well, I'm always remembering your contempt for the artificial whodunit with no knowledge of real crime and real police. Her detective is a Scotland Yard inspector; Scotland Yard oughta sue" (*Bone,* 288). In addition to this, Davidman continued to work on several short stories and nonfiction pieces, hoping to be able to sell them. One story that likely dates from this time is the unpublished "My Two Front Teeth (An Adventure in Socialized Medicine)."[13] This light-hearted, thinly veiled autobiographical story relates the challenges a Miss Jones faces in England after having landed with a mouth full of teeth needing drastic reconstruction. Although she initially resists "taking advantage" of the free dental care she can receive, her aching teeth drive her to see a dentist. However, her hopes are soon dampened by the innumerable forms she has to fill out as well as the arbitrary policies of the National Health

---

12. *The Scandalous Regent: A Life of Philippe, Duc d'Orleans 1674-1723 and His Family* (London: Andre Deutsch, 1961), 7.

13. DP Box 1, Series 5, Folder 60. Davidman suffered greatly with bad teeth, and her letter to Bill of February 4, 1954, details the genesis of "My Two Front Teeth":

> No more news except that I am going to the dentist (for free natch). The guy turned pale when he looked into my mouth and at once began worrying how much he dared stick the National Health Board for. It seems that to do me properly would cost about £45 even here ($150 with us) and daren't risk it for fear of questions in Parliament, or whatever; so he has applied for permission to do crowns and inlays, we'll wait till they call me up for examination, then they'll argue with him and grudgingly permit about half of what he asks, then he'll do the work, and then they'll probably reexamine me and object in triplicate. All of which no doubt will cost nearly as much as the work on the teeth. Socialism yet! When it's all over I plan an article called "My Two Front Teeth" about it. (*Bone,* 175)

Service: the dentist cannot give her crowns — what he wants to do — but instead, in order to follow the dictates of the health system, he must pull her bad teeth and give her dentures instead. The story ends with Miss Jones's parents in America wiring her enough money to go to a private dentist for the crowns instead. Thus the somewhat hackneyed final line of the story: "And that, my dears, is the story of how I got my two front teeth for Christmas."[14]

However, Davidman's most important literary endeavors during the last years of her life concern her collaborations with Lewis.[15] Almost from her first meeting with Lewis, the two of them were given to collaboration. As I noted in the last chapter, in her unpublished letters of October through December 1952 she mentions numerous occasions when she and Lewis were consulting on literary matters.[16] In her January 25, 1953, letter to Chad Walsh about her Christmas stay at the Kilns, she wrote: "[Lewis had] time to go over my own [*Smoke on the Mountain*] with me (about 50,000 words of it) and tell me how to fix it; he liked it quite well, thank heaven" (*Bone,* 138). Later in the letter she added:

> The OHEL volume[17] is going to make people sizzle; it's full of controversial stuff and reversals of conventional judgments. I am the *first* person to see those galleys, and I feel very honored. By the way, I also read a lot of Jack's poetry and I think you're wrong about it. It's quite new and strange and unfashionable, a complete break with the modern conventions of intellectual and bloodless verse, and for that reason rather difficult to appraise; but I thought a lot of it was damn good. Technically it's amazing. He's used very old forms and given them an entirely new twist. (He liked *my* poetry too — so there!) (*Bone,* 139)

This letter also refers to a memorable day-long walk that Davidman and the two Lewis brothers took: "Also there was a lot of walking and talking. One

---

14. For more on her dental problems, see her letters of April 2, 23, and 30, 1954; May 10 and 19, 1954; and June 26, 1954 (*Bone,* 186-88, 190-97).

15. Lewis scholar Diana Pavlac Glyer has written thoughtfully on Davidman's literary influence upon Lewis (and his brother, Warren) in her "Joy Davidman Lewis: Author, Editor, and Collaborator," *Mythlore* 22, no. 2 (Summer 1998): 10-17, 46; and *The Company They Keep: C. S. Lewis and J. R. R. Tolkien as Writers in Community* (Kent, OH: Kent State University Press, 2007). See both of these works for a more detailed discussion of the issues I raise here.

16. For one example, see her "Bread-and-Butter Sestina," *Naked Tree,* 268-69.

17. This refers to Lewis's *English Literature in the Sixteenth Century Excluding Drama.* For more on this, see above, pp. 164-65, note 8.

day the three of us were over Shotover to Horspath and then to Garsington, coming back by way of Wheatley (do you remember all those places?) and getting caught in a savage rain — I blistered my feet, and Jack and Warnie practically had to pull me up Shotover on the last stretch. But it was great fun" (*Bone*, 138-39). Her literary response to this was to compose the "Ballade of Blistered Feet."

> Morning a sparkle of blue
> And air that one breathed with a thrill;
> The world tasted fragrant and new
> When we climbed over Shotover hill.
> Swallows were merry and shrill;
> They cavorted all over the sky,
> And we had the whole day to kill,
> Jack and Warnie and I.
>
> We came to a pub that we knew,
> Whose sign was a queen in a frill,
> And somehow before we were through
> We drank rather more than our fill;
> It *was* a bit careless to spill
> Half of the beer in my eye;
> But we were too gay to sit still,
> Jack and Warnie and I.
>
> What started as delicate dew
> Grew up into rain, dank and chill;
> I got a small lake in my shoe,
> And all down my spine ran a rill;
> There we were, halfway to Brill,
> On ground that was naked and high —
> Wet enough to distill,
> Jack and Warnie and I!
>
> *Envoy*
> Ducks, I got home slightly ill
> And more than ready to die;
> But we'll do it again, so we will,
> Jack and Warnie and I! (*Naked Tree*, 267-68)

Eventually a kind of writers' conclave developed at the Kilns. For instance, on March 23, 1955, Davidman writes Bill: "We're all hard at work here; the house is practically a book factory. Warnie's deep in the life of Gramont (dashing 17th century bloke), I'm putting Mme. M. together, and Jack has started a new fantasy — for grownups" (*Bone*, 242).[18] Although it is impossible to show ways in which she may have had a direct influence upon books such as *Surprised by Joy* (1955), *Till We Have Faces* (1956), *Reflections on the Psalms* (1958), and *The Four Loves* (1960), her letters reveal many instances of Lewis seeking her advice, editorial assistance, and literary insight. Davidman's handling of the manuscript of *Surprised by Joy* appears to have begun as early as July 1954, and by January 19, 1955, she writes friends: "In spite of the move [to Cambridge], he keeps working as hard as usual; has finished his autobiography — I've got the last chapters here now and must set my wits to work on criticism. I think it a first-rate job" (*Bone*, 235).[19] Three weeks later she tells Bill she is typing the manuscript to earn "a little extra dough" (February 8, 1955; *Bone*, 238), and three weeks after that she writes him that she has finished typing the book (February 25, 1955; *Bone*, 240).

Her intimate knowledge of Lewis's autobiography was also critically important during his revision of the galley proofs. On June 23, 1955, Lewis wrote his publisher, Jocelyn Gibb, about needed corrections, advising Gibb to get in touch with Davidman for the quickest way of identifying the needed corrections.[20] On June 24, 1955, Gibb wrote her:

> I understand from Dr. Lewis that you corrected a proof of his book *Surprised by Joy,* and I am now writing to you at his suggestion as I think you may be able to help over one point which has arisen. Unfortunately the "official" proof has now gone back to the printer and it would delay matters for him to send it all the way back here from Somerset, where he operates. Now, Dr. Lewis thinks you will remember some correction two-thirds of the way through the book and I imagine that it was something fairly important. You will realize that I am rather at a disadvantage

18. Lewis's new fantasy was *Till We Have Faces: A Myth Retold* (London: Geoffrey Bles, 1956).

19. *Surprised by Joy: The Shape of My Early Life* (London: Geoffrey Bles, 1955); hereafter *SJ*. In 1955 Lewis moved from Magdalen College, Oxford, to Magdalene College, Cambridge, where he had accepted the Chair of Medieval and Renaissance English Literature.

20. See C. S. Lewis, *Collected Letters* (hereafter *CL*), vol. 3: *Narnia, Cambridge, and Joy, 1950-1963*, ed. Walter Hooper (London: HarperCollins, 2006), 622-23.

because the proof in which he had embodied both yours and his corrections is, as I say, down at the printer's. But if you could tell me the nature of the correction two-thirds of the way through the book I should be most grateful as Dr. Lewis thinks it may have been omitted from the printer's proof copy. I could then telephone the printer and make sure it has duly been made. If it would simplify matters for you to ring me up please do as I shall be here on Monday for all the week. The only thing is that the matter is rather urgent as we are waiting to go ahead with printing the book. (*Bone,* 253-54)

When she writes Bill on October 10, 1955, and tells him that "*Surprised by Joy* is getting good reviews and doing well — 10,000 sold before publication, out two weeks and already being reprinted" (*Bone,* 263), she must have taken some satisfaction in her role in helping Lewis to get the book completed.[21]

However, I believe there is another way — perhaps a much more profound one — in which Davidman contributed to *SJ:* Lewis may have been influenced in writing his autobiographical account of his conversion by reading Davidman's own essay account of her conversion, "The Longest Way Round." Her essay first appeared as the lead piece in *These Found the Way: Thirteen Converts to Protestant Christianity,*[22] and we know Lewis read the essay before he published *SJ,* writing a friend on March 25, 1954: "I happen to have 2 copies of this ugly book in wh. you may find some of the articles worth reading. Joy Davidman's is the best, I think."[23] When we realize that Davidman herself had been influenced by Lewis in the writing of her conversion essay, we may witness in these two works a kind of extraordinary literary cross-fertilization. Lewis's influence upon Davidman's essay is obvious, as she notes how her reading of his books, particularly *The Pilgrim's Regress, The Screwtape Letters,* and *The Great Divorce,* came to inform her

21. After Bill read *SJ* he commented to Joy that Lewis's grief expressed in the book might benefit from insights from dianetics (*Bone,* 283). She replied: "You're right about Jack's autobiography; I don't think he's ever got over his grief and horror at his mother's death — who would? There'd be no point in stirring up trouble by hunting for grief charges, though — even if he'd let me! Why disturb a satisfactory adjustment? Jack's sorrows, instead of breaking him down, seem to have strengthened him, made him something like a saint" (March 14, 1956; *Bone,* 282).

22. *These Found the Way: Thirteen Converts to Protestant Christianity,* ed. David Wesley Soper (Philadelphia: Westminster, 1951), 13-26; citations here are from the version published in *Bone.*

23. *CL,* 3, p. 447.

interior world, and in the end helped to propel her into a personal encounter with Jesus Christ.[24] For instance, she links her own lifelong yearning for spiritual reality — something that as an atheist she claimed to despise on the conscious level — with Lewis's notion of joy:

> There is a myth that has always haunted mankind, the legend of the Way Out. "A stone, a leaf, an unfound door," wrote Thomas Wolfe — the door leading out of time and space into Somewhere Else.[25] We all go out of that door eventually, calling it death. But the tale persists that for a few lucky ones the door has swung open *before* death, letting them through, perhaps for the week of fairy time which is seven long years on earth; or at least granting them a glimpse of the land on the other side. The symbol varies with different men; for some, the door itself is important; for others, the undiscovered country beyond it — the never-never land, Saint Brendan's Island, the Land of Heart's Desire. C. S. Lewis, whose *Pilgrim's Regress* taught me its meaning, calls it simply the Island. (*Bone,* 88)

But in what ways did Lewis's reading of "The Longest Way Round" influence his writing of *SJ*? I believe the evidence is compelling. For example, both writers use a first remembered moment of experiencing beauty to begin their stories. Davidman begins her essay by recounting an early intense encounter with beauty:

> When I was fourteen I went walking in the park on a Sunday afternoon, in clean, cold, luminous air. The trees tinkled with sleet; the city noises were muffled by the snow. Winter sunset, with a line of young maples sheathed in ice between me and the sun — as I looked up they burned unimaginably golden — burned and were not consumed. I heard the voice in the burning tree; the meaning of all things was revealed and the sacrament at the heart of all beauty lay bare; time and space fell away, and for a moment the world was only a door swinging ajar. Then the light faded, the cold stung my toes, and I went home, reflecting that I had had another aesthetic experience. I had them fairly often. That was what beautiful things did to you, I recognized, probably because of some visceral or glandular

24. *The Pilgrim's Regress: An Allegorical Apology for Christianity, Reason and Romanticism* (London: J. M. Dent, 1933); *The Screwtape Letters* (London: Geoffrey Bles, 1942); and *The Great Divorce: A Dream* (London: Geoffrey Bles, 1945).

25. This line appears in the opening paragraph of Thomas Wolfe's first novel, *Look Homeward, Angel: A Story of the Buried Life* (New York: Charles Scribner's Sons, 1929).

reaction that hadn't been fully explored by science just yet. For I was a well-brought-up, right-thinking child of materialism. Beauty, I knew, existed; but God, of course, did not. (*Bone,* 83)

Although she tried to stifle these aesthetic experiences, beauty nonetheless continued to haunt her; no matter how often her hard-nosed, materialist self tried to shut the door on beauty, shafts of beauty's light continued to pierce through the cracks.

Lewis was also deeply moved by an early experience of beauty. Compare what Davidman writes to what Lewis says near the beginning of *SJ,* where he is reflecting on the relative absence of beauty in his parents' home:

My earliest aesthetic experiences, if indeed they were aesthetic . . . were incredibly romantic. . . . Once in those very early days my brother brought into the nursery the lid of a biscuit tin which he had covered with moss and garnished with twigs and flowers so as to make it a toy garden or a toy forest. That was the first beauty I ever knew. What the real garden had failed to do, the toy garden did. . . . I do not think the impression was very important at the moment, but it soon became im-portant in memory . . . [and it] taught me longing — *Sehnsucht.* . . . If aesthetic experiences were rare, religious experiences did not occur at all. (*SJ,* 6-7)

The remarkable parallels in these two passages — both writers recalling in-tense, early encounters with beauty, both identifying and yet downplaying them as aesthetic experiences, and both insisting that such experiences had no link with the spiritual or religious life — suggest that Lewis may have intuitively imitated the structure of Davidman's presentation of these ideas from her autobiographical essay when writing his story of conversion.[26]

26. In " 'Early Prose Joy': C. S. Lewis's Early Draft of an Autobiographical Manuscript," edited by Andrew Lazo, and published in *SEVEN: An Anglo-American Literary Review* 30 (2013): 13-49, Lewis comes near to describing his experience with the toy garden as an aesthetic one by remembering autumn pictures in Beatrix Potter's *Squirrel Nutkin* when he was simultaneously witnessing "real autumn":

Those who remember their nursery days will know that [*Squirrel Nutkin*] is full of pictures of woods in autumn. There was also, opposite our house, a straight road running down hill, over-arched with trees which the real autumn was then colouring. . . . Whether the road reminded me of the pictures, or the pictures of the road, I cannot now remember; but somewhere between the two there arose another such experience as I had had beneath

A second way Lewis may have imitated Davidman is in how he portrays the internal dichotomy he experienced between reason and imagination. In recounting her early commitment to atheism — learned at least in part, she says, from the rationalism of her father — Davidman admits that she could not reconcile her belief that the material world was all there was with her emotions and desires:

> I believed the three-dimensional material world was the only thing that existed, but in literature it bored me. I didn't believe in the supernatural, but it interested me above all else. Only it had to be written as fiction; the supernatural presented as fact outraged my convictions. By disguising heaven as fairyland I was enabled to love heaven. (*Bone,* 88)

Lewis, after several years of studying with his great rationalist and atheist tutor, W. T. Kirkpatrick, found himself torn between his longing to experience joy and the cold, hard logic of his tutor's dialectic:

> Such, then, was the state of my imaginative life; over against it stood the life of my intellect. The two hemispheres of my mind were in the sharpest contrast. On the one side a many-islanded sea of poetry and myth; on the other a glib and shallow "rationalism." Nearly all that I loved I believed to be imaginary; nearly all that I believed to be real I thought grim and meaningless. (*SJ,* 170)

A third evidence of the influence Davidman may have had upon Lewis in *SJ* is the fact that both cite the same authors as being key influences upon them. For instance, both connect their early atheism with reading H. G. Wells. Davidman writes that "I declared my own atheism at the age of eight, after reading [H. G.] Wells's *Outline of History*" (*Bone,* 85), while several times in *SJ* Lewis credits his reading of Wells with his intellectual movement away from Christianity.[27] In addition, to underscore their desperate desire

---

the flowering shrub. It was not what is usually called aesthetic experience. . . . Aesthetic people, if I understand them, would value autumn because it showed certain colours. . . . What I delighted in was autumn itself. (15)

This "Early Prose Joy" passage (which Lazo dates as 1930 or 1931) shows Lewis writing about his own early remembered aesthetic experience, which may have been enhanced, expanded, and refined in *SJ* because of his reading of Davidman's early remembered experience.

27. H. G. Wells, *The Outline of History: Being a Plain History of Life and Mankind* (London: Macmillan, 1920). For Lewis's references to Wells, see *SJ,* 35 and 43.

before their conversions to live autonomously, both writers make use of lines from William Henley's poem "Invictus" (1888):

Out of the night that covers me,
Black as the Pit from pole to pole,
I thank whatever gods may be
For my unconquerable soul.

In the fell clutch of circumstance
I have not winced nor cried aloud.
Under the bludgeonings of chance
My head is bloody, but unbowed.

Beyond this place of wrath and tears
Looms but the Horror of the shade,
And yet the menace of the years
Finds, and shall find, me unafraid.

It matters not how strait the gate,
How charged with punishments the scroll.
I am the master of my fate;
I am the captain of my soul.[28]

Davidman quotes the poem's final lines when she writes:

For the first time in my life I felt helpless; for the first time my pride was forced to admit that I was not, after all, "the master of my fate" and "the captain of my soul." All my defenses — the walls of arrogance and cock-sureness and self-love behind which I had hid from God — went down momentarily. And God came in. (*Bone,* 94)

Similarly, Lewis says:

Remember, I had always wanted, above all things, not to be "interfered with." I had wanted (mad wish) "to call my soul my own." . . . Every step I had taken, from the Absolute to "Spirit" and from "Spirit" to "God," had been a step toward the more concrete, the more imminent, the more

28. The title of the poem means "unconquered."

compulsive. At each step one had less chance "to call one's soul one's own." (*SJ*, 228, 237)

While Lewis rephrases Henley's "I am the captain of my soul" into "To call one's soul one's own," it is clear he has the line from "Invictus" in mind. Earlier in the book, Lewis anticipates the ideas in Henley's poems while not directly quoting from the poem:

> But, of course, what mattered most of all was my deep-seated hatred of authority, my monstrous individualism, my lawlessness. No word in my vocabulary expressed deeper hatred than the word *Interference.* But Christianity placed at the centre what then seemed to me a transcendental Interferer. If its picture were true then no sort of "treaty with reality" could ever be possible. There was no region even in the innermost depth of one's soul (nay, there least of all) which one could surround with a barbed wire fence and guard with a notice No Admittance. And that was what I wanted; some area, however small, of which I could say to all other beings, "This is my business and mine only." (*SJ*, 172)[29]

Here again is another instance where Lewis may have been influenced by the structural pattern of Davidman's conversion story.

Another work both writers draw upon is *The Hound of Heaven* (1893), Francis Thompson's compelling autobiographical poem of his conversion. Davidman refers to the poem early in her account:

> Francis Thompson symbolized God as the "Hound of Heaven," pursuing on relentless feet.[30] With me, God was more like a cat. He had been stalking

---

29. Lewis also echoes the language of "Invictus" in "Early Prose Joy": "Under my old system I had felt that even if I reached 'Heaven' I should never be free, never the master of my soul" (29). In addition, in a later passage that he struck through, he writes: "Not to be ones own man, not to call ones soul ones own" (37).

30. Davidman has in mind these lines:

I fled Him, down the nights and down the days;
   I fled Him, down the arches of the years;
I fled Him, down the labyrinthine ways
   Of my own mind; and in the mist of tears
I hid from Him, and under the running laughter.
       Up vistaed hopes I sped;
       And shot, precipitated,

me for a very long time, waiting for his moment; he crept nearer so silently that I never knew he was there. Then, all at once, he sprang. (*Bone*, 93)

A little later in her essay she refers to the poem again:

I could not doubt the truth of my experience. It was so much the *realest* thing that had ever happened to me! And, in a gentler, less overwhelming form, it went right on happening. So my previous reasoning was at fault, and I must somehow find the error. I snatched at books I had despised before; reread *The Hound of Heaven*, which I had ridiculed as a piece of phony rhetoric — and, understanding it suddenly, burst into tears. (*Bone*, 95)

While Lewis never directly mentions Thompson's poem, the language he uses to refer to God as he closes in on Lewis recalls the poem. Having earlier referred to God as "the great Angler [playing] His fish and I never [dreaming] that the hook was in my tongue" (*SJ*, 211), Lewis shifts his metaphor for God in the penultimate chapter, "Checkmate." Ostensibly suggesting that God is the great chess master maneuvering him into a situation where he has no other play except acquiescence, Lewis equally suggests that God is like a hound ever pursuing him. God is the great Adversary beginning "to make His final moves" (*SJ*, 216), leading Lewis to realize that it was not even Joy that he had been seeking all his life: "Inexorably Joy proclaimed, 'You want — I myself am your want of — something other, outside, not you nor any state of you.' I did not yet ask, Who is the desired? only What is it?" (*SJ*, 221). Here Lewis may be recalling these lines from Thompson's poem: "With unperturbed pace, / Deliberate speed, majestic instancy; / And past those noised Feet / A Voice comes yet more fleet — / 'Lo! naught contents thee, who content'st not Me' " (lines 106-10).

As the great Adversary pursues, Lewis adopts a hunting metaphor, describing himself as a fox "now running in the open, 'with all the wo in the world,' bedraggled and weary, hounds barely a field behind. And nearly ev-

---

Adown Titanic glooms of chasmed fears,
  From those strong Feet that followed, followed after.
        But with unhurrying chase,
        And unperturbed pace,
        Deliberate speed, majestic instancy,
        They beat — and a Voice beat
        More instant than the Feet —
        "All things betray thee, who betrayest Me." (lines 1-15)

eryone was now (one way or another) in the pack; Plato, Dante, [George] MacDonald, [George] Herbert, [Owen] Barfield, [J. R. R.] Tolkien, [Hugo] Dyson, Joy itself" (*SJ*, 225). In the end the Hunter demands that Lewis admit "'I am the Lord'; 'I am that I am'; 'I am,'" and Lewis uses language that echoes Davidman's: "People who are naturally religious find difficulty in understanding the horror of such a revelation. Amiable agnostics will talk cheerfully about 'man's search for God.' To me, as I then was, they might as well have talked about the mouse's search for the cat" (*SJ*, 227).

Lewis further recalls Thompson's Hound in perhaps the most famous passage in *SJ:*

> You must picture me alone in that room in Magdalen [College], night after night, feeling, whenever my mind lifted even for a second from my work, the steady, unrelenting approach of Him whom I so earnestly desired not to meet. That which I greatly feared had at last come upon me. In the Trinity Term [summer] of 1929 I gave in, and admitted that God was God, and knelt and prayed: perhaps, that night, the most dejected and reluctant convert in all England. (*SJ*, 228)

Surely Lewis is recalling at least in part the end of *The Hound of Heaven:*

> Now of that long pursuit
> Comes on at hand the bruit;
> That Voice is round me like a bursting sea:
> "And is thy earth so marred,
> Shattered in shard on shard?
> Lo, all things fly thee, for thou fliest Me!
> Strange, piteous, futile thing,
> Wherefore should any set thee love apart?
> Seeing none but I makes much of naught" (He said),
> "And human love needs human meriting:
> How hast thou merited —
> Of all man's clotted clay the dingiest clot?
> Alack, thou knowest not
> How little worthy of any love thou art!
> Whom wilt thou find to love ignoble thee,
> Save Me, save only Me?
> All which I took from thee I did but take,
> Not for thy harms,

But just that thou might'st seek it in My arms.
   All which thy child's mistake
Fancies as lost, I have stored for thee at home:
   Rise, clasp My hand, and come."
Halts by me that footfall:
Is my gloom, after all,
Shade of His hand, outstretched caressingly?
   "Ah, fondest, blindest, weakest,
   I am He Whom thou seekest!
Thou dravest love from thee, who dravest Me." (lines 155-82)

Both Davidman and Lewis employ the imagery of Thompson's poem to describe their own resistance to but eventual acceptance of the great Hound of Heaven.

The last writer both Davidman and Lewis cite in their conversion accounts is George MacDonald. Davidman notes that early on "what I read, eagerly and untiringly, was fantasy. Ghost stories and superscience stories; George MacDonald in my childhood, [Lord] Dunsany in my teens" (*Bone,* 87-88).[31] MacDonald so influenced her that a recurring dream she had is like one she might have come across while reading MacDonald's *The Princess and the Goblin* (1872) or *The Princess and Curdie* (1883):

> As a child I had a recurring dream: I would walk down a familiar street which suddenly grew unfamiliar and opened onto a strange, golden, immeasurable plain, where far away there rose the towers of Fairyland. If I remembered the way carefully, the dream told me, I should be able to find it when I woke up. . . . The last time I had that dream I was grown up, and so I put it in rhymes, . . . as proof of the hope of heaven, making itself known even to one so willfully blind as I. (*Bone,* 88)

The poem she wrote based on this dream experience is "Fairytale":

> At night, when we dreamed,
> we went down a street,
> and turned a corner;

---

31. George MacDonald (1824-1905) wrote fantasies, fairytales, romantic novels, and poetry; Lord Dunsany (1878-1957), born Edward John Moreton Drax Plunkett, was one of the earliest writers of modern fantasy literature.

we went down the street
and turned the corner,
and there, it seemed,
there was the castle.

Always, if you knew,
if you knew how to go,
you could walk down a street
(the daylight street)
that twisted about
and ended in grass;
there it was
always, the castle.

Remote, unshadowed,
childish, immortal,
with two calm giants
guarding the portal,
stiff in the sunset,
strong to defend,
stood castle safety
at the world's end.

O castle safety,
Love without crying,
honey without cloying,
death without dying!
Hate and heartbreak
all were forgot there;
we always woke,
we never got there. (*Naked Tree*, 221-22)[32]

The love of fairyland entrenched in Davidman's mind because of her early reading of MacDonald prepared the way later for her to cross her atheistic frontier and move to faith in Christ. Lewis's great affection for and debt to MacDonald is well-documented, including the appreciative introduction he

32. The poem first appeared in *War Poems of the United Nations,* ed. Joy Davidman (New York: Dial Press, 1943).

wrote for *George MacDonald: An Anthology.*[33] In *SJ* he mentions MacDonald several times, most famously in the chapter "Check," where at the height of his atheism he describes having rather casually picked up in a train station a copy of *Phantastes: A Fairie Romance for Men and Women* (1858). He was in no way prepared for the shock of reading the novel:

> It was as if I were carried sleeping across the frontier, or as if I had died in the old country and could never remember how I came alive in the new. For in one sense the new country was exactly like the old. . . . But in another sense all was changed. I did not yet know (and I was long in learning) the name of the new quality, the bright shadow, that rested on the travels of [the main character] Anodos. I do now. It was Holiness. (*SJ,* 179)

Like Davidman's, Lewis's pre-conversion engagement with MacDonald set the stage later for a genuine encounter with the Author of holiness. As Lewis puts it: "That night my imagination was, in a certain sense, baptized; the rest of me, not unnaturally, took longer. I had not the faintest notion what I had let myself in for by buying Phantastes" (*SJ,* 181).[34]

A fourth way Davidman's "The Longest Way Round" may have influenced Lewis's writing of *SJ* concerns instances where both use similar expressions or related ideas to state things regarding their conversions. Some of these might be called parallel passages. For example, where Davidman says, "Atheist virtues . . . don't keep very well" (*Bone,* 85), Lewis says, "A young man who wishes to remain a sound Atheist cannot be too careful of his reading" (*SJ,* 191), and "Really, a young Atheist cannot guard his faith too carefully. Dangers lie in wait for him on every side" (*SJ,* 226). Another instance is the way both describe their direct experiences of God. Davidman writes:

> How can one describe the direct perception of God? It is infinite, unique; there are no words, there are no comparisons. Can one scoop up the sea in a teacup? Those who have known God will understand me; the others, I find, can neither listen nor understand. There was a Person with me in the

---

33. *George MacDonald: An Anthology,* ed. C. S. Lewis (London: Geoffrey Bles, 1946; New York: Macmillan, 1947). Lewis cites the profound influence of MacDonald on him in numerous other works in addition to *SJ.*

34. In "Early Prose Joy" (21-23) Lewis also cites the importance of MacDonald's *Phantastes,* but not with the same degree of detail or emphasis that he does in *SJ;* again, he may have brought his reading of Davidman's conversion experience as influenced by MacDonald into greater focus when he was writing *SJ.*

room, directly present to my consciousness — a Person so real that all my previous life was by comparison mere shadow play. And I myself was more alive than I had ever been; it was like waking from sleep. So intense a life cannot be endured for long by flesh and blood; we must ordinarily take our life watered down, diluted as it were, by time and space and matter. My perception of God lasted perhaps half a minute. (*Bone*, 94)

Compare this to Lewis's description:

I know very well when, but hardly how, the final step was taken. I was driven [by his brother] to Whipsnade [zoo] one sunny morning. When we set out I did not believe that Jesus Christ is the Son of God, and when we reached the zoo I did. Yet I had not exactly spent the journey in thought. Nor in great emotion. "Emotional" is perhaps the last word we can apply to some of the most important events. It was more like when a man, after long sleep, still lying motionless in bed, becomes aware that he is now awake. (*SJ*, 237)

Both writers suggest how difficult it is to articulate the nature of their theophany, both use an awakening from sleep metaphor to describe their final realization about their experiencing of God, and both suggest that it all happened in just a moment. Perceptive readers will also note that Davidman's reference to all of her previous life as being like "mere shadow play" recalls Lewis's notion of human life being lived in the "shadow lands," something he especially highlights in the final book of the Chronicles of Narnia, *The Last Battle* (1956).[35]

The last parallel passages may be the most telling in terms of Davidman's influence upon Lewis's conversion narrative. After her encounter with God, she says:

When it was over I found myself on my knees, praying. I think I must have been the world's most astonished atheist. My surprise was so great that for a moment it distracted me from my fear; only for a moment, however. My awareness of God was no comforting illusion, conjured up to reassure me

35. The last lines of "Early Prose Joy" come near to using Joy's "mere shadow play": "Thus I came to know beyond doubt that my surrender to the will of God, however imperfect, was not a mere fantasy: and also to feel by experience the old Platonic truth, that this sensible world is a shadow of the real one, and that the soul is logically prior to the body" (40).

about my husband's safety. I was just as worried afterward as before. No; it was terror and ecstasy, repentance and rebirth. (*Bone*, 94)

The similarity of language that Lewis uses is striking:

In the Trinity Term of 1929 I gave in, and admitted that God was God, and knelt and prayed: perhaps, that night, the most dejected and reluctant convert in all England. (*SJ*, 228)

Perhaps it is little wonder that the world's most astonished atheist won the love of the most dejected and reluctant convert in all England.

Davidman's collaborative role in *Till We Have Faces* is also multi-layered but not as deeply penetrating as her influence upon *SJ*. First, she helped jar Lewis out of a writer's block. On March 23, 1955, she writes to Bill: "One night [Lewis] was lamenting that he couldn't get a good idea for a book. We kicked a few ideas around till one came to life. Then we had another whiskey each and bounced it back and forth between us. The next day, without further planning, he wrote the first chapter! I read it and made some criticisms (feels quite like old times); he did it over and went on with the next" (*Bone*, 242). It is reasonable to assume that Davidman offered similar criticism and suggestions for the remaining chapters of *Till We Have Faces*.

Second, she helped Lewis work through many of the ideas he wanted to include in the book, exercising what Davidman believed was her most valuable attribute as a collaborator, and recalling incidences in the past when she had similarly assisted Bill in his writing:

I don't kid myself in these matters — whatever my talents as an independent writer, my *real* gift is as a sort of editor-collaborator like Max Perkins, and I'm happiest when I'm doing something like that.[36] Though I can't write one-tenth as well as Jack, I can tell him how to write more like himself! He is now about three-quarters of the way through [*Till We Have Faces*] (what I'd give for that energy!) and says he finds my advice indispensable. (April 29, 1955; *Bone*, 246)

Diane Pavlac Glyer believes that Davidman "was involved in each step of [Lewis's] writing process. They would brainstorm ideas together before the

36. Maxwell E. Perkins (1884-1947) was a gifted editor, assisting in critically important ways many writers, including F. Scott Fitzgerald, Ernest Hemingway, and Thomas Wolfe.

text was written. She would carefully read and critique each chapter, making specific suggestions for needed changes. She would problem solve when the writing bogged down. And she would encourage, asking how the project was coming along, expressing ongoing interest in the work and in the writer."[37]

Third, Davidman's female perspective (*Till We Have Faces* was Lewis's only book written from the viewpoint of a woman) served Lewis well as he tested her reaction to his presentation of Orual, the main character. Driven by jealousy, Orual tries to keep her younger sister, Psyche, to herself. In several letters Lewis writes about this, telling Jocelyn Gibb on February 16, 1956, that "every woman reader so far has" understood this jealousy.[38] He confides to another correspondent on March 4, 1956: "I believe I've done what no mere male author has done before, talked thro' the mouth of, & lived in the mind of, an *ugly* woman for a whole book. All female readers so far have approved the feminine psychology of it: i.e. no masculine note intrudes."[39] Furthermore, Glyer argues there is something "of Joy Davidman's character in Orual, in her wise decisions as queen, in her efforts to work things out logically, in her boldness to write out her complaint and face down the gods."[40] Although Glyer does not believe Davidman actually composed portions of *Till We Have Faces,* "the fact that she and Lewis thoroughly discussed the chapters before they were written convinces me that she is in part responsible for their creation."[41] A final point worth noting is that Lewis dedicated *Till We Have Faces* to Davidman, suggesting in part his indebtedness to her.

Davidman's influences upon Lewis when he was writing *Reflections on the Psalms* and *The Four Loves* were probably primarily indirect, in no small part because when these books were being written she was battling the cancer that would eventually take her life. Indeed, after her cancer is first mentioned in her letter of October 19-20, 1956, to Bill, references to her own writing essentially cease. She first mentions Lewis's work on the Psalms in her letter to Chad and Eva Walsh of June 6, 1957, only months after she was given up for dead: "My case is definitely arrested for the time being.

37. Glyer, "Joy Davidman Lewis," 13.

38. *CL,* 3, p. 707.

39. *CL,* 3, p. 716.

40. Glyer, "Joy Davidman Lewis," 14. Similarly, Robert Lancelyn Green and Walter Hooper in *C. S. Lewis: A Biography* (London: Collins, 1974) suggest that "there is a great deal of Joy Davidman in the character of Orual" (263).

41. Glyer, "Joy Davidman Lewis," 15. Glyer also quotes Douglas Gresham who says: "Jack always said that Mother's input was so much and so important that the book was really a collaboration between them" (15).

I may be all right for three or four years, they say. . . . Jack is working on a projected book about the Psalms. Me, I'm superintending the household and working on a crocheted rug!" (*Bone*, 320-21).[42] The next reference comes in her February 4, 1958, letter to Bill: "Jack's finished his book on the Psalms" (*Bone*, 331). George Sayer, Lewis's friend and biographer, says that Austin Farrer convinced Lewis "there was a great need for a book that would deal with things that worried people when they read the Psalms. Joy warmly supported the idea and offered to edit and type the book, if she was well enough."[43] Unfortunately, Davidman's poor health made it impossible for her to type the book, although she almost certainly discussed with Lewis many of the ideas he explores in the book. Indeed, since Lewis had read and advised Davidman about her own Old Testament–inspired *Smoke on the Mountain*, it stands to reason that he was influenced by her ideas as he worked on his personal study of the Psalms.[44] Glyer notes the connections between the two books: "Both are treatments of Old Testament texts, both are quite colloquial in style, and both attempt to answer questions about troublesome passages by putting them in their historical contexts."[45]

In Lewis's letters as early as 1954 he writes about the four Greek words for love: *agape, eros, philia*, and *storge*.[46] So when in 1957 the Episcopal Radio-TV Foundation of America in Atlanta, at the prompting of Chad Walsh, invited Lewis to make a series of tape recordings on any topic of his choice for broadcast on their network, Lewis agreed; he writes on May 1, 1958: "The subject I want to say something about in the near future, in some form or the other, is the four Loves — Storge, Philia, Eros, and Agape. This seems to bring in nearly the whole of Christian ethics."[47] Lewis finished writing the script in the summer of 1958, and he met Caroline Rakestraw of the Episcopal Radio-TV Foundation in London where the recording took place on August 19-20, 1958.

---

42. C. S. Lewis, *Reflections on the Psalms* (London: Geoffrey Bles, 1958).

43. Sayer, *Jack: C. S. Lewis and His Times* (San Francisco: Harper & Row, 1988), 239.

44. As previously noted, in her January 25, 1953, letter to Walsh she writes that Lewis had "time to go over my own Decalogue book with me (about 50,000 words of it) and tell me how to fix it; he liked it quite well, thank heaven" (*Bone*, 138).

45. Glyer, "Joy Davidman Lewis," 16. In addition, Green and Hooper write that "Joy Davidman, with her Jewish background, was proving helpful and an inspiration" (*C. S. Lewis: A Biography*, 267) as Lewis worked on *Reflections on the Psalms*.

46. See, for instance, his letters of January 23, 1954 (*CL*, 3, p. 413), February 18, 1954 (pp. 428-29), and December 4, 1954 (p. 538).

47. *CL*, 3, p. 941.

After these recordings, Davidman's collaboration with Lewis on what came to be *The Four Loves* was more as a guardian than as a catalyst.[48] Apparently during the recordings Rakestraw had tried to coach Lewis on how to improve his delivery, something Davidman writes Walsh about on December 29, 1958:

> We are feeling deeply injured and would dunk you in the pond if you were available for dunking! *Why* did you get my poor Jack mixed up with the ineffable Rakestraw or whatever her name was? She began by criticizing his opening words — "Today I want to discuss . . ." "Professor Lewis, couldn't you say instead '*Let us think together, you and I about . . . ?*' " *No*, he couldn't. "*But* we want you to give the feeling of *embracing* them." Jack said if they wanted an embracer they had the wrong man. "Well, perhaps I mean a feeling of involvement . . ." Ugh! At the end she made him sit absolutely silent before the microphone for a minute and a half "so they could feel his living presence." I told him he oughta charge double rates for that — C. S. Lewis being silent, a unique listening experience. He came home rather shattered with all this; and now we learn — not from the organization, but through a friend — that they've decided to suppress the whole series because of Jack's "startling frankness" on sexual matters! Needless to say he wouldn't have startled anyone over the age of sixteen and the I.Q. of 80. (*Bone,* 341-42)[49]

Chagrined, Walsh replies:

> I'm ready to be dunked. Can you send me this Rakestraw's full name and address? (I failed to keep her letters.) I want to write her and ask for a full explanation, and then I'll be in position to give them the kind of Holy Hell they deserve. Not that this will change anything, but they've asked for it, and I want to have my say. Jack is the one who has been principally betrayed, but in a secondary way I have real reason to be sore. After all, I *was* the go-between, and I served as a go-between on the basis of the

48. C. S. Lewis, *The Four Loves* (London: Geoffrey Bles, 1960).

49. Green and Hooper give Lewis's amusing account of meeting with Rakestraw. According to them, she said to Lewis: "Professor Lewis, I'm afraid you brought sex into your talks on Eros." Astonished, Lewis replied, "My dear Mrs. Cartwheel [his mispronunciation of Rakestraw], how can you talk about Eros and *leave it out?*" Lewis thought it "unthinkable that in a country that peddled so much pornography people could not bear to hear a Christian discussion of sex" (*C. S. Lewis: A Biography*, 231-32).

favorable things I'd heard about that program. If they are a bunch of timid prudes, it was their duty to spell out their taboos in advance. So, for the sake of my blood pressure, do send me that name and address. And ask Jack's Christian forgiveness for me. Strange, strange, how one can act with such unsullied motives and yet contribute to the most stupid situations. I think there is creeping prudery abroad in the land. Last winter some of the faculty at Beloit accused the *Poetry Journal* of being anti-Christian and indecent and kicked up enough of a rumpus so that the trustees, to avoid "controversy," I suppose, withdrew the college support. It is now an independent mag. Then this summer a juvenile writer whom I know found that her recent novel was on the "don't buy" list in the public libraries of a large city because she described an eleven-year-old girl becoming aware that she was developing. (*Bone,* 342-43)

In fact, at first the tapes were not widely broadcast, but according to a mutual agreement Lewis used the script as the basis for his book, *The Four Loves.*[50] He finished the manuscript in June of 1959, and the book was published in March of 1960, just months before Davidman's death. After her death, he writes one correspondent: "My wife died in July, so my married life was very short; it surpassed in happiness all the rest of my life. You'll find everything I have to say about marriage in my *The Four Loves.*"[51] Since Lewis had written in letters as early as 1954 about many ideas that he explored in greater depth in the book, Davidman's influence upon *The Four Loves* was probably an indirect one, although a very powerful one. Indeed, his marriage to Davidman — and the deeply felt experiences of *agape, philia,* and *eros* he had with her — infuses almost every page of the book. One measure of Lewis's love for Davidman is the fact he copyrighted *The Four Loves* in the name of Helen Joy Davidman.

In addition to all this, there is anecdotal evidence of frequent collaboration between the two. For instance, Glyer reports that Douglas Gresham said his mother was involved in helping Lewis with his unfinished novel about the fall of Troy.[52] Gresham says his mother helped with "generating ideas and doing re-writes of the story," and he recalls Lewis "reading us parts of it, and my mother's comments, which were, it was good stuff, it was very good."[53]

50. In 1970 the tapes were published by the Foundation.

51. July 10, 1961; *CL,* 3, p. 1226.

52. Published as "After Ten Years" in *The Dark Tower and Other Stories,* ed. Walter Hooper (London: Collins, 1977).

53. Glyer, "Joy Davidman Lewis," 16.

In addition, there were instances when Davidman and Lewis collaborated on poems. Some have suggested that the two collaborated on "Evolution-ary Hymn," even singing it as a joyful parody to the tune of "Joyful, Joyful We Adore Thee" or "Lead Us, Heavenly Father, Lead Us."[54] Robert Lance-lyn Green and Walter Hooper give an account of a poem composed on the evening of April 10, 1960, when Davidman and Lewis were visiting Greece along with Green and his wife, June. After waiting a considerable time for their evening meal, "Joy finally began flicking bread-pellets at the nearest musician, and the four of us whiled away the time by writing alternate lines of the following doggerel:

[Jack]   A pub-crawl through the glittering isles of Greece,
[Joy]   I wish it left my ears a moment's peace!
[June]   If once the crashing Cretans ceased to bore,
[Roger]   The drums of England would resist no more.
[Jack]   No more they *can* resist. For mine are broken!
[Roger]   To this Curates' shields were but a token,
[June]   *Our* cries in silence still above the noise —
[Joy]   He has been hit by a good shot of Joy's!
[Jack]   What aim! What strength! What purpose and what poise![55]

Gresham recalls other instances of "rhyming competitions" when his mother and Lewis would compose alternating lines of poetry together: "One after-noon, they sat at the Trout Inn in Godstow. This pub features a patio over-looking a stream filled with fish known as chavender, or chub. There Jack and Joy composed a serial poem that included the line 'Pavender or Pub,' giving rise to the Narnian fish known as the pavender."[56]

Perhaps we will never fathom the many ways in which Davidman influ-enced Lewis's later writings. For instance, it goes without saying that David-man's spirit completely envelops *A Grief Observed*. However, it is now time to turn to a final assessment of her literary corpus. As the preceding chapters have demonstrated, she was a dedicated writer, cognizant of the time, energy, and commitment necessary to produce good work. Her early short stories, "Reveal the Titan" and "Apostate," are apprentice works, yet both suggest

54. Published in *The Cambridge Review* 79 (November 30, 1957): 227; see also *The Collected Poems of C. S. Lewis: A Critical Edition*, ed. Don W. King (Kent, OH: Kent State University Press, 2015), 384.

55. Green and Hooper, *C. S. Lewis: A Biography*, 274.

56. Cited in Glyer, *The Company They Keep*, 162.

the mature fiction writer who later publishes *Anya* and *Weeping Bay.* The book and film reviews she writes for *NM* are penetrating, cogent, insightful, and articulate — if at times biased toward the Communist principles she espoused at the time. Her autobiographical essay, "The Longest Way Round," is critical for understanding the profound political, personal, and spiritual transformation she realized as a result of her rejection of Communism and her conversion to Christianity.[57] *Smoke on the Mountain* is her most mature piece of writing as a Christian, and in it she calls upon her heritage as a Jew to inform her Christian understanding of the Decalogue. However, Davidman's literary legacy rests, I believe, on her work as a poet. Although she published only one volume of verse, *Letter to a Comrade,* I have shown that she worked on at least two other volumes, *Red Primer* and *Courage;* moreover, the recent discovery of over two hundred heretofore unknown poems, including the sequence of forty-five love sonnets to C. S. Lewis, demonstrates that her most natural, compelling, and effective literary medium is poetry.

Ironically, however, Davidman decided to abandon her focus on writing poetry in favor of prose. Evidence of this abandonment can be readily seen in her letters. Until the late 1940s, her letters reflect a stubborn commitment to writing and publishing poetry. For example, she writes several letters to her mentor, Stephen Vincent Benét, earnestly soliciting his advice and criticism (*Bone,* 11-14, 18-19, and 29-30). In addition, after she becomes poetry editor at *NM,* she writes lengthy letters giving advice to aspiring poets, including Harold Harewell Lewis (*Bone,* 34-39), Aaron Kramer (*Bone,* 43-47 and 55-76), and Kenneth Porter (*Bone,* 117-28). However, after her marriage to Bill Gresham and the birth of her two sons, Davidman's concerns become increasingly practical. For instance, she tells Chad Walsh on June 21, 1949, that "I used to be a poet myself, but I'm afraid my inspiration gave out when I discovered that people would *pay* for prose" (*Bone,* 105); on January 27, 1950, she tries to encourage Walsh's efforts at writing clear, accessible verse, noting that "I was well on the way to a simple style myself, I think, when I turned completely professional and concentrated on prose" (*Bone,* 114). Perhaps she records the death of her efforts to make a career as a poet when she writes Porter on May 29, 1951: "Are you still writing poetry? I hardly either write or read it any more, and I don't follow the critics, so I wouldn't know.

---

57. I do not address Davidman as a letter writer in this study since letters tend to be private and not intended for general consumption. That said, readers will notice how frequently I have referred to her letters, and they would be well-advised to read them for additional insight into Davidman's aspirations, thoughts, changing political, personal, and spiritual beliefs, and engaging prose style.

Bill and I, being free-lance writers with two kids, have become severely professional — we write for money, damn it" (*Bone,* 118). Yet her claims are somewhat disingenuous since the newly discovered poems show she was still actively writing poetry if not trying to get it published.[58]

Accordingly, I believe her diminished status as a twentieth-century American writer was not the result of literary failure; rather, it was because she made a practical decision to earn a living as a prose writer. Hard experience had shown her that earning an income as a poet was not possible. Thus she made a pragmatic choice; believing that she could earn a living as a prose writer, she gave up attempting to publish her poetry. Perhaps it would be uncharitable to claim that she sold out — exchanging the literary equivalent of her birthright for a mess of porridge — but such an argument may be close to the truth. Although we will have to wait for other scholars to assess the literary merit of these new poems, I am confident that Davidman's status as a twentieth-century American writer will rise considerably because of what these poems reveal about her as a writer. In her Sonnet XIV to Lewis she hinted that she knew poetry was her main literary gift, so it is fitting to conclude with this sonnet:

> When I have said all the words, what shall I do?
> When all the rhymes are paired and I have sung
> Whatever tunes are nested in my tongue,
> And have made all the promises, false and true —
>
> When the sonnets are written and the night
> Burns black to moonset and bright to sunrise,
> And dawn strikes like murder at my aching eyes
> With its intolerable bruise of light —
>
> Always, after the praying and the poor gabble
> Of sobs, and the twisting in the lonely bed,
> And the clever spiderwebs I weave in my head
> To catch you with, I sit down at my table
>
> And stare at nothing, neither God nor you;
> Sir, at the end of words, what shall I do? (*Naked Tree,* 290-91)

---

58. And certainly she was not ashamed of her poetry, using it in fact to make an early literary connection to Lewis.

Table of Contents for *Courage*

I indicate poems that do not appear in DP with italics. All the remaining poems appear in *A Naked Tree* except those noted by an asterisk.

Time Is

1. Tragic Muse
2. For the Happy Man
3. How about It?
4. Tourist Folder
5. *What the Holy Ghost Said*
6. Game with Children
7. Next Step
8. In Memory of H. Bottcher
9. Moral Lesson
10. Quisling at Twilight
11. Dayspring
12. Trojan Women
13. In the Atomic Year [This Year of the Atom in *A Naked Tree*]
14. Roncesvailes [Poem for Liberation in *A Naked Tree*]
15. Unknown Soldier
16. Religious Education
17. Everytown
18. *Memorandum for Fighters*
19. Frankenstein's Nursery Rhymes*
20. Peter the Plowman

Appendix

Time Was

Time Is Past

1. The poem's structure has in it the phrases "time is," "time was," and "time past."

Bibliography

A Chronological Bibliography of Joy Davidman's Publications

"Clair de Lune" (translation of Verlaine) and "Odelette" (translation of H. De Regnier). *Hunter College Echo* (Christmas 1932).

"I Hate You for Your Kind Indifference." *Hunter College Echo* (Christmas 1933).

"Reveal the Titan." *Hunter College Echo* (May 1934): 26-36.

"Apostate." *Hunter College Echo* (November 1934): 17-26. Winner of the Bernard Cohen Prize Story.

"Cristal." *Hunter College Notre Revue Française* (1934): 11.

"Âmes ExQuises." *Hunter College Notre Revue Française* (1934): 19-23.

"My Lord of Orrery." MA Thesis. Columbia University, 1935 (unpublished).

"Resurrection" and "Amulet." *Poetry* 47 (January 1936): 193-95.

"Variations on a Theme," "The Half-Hearted," "Shadow Dance," and "Odi et Amo." *Poetry* 49 (March 1937): 323-27.

"Strength through Joy." *New Masses* 27 (April 5, 1938): 5.

"Spartacus — 1938." *New Masses* 27 (May 24, 1938): 19. Reprinted in *Letter to a Comrade,* 22-23.

"Prayer Against Indifference." *New Masses* 28 (August 9, 1938): 17. Reprinted in *Letter to a Comrade,* 31.

"Apology for Liberals." *New Masses* 28 (August 16, 1938): 4. Reprinted in *Letter to a Comrade,* 90.

"Near Catalonia." *New Masses* 29 (October 18, 1938): 18. Reprinted in *Letter to a Comrade,* 67.

Letter to a Comrade. New Haven: Yale University Press, 1938. Winner of the Russell Loines Memorial award for poetry given by the National Institute of Arts and Letters.

"Arcadia, Kentucky" (book review of *Black Is My Truelove's Hair* by Elizabeth Madox Roberts). *New Masses* 30 (December 27, 1938): 25.

"About Spain" (book review of *Salud! Poems, Stories, and Sketches of Spain by American Writers,* edited by Alan Calmer). *New Masses* 30 (January 31, 1939): 24-25.

"Kansas Poet" (book review of *The High Plains* by Kenneth Porter). *New Masses* 30 (February 7, 1939): 26-27.

"Nazi Classroom" (book review of *The Age of the Fish* by Odon von Horvath). *New Masses* 30 (March 14, 1939): 24-25.

"The Power-House" (book review of *The Power-House* by Benjamin Appel). *New Masses* 31 (May 16, 1939): 23-24.

"The Devil Will Come." *New Masses* 32 (June 27, 1939): 6.

"Jews of No Man's Land." *New Republic* 99 (July 5, 1939): 248.

"Office Windows." *Fantasy: A Literary Quarterly with an Emphasis on Poetry* 6, no. 3 (1939): 5-7.

Anya. New York: Macmillan, 1940.

"In All Humility." *Fantasy: A Literary Quarterly with an Emphasis on Poetry* 6, no. 4 (1940): 27.

"Though Transitory." *Fantasy: A Literary Quarterly with an Emphasis on Poetry* 6, no. 4 (1940): 26-27.

"Amateur Night in Harlem," comprised of "High Yellow," "New Spiritual," and "So We Can Forget Our Troubles." *Fantasy: A Literary Quarterly with an Emphasis on Poetry* 7, no. 1 (1941): 21-22.

"For the Gentlemen." *New Masses* 38 (December 31, 1940): 23.

"Prophet without Honor." *New Masses* 38 (January 14, 1941): 14.

"For the Happy Man." *New Masses* 38 (February 18, 1941): 36.

"Marxist Mania" (movie review of *Go West*). *New Masses* 38 (March 4, 1941): 27-28.

"Blunted Edge" (movie reviews of *Tobacco Road* and *The Lady Eve*). *New Masses* 38 (March 11, 1941): 30-31.

"Humdrum Cinema" (movie reviews of *Come Live with Me* and *So Ends Our Night*). *New Masses* 38 (March 18, 1941): 29-30.

"Pacific Shore." *New Masses* 39 (March 25, 1941): 24.

"Pepe le Moko" (movie reviews of *Pepe le Moko, Andy Hardy's Private Secretary, The Mad Doctor,* and *Cheers for Miss Bishop*). *New Masses* 39 (March 25, 1941): 29.

"Huey Hooey" (movie reviews of *Meet John Doe* and *Rage in Heaven*). *New Masses* 39 (April 1, 1941): 30-31.

"Rover Boys on Wings" (movie reviews of *I Wanted Wings* and *Topper Returns*). *New Masses* 39 (April 8, 1941): 28-29.

"Soviet Love Story" (movie reviews of *The New Teacher* and *That Hamilton Woman*). *New Masses* 39 (April 22, 1941): 28-29.

"Citizen Kane" (movie reviews of *Citizen Kane* and *The Sea Wolf*). *New Masses* 39 (May 13, 1941): 28-29.

"Three Films" (movie reviews of *That Uncertain Feeling, The Flame of New Orleans,* and *Penny Serenade*). *New Masses* 39 (May 20, 1941): 30-31.

"Volga-Volga" (movie review of *Volga-Volga*). *New Masses* 39 (May 27, 1941): 25.

"St. George Pets the Dragon" (movie reviews of *Major Barbara, A Woman's Face,* and *Proud Valley*). *New Masses* 39 (June 3, 1941): 28-29.

"Poet of the Poor." *New Masses* 39 (June 10, 1941): 12.

"Neptune's Pets" (movie reviews of *Washington Murderdrama, Power Dive,* and *Border Vigilantes*). *New Masses* 39 (June 10, 1941): 28-29.

"Dayspring." *New Masses* 39 (June 17, 1941): 17.

Bibliography

"Shining Screwballs" (movie reviews of *Love Crazy* and *Shining Victory*). *New Masses* 39 (June 17, 1941): 28.

"Monopoly Takes a Screen Test." *New Masses* 39 (June 24, 1941): 28-30.

"Tripe and Taylor" (movie reviews of *Billy the Kid, She Knew All the Answers,* and *The Face Behind the Mask*). *New Masses* 40 (July 1, 1941): 30-31.

"Here in the City." *New Masses* 40 (July 8, 1941): 20.

"The Face of China" (movie reviews of *Ku Kan* and *Out of the Fog*). *New Masses* 40 (July 8, 1941): 27, 29.

"Soviet Frontiers" (movie reviews of *Soviet Frontiers on the Danube* and *Underground*). *New Masses* 40 (July 15, 1941): 27-28.

"Coldwater Canyon," "Game with Children," and "Trojan Women." *Accent: A Quarterly of New Literature* 2 (Summer 1941): 200-201. "Trojan Women" was also reprinted in *War Poems of the United Nations*. Edited by Joy Davidman, 300-301. New York: Dial Press, 1943.

"Three Movies" (movie reviews of *The Big Store, Blossoms in the Dust,* and *Tight Shoes*). *New Masses* 40 (July 22, 1941): 29-30.

"The Movies: Stern, Gay, and Otherwise" (movie reviews of *The Bride Came COD, In the Navy,* and *They Met in Bombay*). *New Masses* 40 (August 5, 1941): 28-29.

"Fantasy and Fun" (movie reviews of *Million Dollar Baby* and *Singapore Woman*). *New Masses* 40 (August 19, 1941): 30.

"Studies in Pathos" (movie reviews of *Honky Tonk* and *Hold Back the Dawn*). *New Masses* 41 (October 14, 1941): 27.

"The Maltese Falcon" (movie reviews of *The Maltese Falcon, It Started with Eve,* and *The Man Who Seeks the Truth*). *New Masses* 41 (October 21, 1941): 28.

"Recent Movies" (movie reviews of *Musical Story* and *This Woman Is Mine*). *New Masses* 41 (October 28, 1941): 28-30.

"Other Movies" (movie reviews of *Dumbo, All That Money Can Buy,* and *Target for To-night*). *New Masses* 41 (November 4, 1941): 27-28.

"Scorched Valley" (movie reviews of *How Green Was My Valley* and *Le Roi*). *New Masses* 41 (November 11, 1941): 26-27.

"Horror with Subtlety" (movie reviews of *Ladies in Retirement, The Chocolate Soldier, Never Give a Sucker an Even Break,* and *My Life with Caroline*). *New Masses* 41 (November 18, 1941): 28-29.

"Perfect Landing" (movie reviews of *Wings of Victory* and *The Land Is Bright*). *New Masses* 41 (November 25, 1941): 26-27 and 28-29.

"Forgotten Village" (movie reviews of *The Forgotten Village, International Lady,* and *This England*). *New Masses* 41 (December 2, 1941): 27-28.

"A Rake Reforms" (movie reviews of *Suspicion* and *Skylark*). *New Masses* 41 (December 9, 1941): 27-29.

"New Movies" (movie reviews of *The Feminine Touch* and *The Men in Her Life*). *New Masses* 41 (December 23, 1941): 28.

"B Becomes A" (movie reviews of *Among the Living, Birth of the Blues,* and *Blues in the Night*). *New Masses* 41 (December 30, 1941): 26.

"The Girl from Leningrad" (movie review of *The Girl from Leningrad*). *New Masses* 42 (January 6, 1942): 26-27.

"Thumbs Down" (movie reviews of *Two-Faced Woman, The Shanghai Gesture,* and *The Wolf Man*). *New Masses* 42 (January 13, 1942): 26-28.

"Dinner Knives" (movie reviews of *The Man Who Came to Dinner* and *Louisiana Purchase*). *New Masses* 42 (January 20, 1942): 29-30.

"Ingratiating Comedy" (movie reviews of *Ball of Fire* and *Pacific Blackout*). *New Masses* 42 (January 27, 1942): 27-28.

"Paris Calling" (movie reviews of *Paris Calling, I Wake Up Screaming*, and *Mr. and Mrs. North*). *New Masses* 42 (February 3, 1942): 27-28.

"Quack, Quack" (book review of *Hollywood: The Movie Colony — The Movie Makers* by Leo Rosten). *New Masses* 42 (February 10, 1942): 24.

"This Week's Films" (movie reviews of *Sullivan's Travels* and *Joan of Paris*). *New Masses* 42 (February 10, 1942): 28-29.

"Cabbages and Kings" (movie reviews of *King's Row* and *All through the Night*). *New Masses* 42 (February 17, 1942): 28.

"Our Russian Front" (movie reviews of *One Day in Soviet Russia* and *Woman of the Year*). *New Masses* 42 (February 24, 1942): 29-30.

"The Shadow" (movie reviews of *Mr. V, Nine Bachelors*, and *Design for Scandal*). *New Masses* 42 (March 3, 1942): 28-29.

"Superb Screen Satire" (movie reviews of *Roxie Hart, Crime and Punishment*, and *The Brothers Karamazov*). *New Masses* 42 (March 10, 1942): 28-29.

"Tanya's Glass Slipper" (movie reviews of *Tanya* and *Invaders*). *New Masses* 42 (March 17, 1942): 29-30.

"Zola Revival" (movie review of *Zola* and further discussion of *How Green Was My Valley*). *New Masses* 42 (March 24, 1942): 30.

"A Spirited Ghost" (movie reviews of *The Remarkable Andrew* and *Alexander Nevsky*). *New Masses* 42 (March 31, 1941): 29-30.

"Tragic Laughter" (movie review of *To Be or Not to Be*). *New Masses* 43 (April 7, 1942): 29-30.

"Fourth Down" (movie reviews of *The Male Animal, The Bugle Sounds*, and comments on the reissuing of *Gone with the Wind*). *New Masses* 43 (April 14, 1942): 28-30.

"Guerrilla Brigade" (movie reviews of *Guerrilla Brigade* and *The Ghost of Frankenstein*). *New Masses* 43 (April 21, 1942): 28-29.

"Shadows and Percy" (movie reviews of *Joe Smith, American, Dangerously They Live*, and *My Favorite Blonde*). *New Masses* 43 (April 28, 1942): 30.

"Before the Talkies" (movie review of the reissue of *The Gold Rush*). *New Masses* 43 (May 5, 1942): 28-29.

"Low Ebb" (movie review of *Moontide*). *New Masses* 43 (May 12, 1942): 30.

"Native Land" (movie review of *Native Land*). *New Masses* 43 (May 19, 1942): 28-29.

"Shadows in a Fog" (movie reviews of *Tortilla Flat, This above All*, and *The Thirty-Nine Steps*). *New Masses* 43 (June 2, 1942): 29-31.

"This One's a Dud" (movie review of *Ships with Wings*). *New Masses* 43 (June 9, 1942): 31.

"Exciting Soviet Film" (movie reviews of *Red Tanks* and *Take a Letter, Darling*). *New Masses* 43 (June 16, 1942): 27-29.

"Under the Bombs" (movie reviews of *Mrs. Miniver, Nazi Agent*, and *Ring of Steel*). *New Masses* 43 (June 30, 1942): 29-30.

"This Is the Enemy" (movie reviews of *This Is the Enemy* and *Laugh, Town, Laugh*). *New Masses* 44 (July 7, 1942): 30-31.

"Women: Hollywood Style." *New Masses* 44 (July 14, 1942): 28-31.

"Peter the Plowman." *New Masses* 44 (September 15, 1942): 15.

Bibliography

"Heroes Are Human Beings" (movie reviews of *In the Rear of the Enemy, Desperate Journey, Manila Calling,* and *Tales of Manhattan*). *New Masses* 45 (October 13, 1942): 30-31.

"Two Films, One Revue" (movie reviews of *Inside Britain* and *Panama Hattie*). *New Masses* 45 (October 20, 1942): 28.

"The Will and the Way." *New Masses* 45 (October 27, 1942): 28, 30-31.

"Fun with Russell" (movie reviews of *My Sister Eileen* and *The Devil with Hitler*). *New Masses* 45 (November 3, 1942): 29-30.

"The Moon and Sixpence" (movie reviews of *The Moon and Sixpence* and *Now, Voyager*). *New Masses* 45 (November 10, 1942): 29-30.

"Dutch Underground" (movie reviews of *One of Our Aircraft Is Missing, George Washington Slept Here, A Yank at Eton,* and *Iceland*). *New Masses* 45 (November 17, 1942): 29-31.

"The War Film: An Examination." *New Masses* 45 (November 24, 1942): 29-30.

"Those Fighting Britons" (movie reviews of *Target for Tonight, Soviet School Child,* and *Listen to Britain*). *New Masses* 45 (December 1, 1942): 29-30.

"Cameras as Weapons." *New Masses* 45 (December 8, 1942): 28-29.

"Real Boy Meets Real Girl" (movie reviews of *Mashenka, Casablanca, The Avengers,* and *I Married a Witch*). *New Masses* 45 (December 15, 1942): 29-30.

"Screen Spookery" (movie review of *The Cat People*). *New Masses* 45 (December 22, 1942): 31.

"Poems against Hitler" (book review of *Untergrund* by Hans Marchwitza). *New Masses* 45 (December 29, 1942): 25-26.

"Battered Formulas" (movie reviews of *The Palm Beach Story* and *Life Begins at Eight-Thirty*). *New Masses* 45 (December 29, 1942): 29-31.

"Little Margaret's Journey" (movie reviews of *Journey for Margaret* and *Fortress on the Volga*). *New Masses* 46 (January 5, 1943): 29-30.

"Crowds in the Rain" (movie reviews of *The World in Action* and *Flying Fortresses*). *New Masses* 46 (January 12, 1943): 29-30.

"In Which We Serve" (movie reviews of *In Which We Serve* and *Arabian Nights*). *New Masses* 46 (January 19, 1943): 29-30.

"A Film Goebbels Would Love" (movie review of *Tennessee Johnson*). *New Masses* 46 (January 26, 1943): 29-30.

"The Camera as Narrator" (movie reviews of *The Black Room* and *Shadow of a Doubt*). *New Masses* 46 (February 2, 1943): 29-31.

"Commandos Strike at Dawn" (movie reviews of *Commandos Strike at Dawn* and *China Girl*). *New Masses* 46 (February 9, 1943): 27-28.

"Drama Roundup" (play review of *The Barber Had Two Sons* and movie reviews of *Air Force* and *Random Harvest*). *New Masses* 46 (February 16, 1943): 27-28.

"Margaret Walker: Negro Poet." *New Masses* 46 (February 23, 1943): 24-25.

"Siege of Leningrad" (movie review of *The Siege of Leningrad*). *New Masses* 46 (February 23, 1943): 29-31.

"Saludos Amigos" (movie review of *Saludos Amigos*). *New Masses* 46 (March 2, 1943): 30.

"Mr. Chadband's Ghost" (movie reviews of *The Human Comedy* and *Counterattack*). *New Masses* 46 (March 16, 1943): 29-31.

"Goebbels's Missing Link" (comment on forthcoming movie *Captive Wild Women*). *New Masses* 46 (March 23, 1943): 29.

"False History" (movie review of *Young Mr. Pitt*). *New Masses* 46 (March 23, 1943): 30-31.

"Stephen Vincent Benét." *New Masses* 46 (March 30, 1943): 23-24.

"Keeper of the Flame" (movie reviews of *Keeper of the Flame, Chetniks,* and *Hitler's Children*). *New Masses* 46 (March 30, 1943): 28-29.

"With Bullet and Whip" (movie reviews of *Diary of a Nazi* and *Forever and a Day*). *New Masses* 47 (April 6, 1943): 28-30.

"The Moon Is Up" (movie review of *The Moon Is Down*). *New Masses* 47 (April 13, 1943): 29-30.

"Script and Screen" (commentary by screenwriter Lester Cole disagreeing with Davidman's earlier article "Camera as Narrator"; Davidman answers). *New Masses* 47 (April 20, 1943): 28-30.

"Prayer for Every Voyage." *New Masses* 47 (April 27, 1943): 16.

"Sword's Edge" (movie reviews of *Edge of Darkness, Desert Victory,* and *Heart of a Nation*). *New Masses* 47 (April 27, 1943): 28-30.

"But the People Live" (movie review of *Hangmen Also Die*). *New Masses* 47 (May 4, 1943): 28-29.

"Journey into Truth" (movie review of *Mission to Moscow*). *New Masses* 47 (May 11, 1943): 28-30.

"Deaths and a Warning" (movie reviews of *The Ox-Bow Incident* and *Next of Kin*). *New Masses* 47 (May 18, 1943): 30-31.

"Mission of Sabotage." *New Masses* 47 (May 25, 1943): 29.

"Assignment in Brittany" (movie review of *Assignment in Brittany*). *New Masses* 47 (May 25, 1943): 31.

"Let the People Sing" (book review of Aaron Kramer's *Till the Grass Is Ripe for Dancing*). *New Masses* 47 (June 1, 1943): 26-27.

"Masquerade" (movie review of *Masquerade* and continuing discussion of *Mission to Moscow*). *New Masses* 47 (June 1, 1943): 29-31.

"Canvas and Film" (movie reviews of *The More the Merrier, Desperados, I Walked with a Zombie, Leopard Man*). *New Masses* 47 (June 8, 1943): 29-31.

"Seamen in Battle" (movie reviews of *Action in the North Atlantic, This Land Is Mine,* and *Five Graves to Cairo*). *New Masses* 47 (June 15, 1943): 29-31.

"The Russian Story" (movie review of *The Russian Story*). *New Masses* 47 (June 22, 1943): 30-31.

"Entertainment Goes to War." *New Masses* 47 (June 29, 1943): 30.

"Young Defenders" (movie review of *Boy from Stalingrad*). *New Masses* 48 (July 6, 1943): 28-29.

"Two Films about Bataan" (movie reviews of *So Proudly We Hail* and *Bataan*). *New Masses* 48 (July 13, 1943): 29-31.

"At the Canteen" (movie reviews of *Stage Door Canteen* and *Background to Danger*). *New Masses* 48 (July 20, 1943): 31.

"The Equivocal Bell" (movie review of *For Whom the Bell Tolls*). *New Masses* 48 (July 27, 1943): 30-31.

"For Odessa" (by Boris Veselchakov, adapted by Joy Davidman). *New Masses* 48 (August 10, 1943): 14. Reprinted in *War Poems of the United Nations,* 216-17.

"The Young Pioneers" (by A. Bezmensky, adapted by Joy Davidman). *New Masses* 48 (September 7, 1943): 12. Reprinted in *War Poems of the United Nations,* 195.

Bibliography

"Anti-Fascist Vignettes" (book review of *A Garland of Straw* by Sylvia Townsend Warner). *New Masses* 49 (October 19, 1943): 28-29.

War Poems of the United Nations. Edited by Joy Davidman. New York: Dial Press, 1943. Davidman's contributions to the volume: "Fairytale" (299-300); "Trojan Women" (300-301) (first published in *Accent: A Quarterly of New Literature* 2 [Summer 1941]: 200-201); "For My Son" (under the name Megan Coombes-Dawson) (24-25); "Four Years After Munich" and "Peccavimus" (both under the name Haydon Weir) (49-51); "For Odessa" (14) (by Boris Veselchakov, adapted by Joy Davidman); "The Young Pioneers" (12) (by A. Bezmensky, adapted by Joy Davidman); and "Snow in Madrid" (301-2) (reprinted from *Letter to a Comrade*).

"The Language Men Speak" (book review of *The Fourth Decade* by Norman Rosten). *New Masses* 49 (November 30, 1943): 26-27.

"Foreword." In *They Look Like Men,* by Alexander F. Bergman. Edited by Joy Davidman. New York: Bernard Ackerman, 1944.

Seven Poets in Search of an Answer. Edited by Thomas Yoseloff. New York: Bernard Ackerman, 1944. Davidman contributed seven poems: "Spartacus 1938" (from *Letter to a Comrade*), "The Dead Partisan," "Dirge for the Suicides," "For the Nazis" (first published as "For the Gentlemen," *New Masses* 38 [December 31, 1940]: 23), "Elegy for Garcia Lorca," "Trojan Women" (first published in *Accent: A Quarterly of New Literature* 2 [Summer 1941]: 200-201), and "New Spiritual" (first published in *Fantasy: A Literary Quarterly with an Emphasis on Poetry* 7, no. 1 [1941]: 21-22).

"Dialogue for D-Day." *New Masses* 51 (June 20, 1944): 15.

"No Sun, No Stars" (book review of *No Beautiful Nights* by Vassili Grossman). *New Masses* 52 (August 1, 1944): 28.

"Poem for Liberation." *New Masses* 52 (September 12, 1944): 8.

"The Nessus-shirt" (book review of *The Mocking Bird Is Singing* by Louise Malley). *New Masses* 52 (September 12, 1944): 26-27.

"Sonnet to Various Republicans." *New Masses* 53 (December 19, 1944): 10.

"Without the Reason Why" (book review of *The Journal of Mary Hervey Russell* by Storm Jameson). *New Masses* 55 (April 10, 1945): 24-25.

"Life with Mother" (book review of *The Ballad and the Source* by Rosamund Lehman). *New Masses* 56 (July 10, 1945): 26-27.

"Quisling at Twilight." *New Masses* 56 (July 31, 1945): 4.

[The last time Davidman appears on the masthead of *New Masses* as a "contributing editor." *New Masses* 59 (April 16, 1946): 1.]

"Materialism vs. Romance" (letter to editor). *The Saturday Review of Literature* 31 (December 25, 1948): 23.

"Theater Party." *Bluebook* 88 (February 1949): 16-17.

Weeping Bay. New York: Macmillan, 1950.

"The Longest Way Round." In *These Found the Way: Thirteen Converts to Protestant Christianity.* Edited by David Wesley Soper. Philadelphia: Westminster, 1951.

"A Little Bird Told Her." *McCall's* (February 1951): 44, 112, 115-17.

"It's Right to Marry Young." *Redbook* (November 1952): 40-41, 72-73. With William Lindsay Gresham.

"Into the Full Light." *Presbyterian Life* 6 (April 4, 1953): 12-13, 26-29.

"God Comes First." *Presbyterian Life* 6 (May 2, 1953): 12-14.

Smoke on the Mountain: An Interpretation of the Ten Commandments. Philadelphia: Westminster, 1953; London: Hodder & Stoughton, 1955.
Out of My Bone: The Letters of Joy Davidman. Edited by Don W. King. Grand Rapids: Eerdmans, 2009.

Critical Bibliography

Book Reviews

Letter to a Comrade

Blackmur, R. P. "Nine Poets." *Partisan Review,* Winter 1939, p. 112.
Emerson, Dorothy. "Three Young Poets." *Scholastic* 34 (May 27, 1939): 27E.
Hawkins, Desmond. Review of Joy Davidman's *Letter to a Comrade. Spectator* 162 (May 19, 1939): 868.
Lechlitner, Ruth. Review of Joy Davidman's *Letter to a Comrade. New York Herald Tribune Books,* December 25, 1938, p. 2.
Millspaugh, C. A. "Among the New Books of Verse." *Kenyon Review* 2 (1940): 363.
Review of Joy Davidman's *Letter to a Comrade. Times Literary Supplement* [London], October 14, 1939, p. 599.
Rukeyser, Muriel. Review of Joy Davidman's *Letter to a Comrade. New Republic* 98 (March 8, 1939): 146.
Ulrich, Dorothy. Review of Joy Davidman's *Letter to a Comrade. New York Times Book Review,* August 6, 1939, p. 4.
Williams, Oscar. Review of Joy Davidman's *Letter to a Comrade. Poetry* 54 (April 1939): 33.

Anya

Cournos, John. Review of Joy Davidman's *Anya. New York Times,* July 14, 1940, p. 7.
Frye, Dorothy. Review of Joy Davidman's *Anya. Boston Transcript,* August 10, 1940, p. 2.
Kazin, Alfred. Review of Joy Davidman's *Anya. New York Herald Tribune Books,* July 14, 1940, p. 2.
Review of Joy Davidman's *Anya. Christian Century* 57 (July 10, 1940): 879.
Review of Joy Davidman's *Anya. New Republic* 103 (August 12, 1940): 222.
Rothman, N. L. Review of Joy Davidman's *Anya. Saturday Review of Literature* 22 (July 13, 1940): 10.

Weeping Bay

Breaden, R. P. Review of Joy Davidman's *Weeping Bay. Library Journal* 75 (February 1, 1950): 171.
Derleth, August. Review of Joy Davidman's *Weeping Bay. Sunday Chicago Tribune,* March 12, 1950, p. 4.

Bibliography

Hicks, Granville. Review of Joy Davidman's *Weeping Bay*. *New York Times,* March 5, 1950, p. 30.

Hilton, James. Review of Joy Davidman's *Weeping Bay*. *New York Herald Tribune Book Review,* March 12, 1950, p. 6.

Jackson, J. H. Review of Joy Davidman's *Weeping Bay*. *San Francisco Chronicle,* March 7, 1950, p. 18.

Review of Joy Davidman's *Weeping Bay*. *Kirkus* 18 (January 1, 1950): 8.

Review of Joy Davidman's *Weeping Bay*. *New Yorker* 26 (March 11, 1950): 103.

Review of Joy Davidman's *Weeping Bay*. *United States Quarterly Booklist* 6 (June 1950): 156.

Sandrock, Mary. Review of Joy Davidman's *Weeping Bay*. *Catholic World* 171 (June 1950): 171.

Walsh, Chad. "First Things First: How Does One Come to Know God?" *Presbyterian Life* 3 (May 27, 1950): 36-38.

Wolfe, A. F. Review of Joy Davidman's *Weeping Bay*. *Saturday Review of Literature* 33 (March 18, 1950): 16.

Smoke on the Mountain

Miller, L. R. Review of Joy Davidman's *Smoke on the Mountain*. *Library Journal* 79 (September 1, 1954): 1496.

Review of Joy Davidman's *Smoke on the Mountain*. *Christian Century* 72 (February 16, 1955): 72.

Review of Joy Davidman's *Smoke on the Mountain*. *Journal of Bible and Religion* 23 (April 1955): 157.

Review of Joy Davidman's *Smoke on the Mountain*. *Kirkus* 22 (September 15, 1954): 661.

Review of Joy Davidman's *Smoke on the Mountain*. *Saturday Review of Literature* 38 (March 5, 1955): 31.

Review of Joy Davidman's *Smoke on the Mountain*. *Times Literary Supplement* [London], May 6, 1955, p. iii.

Articles and Books

Aaron, Daniel. *Writers on the Left.* New York: Harcourt, 1961.

Allego, Donna M. "The Construction and Role of Community in Political Long Poems by Twentieth-Century American Poets: Lola Ridge, Genevieve Taggard, Joy Davidman, Margaret Walker, and Muriel Rukeyser." Diss. Southern Illinois University at Carbondale, 1997.

Belknap, Michal R. *Cold War Political Justice: The Smith Act, the Communist Party, and American Civil Liberties.* Westport, CT: Greenwood Press, 1977.

Benét, Stephen Vincent. *Burning City.* New York: Farrar & Rinehart, 1936.

Benét, William Rose. "Assumption." *The Saturday Review of Literature* 30 (May 10, 1947): 35.

————. "The Phoenix Nest" (column). *The Saturday Review of Literature* 32 (January 29, 1949): 42-43.

———. "The Phoenix Nest" (column). *The Saturday Review of Literature* 32 (July 23, 1949): 28-29.

———. "To a Communist." *The Saturday Review of Literature* 31 (October 23, 1948): 39.

Bergen, Doris L. "Catholics, Protestants, and Christian Antisemitism in Nazi Germany." *Central European History* 27, no. 3 (1994): 329-48.

Bergman, Alexander. *They Look Like Men.* New York: Bernard Ackerman, 1944.

Berman, Jeffrey. *Companionship in Grief: Love and Loss in the Memoirs of C. S. Lewis, John Bayley, Donald Hall, Joan Didion, and Calvin Trillin.* Amherst, MA: University of Massachusetts Press, 2010.

Blackbourn, David. "Roman Catholics, the Centre Party and Anti-Semitism in Imperial Germany." In *Nationalist and Racialist Movements in Britain and Germany before 1914,* edited by Paul Kennedy and Anthony Nicholls. London: Palgrave Macmillan, 1981.

Borhek, Mary. "A Grief Observed: Fact or Fiction?" *Mythlore* 16 (Summer 1990): 4-9, 26.

Bradley, George, ed. *The Yale Younger Poets Anthology.* New Haven, CT: Yale University Press, 1998.

Calmer, Alan. "Portrait of the Artist as a Proletarian." *Saturday Review of Literature,* July 1937, pp. 3-4, 17.

———. "The Proletarian Short Story." *New Masses* 16 (July 2, 1935): 17-19.

Ceplair, Larry, and Steven Englund. *The Inquisition in Hollywood: Politics in the Film Industry, 1930-1960.* Garden City, NY: Anchor, 1980.

Christopher, Joe. "Joy Davidman, Laundress?" *Lamp-Post of the Southern California C. S. Lewis Society* 27 (Summer 2003): 26-27.

Christopher, John. "Notes on Joy." *Encounter* 68 (April 1987): 41-43.

Conrad, Joseph. *Youth.* Baltimore: Penguin, 1975.

Conway, John S. *The Nazi Persecutions of the Churches, 1933-45.* New York: Weidenfeld & Nicolson, 1968.

Davidman, Joy. Joy Davidman Papers, 1926-1964, The Marion E. Wade Center, Wheaton College, Wheaton, IL.

———. "The Longest Way Round." In *These Found the Way: Thirteen Converts to Protestant Christianity,* edited by David Wesley Soper. Philadelphia: Westminster, 1951. Reprinted in *Out of My Bone: The Letters of Joy Davidman,* edited by Don W. King, 83-97. Grand Rapids: Eerdmans, 2009.

———. *A Naked Tree: Love Sonnets to C. S. Lewis and Other Poems.* Edited by Don W. King. Grand Rapids: Eerdmans, 2015.

Dietrich, Donald J. *Catholic Citizens in the Third Reich: Psycho-Social Principles and Moral Reasoning.* New Brunswick, NJ: Transaction, 1988.

Dorsett, Lyle W. *And God Came In: The Extraordinary Story of Joy Davidman.* New York: Macmillan, 1983.

———. "The Search for Joy Davidman." *Bulletin of the New York C. S. Lewis Society* 14 (October 1983): 1-7.

Edwards, Bruce, ed. *C. S. Lewis — Life, Works, and Legacy.* 4 vols. Westport, CT: Praeger, 2007.

Engels, Frederick. *Ludwig Feuerbach and the Outcome of Classical German Philosophy.* New York: International Publishers, 1941.

Ferrari, Arthur C. "Proletarian Literature: A Case of Convergence of Political and Literary Radicalism." In *Cultural Politics: Radical Movements in Modern History,* edited by Jerold M. Starr. New York: Praeger, 1985.

Foley, Barbara. "Women and the Left in the 1930s." *American Literary History* 2 (Spring 1990): 150-69.

Folsom, Franklin. *Days of Anger, Days of Hope: A Memoir of the League of American Writers, 1937-1942.* Boulder: University Press of Colorado, 1994.

Frye, Northrop. *A Natural Perspective.* New York: Columbia University Press, 1965.

Gold, Mike. "Go Left, Young Writer." *New Masses* 4 (January 1929): 3-4. Reprinted in *Mike Gold: A Literary Anthology,* edited by Michael Folsom, 186-89. New York: International, 1972.

———. *Mike Gold: A Literary Anthology.* Edited by Michael Folsom. New York: International, 1972.

———. "Notes of the Month [On Proletarian Realism]." *New Masses* 5 (September 1930): 4-5. Reprinted in *Mike Gold: A Literary Anthology,* edited by Michael Folsom, 203-8. New York: International, 1972.

Glyer, Diana Pavlac. *The Company They Keep: C. S. Lewis and J. R. R. Tolkien as Writers in Community.* Kent, OH: Kent State University Press, 2007.

———. "Helen Joy Davidman Gresham Lewis." In *The C. S. Lewis Reader's Encyclopedia,* edited by Jeffrey Schultz and John West, 248-49. Grand Rapids: Zondervan, 1998.

———. "Joy Davidman Lewis: Author, Editor and Collaborator." *Mythlore* 22 (Summer 1998): 10-17, 46.

Gornick, Vivian. *The Romance of American Communism.* New York: Basic Books, 1977.

Green, Roger Lancelyn, and Walter Hooper. *C. S. Lewis: A Biography.* London: Collins, 1974.

Greenfield, Dean Robert. Recollection of Joy Davidman Lecture. *The Chronicle of the Portland C. S. Lewis Society* 5 (January-March 1976): 4-5.

Gresham, Douglas. *Jack's Life: A Memoir of C. S. Lewis.* New York: Broadman & Holman, 2005.

———. *Lenten Lands: My Childhood with Joy Davidman and C. S. Lewis.* New York: Macmillan, 1988.

Gresham, William L. "From Communist to Christian, Part 1." *Presbyterian Life* 3 (February 18, 1950): 20-22 and 35-36; "From Communist to Christian, Part 2." *Presbyterian Life* 3 (March 4, 1950): 22-23, 46; and "From Communist to Christian, Part 3." *Presbyterian Life* 3 (March 18, 1950): 21-24. The articles were later combined as "From Communist to Christian" and appeared in *These Found the Way: Thirteen Converts to Protestant Christianity,* edited by David W. Soper, 63-82. Philadelphia: Westminster, 1951.

———. *Houdini: The Man Who Walked through Walls.* New York: Henry Holt, 1959.

———. *Limbo Tower.* New York: Rinehart & Co., 1949.

———. *Nightmare Alley.* New York and Toronto: Rinehart, 1946.

———. *Monster Midway: A Book about Circus Life and Sideshows.* New York: Rinehart & Co., 1953.

Healey, Dorothy, and Maurice Isserman. *Dorothy Healey Remembers: A Life in the American Communist Party.* Oxford: Oxford University Press, 1990.

Helmreich, Ernst Christian. *The German Churches under Hitler: Background, Struggle, and Epilogue.* Detroit: Wayne State University Press, 1979.

Hemingway, Ernest. "Fascism Is a Lie." *New Masses* 23 (June 22, 1937): 4.

Hicks, Granville. *Granville Hicks in the* New Masses. Port Washington, NY: Kennikat Press, 1974.

Hooper, Walter. *C. S. Lewis: A Companion and Guide.* London: HarperCollins, 1996.

Howe, Irving, and Lewis Coser. *The American Communist Party: A Critical History.* New York: Praeger, 1957.

Isserman, Maurice. *Which Side Were You On? The American Communist Party During the Second World War.* Middletown, CT: Wesleyan University Press, 1982.

Jerome, V. J. *Culture in a Changing World.* New York: New Century Publishers, 1947.

Kaufman, Bel. "A Joy Observed." *Commonweal,* March 25, 1994, pp. 6-7.

Kidd, Noelene. "*A Grief Observed:* Art, Apology, or Autobiography?" *The Canadian C. S. Lewis Society* 97 (Spring 2000): 4.

King, Don W. "The Early Writings of Joy Davidman." *The Journal of Inklings Studies* 1, no. 1 (March 2011): 47-67.

———. "Finding Joy: A Comprehensive Bibliography of the Works of Joy Davidman." *SEVEN: An Anglo-American Literary Review* 23 (2006): 69-80.

———. "Fire and Ice: C. S. Lewis and the Love Poetry of Joy Davidman and Ruth Pitter." *SEVEN: An Anglo-American Literary Review* 22 (2005): 60-88.

———. *Hunting the Unicorn: A Critical Biography of Ruth Pitter.* Kent, OH: Kent State University Press, 2008.

———. "Into the Lion's Den: Joy Davidman and Metro-Goldwyn-Mayer." *Mythlore* 30 (Fall/Winter 2011): 91-106.

———. "Joy Davidman and the *New Masses:* Communist Poet and Reviewer." *The Chronicle of the Oxford C. S. Lewis Society* 4, no. 1 (February 2007): 18-44.

———. "Joy Davidman, Poet: *Letter to a Comrade.*" *Christianity and Literature* 62, no. 1 (Autumn 2012): 63-94.

———. "A Naked Tree: The Love Sonnets of Joy Davidman to C. S. Lewis." *SEVEN: An Anglo-American Literary Review* 29 (2012): 79-102.

Kirkpatrick, Ken, and Sidney F. Hunter. "Women Writers in the Proletarian Literature Collection, McFarlin Library." *Tulsa Studies in Women's Literature* 8 (Spring 1989): 143-53.

Klehr, Harvey. *The Heyday of American Communism: The Depression Decade.* New York: Basic Books, 1984.

Kramer, Aaron. *The Thunder of the Grass.* New York: International Publishers, 1948.

Lazo, Andrew. "Correcting the Chronology: Some Implications of 'Early Prose Joy.'" *SEVEN: An Anglo-American Literary Review* 29 (2012): 51-62.

———. "'Early Prose Joy': A Brief Introduction." *SEVEN: An Anglo-American Literary Review* 30 (2013): 5-12.

Lenin, V. I. *Materialism and Empirio-Criticism: Critical Comments on a Reactionary Philosophy.* New York: International Publishers, 1927.

Leopold, Paul. "The Writings of Joy Davidman Lewis, Part 1." *Bulletin of the New York C. S. Lewis Society* 14 (February 1983): 1-10; "The Writings of Joy Davidman Lewis, Part 2." *Bulletin of the New York C. S. Lewis Society* 14 (March 1983): 1-9.

Lewis, C. S. *The Allegory of Love: A Study in Medieval Tradition.* Oxford: Clarendon Press, 1936.

———. *The Case for Christianity.* New York: Macmillan, 1943.

———. *The Collected Letters of C. S. Lewis,* volume 2: *Books, Broadcasts and the War, 1931-1949.* Edited by Walter Hooper. London: HarperCollins, 2004.

———. *The Collected Letters of C. S. Lewis,* volume 3: *Narnia, Cambridge, and Joy, 1950-1963.* Edited by Walter Hooper. London: HarperCollins, 2006.

———. *The Collected Poems of C. S. Lewis: A Critical Edition*. Edited by Don W. King. Kent, OH: Kent State University Press, 2015.

———. *"De Descriptione Temporum."* In *Selected Literary Essays*. Cambridge: Cambridge University Press, 1969.

———. " 'Early Prose Joy': C. S. Lewis's Early Draft of an Autobiographical Manuscript." Edited by Andrew Lazo. *SEVEN: An Anglo-American Literary Review* 23 (2013): 13-49.

———. "The Efficacy of Prayer." *The Atlantic Monthly* 203 (January 1959): 59-61. Reprinted in *The World's Last Night: And Other Essays*. New York: Harcourt, Brace & Co., 1960.

———. *English Literature in the Sixteenth Century Excluding Drama*. The Oxford History of English Literature, vol. 3. Oxford: Clarendon, 1954.

———. *The Four Loves*. London: Geoffrey Bles, 1960.

———. *The Great Divorce: A Dream*. London: Geoffrey Bles, 1945.

———. *A Grief Observed*. London: Faber and Faber, 1961.

———. *Letters to Malcolm: Chiefly on Prayer*. London: Geoffrey Bles, 1964.

———. *The Pilgrim's Regress: An Allegorical Apology for Christianity, Reason and Romanticism*. London: J. M. Dent, 1933.

———. *Reflections on the Psalms*. London: Geoffrey Bles, 1958.

———. *The Screwtape Letters*. London: Geoffrey Bles, 1942.

———. *Surprised by Joy: The Shape of My Early Life*. London: Geoffrey Bles, 1955.

———. *That Hideous Strength: A Modern Fairy-tale for Grown-ups*. London: Bodley Head, 1945.

———. *Till We Have Faces: A Myth Retold*. London: Geoffrey Bles, 1956.

Lewis, Warren. *Brothers and Friends: The Diaries of Major Warren Hamilton Lewis*. Edited by Clyde S. Kilby and Marjorie Lamp Mead. San Francisco: Harper & Row, 1982.

———. *The Splendid Century: Some Aspects of French Life in the Reign of Louis XIV*. London: Eyre & Spottiswoode, 1953.

———. *The Sunset of the Splendid Century: The Life and Times of Louis Auguste de Bourbon, Duc de Maine, 1670-1736*. London: Eyre & Spottiswoode, 1955.

Lewy, Guenter. *The Catholic Church and Nazi Germany*. New York: McGraw-Hill, 1964.

Littell, Franklin H. "Christian Anti-Semitism and the Holocaust." In *Perspectives on the Holocaust*, edited by Randolph L. Braham. Boston: Kluwer-Nijhoff, 1983.

———. *The Crucifixion of the Jews: The Failure of Christians to Understand the Jewish Experience*. New York: Harper & Row, 1975.

Madden, David, ed. *Proletarian Writers of the Thirties*. Carbondale, IL: Southern Illinois University Press, 1968.

McGuire, Damaris Walsh. "Memories of Joy, Jack, and Chad [Walsh]." In *Chad Walsh Reviews C. S. Lewis*. Altadena, CA: Mythopoeic Press, 1998.

Murphy, James E. *The Proletarian Moment: The Controversy over Leftism in Literature*. Chicago: University of Illinois Press, 1991.

Musacchio, George. "C. S. Lewis' *A Grief Observed* as Fiction." *Mythlore* 12 (Spring 1986): 24-27.

Newton, Arvin. "A Letter on Proletarian Literature." *Partisan Review*, February 1936, p. 14.

North, Alfred, ed. *New Masses: An Anthology of the Rebel Thirties*. New York: International Publishers, 1969.

Ottanelli, Fraser M. *The Communist Party of the United States: From the Depression to World War II.* New Brunswick, NJ: Rutgers University Press, 1991.

Pilat, Oliver. "Girl Communist [Joy Davidman]: An Intimate Story of Eight Years in the Party." *The New York Post,* October 31; November 1-4, 6-11, and 13, 1949.

Porter, Kenneth. *The High Plains.* New York: John Day Co., 1938.

———. *Pilate before Jesus and Other Biblical and Legendary Poems.* North Montpelier, VT: Driftwood, 1936.

Prendergast, Alan. "One Man's Nightmare: The Noir Journey of William Lindsay Gresham." *The Writer's Chronicle* 38 (May/Summer 2006): 14-19.

Rahv, Philip. "Proletarian Literature: A Political Autopsy." *Southern Review,* Spring 1939, pp. 616-28.

Rideout, Walter. *The Radical Novel in the United States, 1900-1954.* Cambridge: Harvard University Press, 1956.

Rollins, William. "What Is a Proletarian Writer?" *New Masses* 15 (January 29, 1935): 22-23.

Rosten, Leo C. *Hollywood: The Movie Colony — The Movie Makers.* New York: Harcourt, Brace, 1941.

Rubenstein, Richard L. *After Auschwitz: History, Theology, and Contemporary Judaism.* 2nd ed. Baltimore: Johns Hopkins University Press, 1992.

Santamaria, Abigail. "Joy Davidman: The Honest Fingers of My Hand." *Sacred History,* December 2005, pp. 32-34.

———. *Joy: Poet, Seeker, and the Woman Who Captivated C. S. Lewis.* New York: Houghton Mifflin Harcourt, 2015.

Sarrocco, Clara. "The Three Phases of Joy Davidman." *Bulletin of the New York C. S. Lewis Society* 34 (May-June 2003): 1-9.

Sayer, George. "C. S. Lewis and Adultery." *Bulletin of the New York C. S. Lewis Society* 21 (June-July 1990): 4-7.

———. *Jack: C. S. Lewis and His Times.* San Francisco: Harper & Row, 1988.

Sibley, Brian. *C. S. Lewis, Through the Shadowlands: The Story of His Life with Joy Davidman.* New York: Macmillan, 1985.

Soper, David Wesley, ed. *These Found the Way: Thirteen Converts to Protestant Christianity.* Philadelphia: Westminster, 1951.

Still, James. "Bat Flight." *Saturday Evening Post* 211, no. 10 (September 3, 1938): 12-13, 50-51.

Turney, Ruth. "Joy Davidman's *Weeping Bay.*" *Bulletin of the New York C. S. Lewis Society* 17 (January 1986): 1-3.

Wald, Alan M. *Exiles from a Future Time: The Forging of the Mid-Twentieth-Century Literary Left.* Chapel Hill: University of North Carolina Press, 2002.

Walsh, Chad. *C. S. Lewis: Apostle to the Skeptics.* New York: Macmillan, 1949.

———. *The Literary Legacy of C. S. Lewis.* New York: Harcourt Brace Jovanovich, 1979.

Wixson, Douglas. "In Search of the Low-Down Americano: H. H. Lewis, William Carlos Williams, and the Politics of Literary Reception, 1930-1950." *William Carlos Williams Review* 26, no. 1 (2006): 75-100.

Wolfe, Thomas. *Look Homeward, Angel: A Story of the Buried Life.* New York: Charles Scribner's Sons, 1929.

Zinberg, Len. "Quiet and Safe." *New Masses* 28 (July 12, 1938): 152.

Index

Boldface indicates at-length discussion of the item.

Index

Index